THEODORE

WELD

CRUSADER

FOR

FREEDOM

Theodore D. Weld

THEODORE
WELD
Crusader for Freedom

Benjamin P. Thomas

OCTAGON BOOKS

A DIVISION OF FARRAR, STRAUS AND GIROUX

New York   1973

Reprinted 1973
by special arrangement with Rutgers University Press

OCTAGON BOOKS
A DIVISION OF FARRAR, STRAUS & GIROUX, INC.
19 Union Square West
New York, N. Y. 10003

Library of Congress Cataloging in Publication Data

Thomas, Benjamin Platt, 1902-1956.
Theodore Weld, crusader for freedom.

Reprint of the ed. published by Rutgers University Press, New Brunswick, N. J.

Bibliography: p.
1. Weld, Theodore Dwight, 1803-1895. I. Title.
[E449.W46T48   1973]   326'.092'4   [B]   73-4479
ISBN 0-374-97857-3

Printed in USA by
Thomson-Shore,Inc.
Dexter, Michigan

Not *often does a man whose labors*
shape the course of human history seek deliberately to efface
himself from history's pages, yet this seems to have been the
purpose of Theodore Weld.

The *Dictionary of American Biography* declares that "Meas-
ured by his influence, Weld was not only the greatest of the
abolitionists; he was also one of the greatest figures of his time,"
and the testimony of Weld's contemporaries bears out the estimate.

Wendell Phillips affirmed that "In the first years of the antislavery cause, he was our foremost advocate." William Lloyd
Garrison described Weld's work as indispensable. The Reverend
Samuel J. May said that "Wendell Phillips as an orator, was his
only rival in the cause of liberty." Frederick Douglass testified
that one of Weld's books, *Slavery As It Is*, was as influential in
the earlier period of the antislavery movement as Harriet Beecher
Stowe's *Uncle Tom's Cabin* was in a later day.

Yet this man is totally unknown to most Americans, and he was
little more than a name even to historians until a few years ago.

His obscurity was of his own choosing. Weld would never accept an office of authority or honor in any antislavery organization. He refused to speak at antislavery conventions or anniversaries, or even to attend them if he could avoid it. He shunned the cities, and chose to labor in the country districts, where newspapers were few, and his activities were seldom reported except by abolition journals. His writings were published anonymously, and he would seldom allow the content of his speeches or his letters from the field to appear in print at all.

The manner of his discovery is as astonishing as the man himself. The late Gilbert H. Barnes, a student of the antislavery movement, delving into the source materials of abolitionism, encountered fugitive references to Weld which were of such significance as to indicate that this unknown personality was abolition's "man of power, the greatest individual factor in its triumph." Still the man himself eluded all Barnes' seeking until, after tracing every clue, his search led at last to a trunkful of old family letters in a farmhouse attic near Allston, Massachusetts. They were a rich discovery, and they gave a complete reorientation to the history of the antislavery movement by proving that the really effective antislavery impulse came not nearly so much from William Lloyd Garrison and his New England coterie as from a western group which set up its headquarters in New York City and derived its most puissant motivation from Weld.

The present writer hopes that this first published biography of Theodore Weld will not only depict him as the appealing and extraordinary man that he was, but will also give the reader a new conception of the abolitionists. For we need a reappraisal of these people. It has too long been the fashion to scoff at them, to write them off as humorless fanatics, to ignore their rich humanity, and to minimize the tremendous impact of the moral convictions they avowed. And to misjudge the force of moral humanism invites distortion of history.

With all their faults and errors, we must credit the abolitionists with striving to perfect the American ideal, and to vitalize the precepts of our Declaration of Independence. "Abolition is essentially a revival," an antislavery paper explained, "a revival of the principles of liberty and social religion. . . . The reformation was a revival of the entire system of Christianity, which in the lapse of centuries, had been transformed into a sort of idolatry. . . . The American Revolution was a political revival—a new and striking exemplification of the great doctrine of human rights. Abolitionism is a two-fold revival; first, of the law of love in relation to man, 'Love thy neighbor as thyself,' and then, of the principles of liberty, as proclaimed by our forefathers. Its necessity has arisen from the national violation of this law, a national departure from these principles."

Slavery was more than a legal relationship; it also involved a code of human values and an ethical philosophy. Our present sensitivity to the rights of racial and religious minorities and so-called backward peoples is in no small degree a heritage from the antislavery impulse, and the very life blood of our political philosophy is the ideal of the worth and kinship of every human individual. In every country that has recognized the moral responsibility of man to man, slavery has succumbed peaceably; whereas, where the doctrine has been denied, freedom has come by cataclysm, if at all. Acceptance of the idea of the spiritual equality of men makes for peaceable social, political, and economic adjustment; its denial brings convulsions.

A reappraisal of the abolitionists is all the more in order inasmuch as the struggle for equal human rights is still a vital issue in our day. Human thralldom still exists in diverse guises, and men are still denied full human fellowship because of race or creed or color. The cult of the master race still mouths seductive shibboleths and coins new catchwords to sustain its philosophy of dominance and exploitation. Nevertheless, there is a restless stirring in the land, reminiscent of the antislavery days, testifying to the eternal validity of the equalitarian principles to which the abolitionists were dedicated, foretokening, we may hope, a new era of enlightenment in human relationships.

Modern antiabolition prejudice stems largely from a misconception—from accepting William Lloyd Garrison as typical of the antislavery agitator. Actually, only a relatively small number of the antislavery crusaders embraced Garrison's extreme beliefs or advocated his radical measures. All sorts of men enlisted in the abolition ranks: quiet men and ranters, broad-minded thinkers and narrow bigots, passive resistants and direct actionists, respecters of law and order and some whose sole allegiance was to "a higher law," exhibitionists and men of humble modesty. Eccentricity was prevalent among them, but their one common and emblematic quality was unselfish consecration to a high ideal. They were dangerous, to be sure, dangerous to counterfeit democracy, dangerous to all institutions and concepts that denied a portion of mankind its natural birthright.

But to what purpose do we seek to justify them? In the case of Theodore Weld, at least, the man's life speaks for itself.

ACKNOWLEDGMENTS

The *writing of any biographical or* historical work has come to be almost a coöperative undertaking, and the author soon finds himself no less impressed by the number of persons to whom he has come under obligation than by their eagerness to help him.

The task of gathering material for this book was materially lightened by the kindness of Paul A. Carmack of the Department of Speech, Ohio State University. He has recently completed a doctoral dissertation on Theodore Weld as an orator and schoolmaster, and in the course of his investigations most graciously sent me copies of his notes to supplement my own researches.

The major collection of Weld letters is now at the William L. Clements Library at the University of Michigan. There Randolph G. Adams, the director, and Colton Storm, his assistant, not only gave me access to this material, but rendered every courtesy, as did also Miss Margaret Larson, who is in immediate charge of the collection.

In 1934 the American Historical Association sponsored the publication of a two-volume selection of these Weld letters covering the period from 1822 to 1844, through the instrumentality of the Beveridge Fund and under the editorship of Professor Dwight L. Dumond and their discoverer, the late Professor Gilbert H. Barnes (*Letters of Theodore Dwight Weld, Angelina Grimké Weld and Sarah Grimké, 1822–1844*). Guy Stanton Ford, executive secretary of the American Historical Association, kindly gave me permission to quote from these published selections, as well as from Dwight L. Dumond, ed., *Letters of James Gillespie Birney, 1831–1857*, published under the same auspices; and during my visit to Ann Arbor, Professor Dumond drew upon his intimate knowledge of Weld and the whole abolition movement in imparting useful information. Later he also sent me pictures of Weld's father and mother from his files.

David C. Mearns, assistant librarian and director of the reference department of the Library of Congress, accorded me every facility for research at that great repository, and Percy Powell of the division of manuscripts was both helpful and hospitable. William P. Kilroy and John J. DePorry assisted in my search for material, and others of the library staff also rendered willing aid.

When I wrote to F. Lauriston Bullard of Melrose Highlands, Massachusetts, for the name of someone who might help me in obtaining material in Boston and vicinity, Mr. Bullard, with a generosity which is not unusual in him but is appreciated all the more by reason of that fact, took it upon himself to check for Weld letters at the Harvard Library, the Boston Public Library, and the Massachusetts Historical Society.

At Oberlin College I profited from an interview with Professor Robert S. Fletcher, and was most graciously piloted through the rich resources of the Oberlin Library by Julian S. Fowler, librarian, and Mary C. Venn. At the Virginia Library, McCormick Theological Seminary, Chicago, John F. Lyons, librarian, and Miss Eleanor Wells were helpful beyond the call of duty, and similar courtesies were extended by Russell H. Anderson, director, and Mrs. Alene Lowe White, librarian, at the Western Reserve Historical Society; by Mrs. Curtis B. Lyon, librarian of the Hyde Park Branch of the Boston Public Library; by Frances

W. Lauman, assistant reference librarian of the Cornell University Library; Foster M. Palmer, reference assistant at the Harvard College Library; Dorothea Abbott of the Norfolk County Probate Court, Dedham, Massachusetts; and Ruth Nichols of the Illinois State Library, Springfield. Hazel C. Wolf of Peoria, Illinois, granted me a preview of her comments on Weld in her forthcoming book on the martyr complex in the abolitionists.

Margaret A. Flint, reference librarian at the Illinois State Historical Library, gave her customary willing assistance in the use of that library's facilities and obtained rare books for me on interlibrary loans. Anna L. Cladek, librarian of the Perth Amboy (New Jersey) Public Library, sent me copies of much useful material from that institution. Mrs. Dorothy B. Porter, supervisor of the Negro collection, Howard University Library, Washington, D. C., and her assistant, Mrs. Constance R. Barber, enabled me to obtain items from newspaper files.

Suggestions regarding the whereabouts of information of one sort or another came from Marion Dolores Bonzi and Lloyd Dunlap of the Abraham Lincoln Association, Springfield, Illinois; from Mrs. H. C. Borchardt of Alpaugh, California, granddaughter of Marcus Spring, with whom the reader will become acquainted in due time; from the late Lloyd Lewis of the Newberry Library, Chicago; and from William B. Hesseltine, professor of American history at the University of Wisconsin.

Robert L. Huttner of Chicago combed his superb collection of abolition material for letters and pictures. Professor Quincy Wright of the University of Chicago sent me a biography and pictures of his great-grandfather, Elizur Wright.

The manuscript has benefited from the careful scrutiny of my friends Roy P. Basler and George W. Bunn, Jr., both of whom have made valuable suggestions regarding content and form. The enthusiasm and critical judgment of Albert and Alice Kurrus helped to improve the earlier chapters. My wife has read and listened to what must have been the point of weariness, and has undergone without complaint the usual hardships of an author's spouse. Professor Jeter A. Isely, of Princeton University, and Mrs. Isely gave helpful criticism and advice. Carl Sandburg suggested stylistic improvements.

Nira Irwin and James N. Adams typed the manuscript with expertness and alertness for my slips.

With the benefit of such ample and ungrudging assistance, I have no one but myself to blame for mistakes.

Benjamin P. Thomas

Springfield, Illinois
April 1950

THEODORE

WELD

CRUSADER

FOR

FREEDOM

1

A MAN OF

RECKLESS

RIGHTEOUSNESS

*t was almost midnight as the stage-*coach lurched and slithered along the miry road eight miles east of Columbus. The driving rain had stopped; and the gusty south-west wind, which had brought Ohio a mid-February thaw, was working back to the north. Already the air had a tangy bite, and the four-horse team snorted steam as the driver pulled up short at the ford of Alum Creek. Ordinarily a shallow, peaceful stream, the creek was now a torrent from the long-continued rain and melting snow. As the driver and his helper swung down stiffly from their seat, they were joined by the two passengers, one a tall, spare white man, the other a brawny Negro.

The four men examined the slope and footing of the bank, then tried to pierce the darkness above the sucking eddies, seeking where the wagon ruts emerged on the opposite bank. The driver decided to risk a crossing, and the passengers, yielding to his judgment with some misgivings, clambered back into the coach. The driver and his helper climbed up to their seat, and with shouts, curses and slashing whip urged the nervous horses forward. The reluctant animals pulled, then braced, as they skidded down the treacherous slope with the coach plunging down behind them. The full force of the current struck them; but they were powerful and accustomed to deep fording; lunging and driving through the swirling water, they pulled out safely on the farther bank. The stage regained the rutted road and rocked on, until, some three miles farther on, the meandering torrent blocked the road again.

Once more the driver flogged the horses in. But the water was deeper here. Almost at once the animals were swimming and the stagecoach was afloat. The power of the current swept horses and coach downstream, and as the two lead horses wrenched around suddenly in an effort to regain the shallow water of the ford the coach tipped dangerously, then went completely over on its side, tossing drivers and passengers into the flood. The water was bitterly cold.

Instinctively, the white passenger drew a deep breath as he felt himself hurled from the coach. But as he broke the surface of the water coming up, he was horrified to find himself directly in the path of the snorting horses, and so close that their breath was in his face. To prevent their swimming over him, he grasped the bit of the nearest horse, but a sharp blow from its hoofs made him let go and sink again. Once more he came up, this time between the lead horses and the wheel horses, and again he was knocked under by a paralyzing kick. Rising again, he was still entangled with the beasts, which were thrashing, plunging and screaming in frenzied fright. At last, somehow, he was free of them, and thinking only of keeping clear of the dangerous hoofs, he struck out downstream with all his might.

But now new danger threatened. Already he was benumbed with cold; his water-logged boots and sodden clothes and overcoat made swimming difficult. As the racing water carried him along, he saw no place where he could land along the steep, dark banks. Working his way toward shore, he grasped desperately at a projecting root, only to feel his hand slip slowly off its slimy surface. Once more he was whirled out into the channel, bruised by submerged rocks, conscious of the increasing intensity of the cold and the weight of his soaked garments.

Fighting with waning strength to keep afloat, he worked out of his overcoat and boots; and then ahead he spied a fallen tree, its branches lying in the water. With his last remaining strength he fought to reach it, trying to push across stream before the current carried him by. He clutched the tree, hung on, finally worked his way to shore along its branches, and then lay there exhausted, his body half in, half out of the water, on a little shelf of land below the steep bank. Between his sucking gasps for breath he called for help, realizing as he sank into unconsciousness that his cries could never penetrate the forest walls that hemmed him in.

Later, in recounting his adventure, he gave thanks to God for the strength that enabled him to reach the bank; and he saw God's mercy in his deliverance at the hands of three men, who, living in a log cabin on the opposite shore some eighty rods from where he was, had heard his cries and searched until they found him. Theirs was the only habitation along that stream for miles.[1]

It was characteristic of Theodore Dwight Weld to draw increased devotion to God from such an experience. Already he thought of himself as God's instrument; and now, in thanks for his miraculous deliverance, he would devote himself with even greater consecration to God's purposes. This event, in fact, was to provide a major propulsion of his career. It left him with a sense of indestructibility, a belief in an omnipotent Providence constantly watching over his personal welfare, and a feeling of indebtedness to God that was beyond his power ever fully to repay.

Twenty-eight years old at the time of this mishap, Weld had

been born in Hampton, Connecticut, on November 23, 1803. His father, Ludovicus Weld, a graduate of Harvard, was pastor of the Congregational Church at Hampton for thirty years. His mother's maiden name was Elizabeth Clark. Both of his grandfathers were also ministers, and among his forebears were Dwights, Edwardses, and Hutchinsons.[2] He had three elder brothers, Lewis, Charles, and Ezra, and a younger sister, Cornelia.[3]

As a boy, young Weld was daring to the point of recklessness. He delighted to run, jump, wrestle, leap fences and chasms, dive into deep water from high rocks or overhanging trees. He seemed to hold a strange communion with the elements; the rolling thunder that frightened other children touched his soul like music. In his later years he recalled how, before he was six years old, his mother had tingled his legs with switches many times because, whenever a thunderstorm came up, he would rush out into it and run whooping and hallooing through the fields like a wild Indian. Before he was ten, he had accumulated an uncommon list of injuries—a broken hand, a broken foot, at least four dislocated bones, the cords of a finger severed, and an eye almost hooked out of its socket.

This recklessness stayed with him as he matured. In his middle age he confessed, "*I must cut capers*"; and every day the chance afforded he would seek a secluded spot where he might "jump and hop and scream like a loon and run on all fours and wrestle and throw stones and play 'tag' and 'hide and seek' and 'blind man's buff' and all those childish rompings." [4]

Too occupied with higher thoughts to care about his personal appearance, Weld was a slovenly man of slouching gait with unblacked boots and unbrushed coat. His hair was as unkempt as a hermit's, and he allowed his beard to grow until his friends begged him to shave for decency's sake, or until the discomfort of its chafing against his collar brought him to his razor in self-defense.

"Every morning, I put my head into cold water half a dozen

times," he wrote when confessing his personal idiosyncrasies, "then frictionize it with a stiff hair brush after wiping it dry and then let it straggle in all directions like the quills of a porcupine." [5]

Added to these peculiarities was a strange defect of memory. Weld could not remember people; he had difficulty keeping account of the days of the week or even the months. "Many a time when sitting in my room I have got up and gone to the window to determine by the face of nature what season of the year it was," he admitted. He searched his room for his pen, when he had it gripped in his teeth, or for his knife, when it was in his hand. He forgot to wind his watch; and, paring an apple, he might throw it away, then several minutes later be surprised to find the parings clutched in his hand. "I very often swing like a pendulum in a dreamy totally abstracted revery," he said, "don't hear questions that are asked me, and sometimes I am told that I go on making a sort of inarticulate um, um, um, um, as a sort of unconscious mechanical assent to someone talking to me, and keep this up for five minutes perhaps without knowing or even hearing a single word he has said." [6]

Weld's face reflected the reformer's conscience. Meeting him for the first time, strangers were invariably impressed with his stern expression. To one he suggested a pirate; another was reminded of the Inquisitor-General. Weld himself recalled how a child of four once came into a room where he was, and, after one glance at him, ran screaming to her mother. His hair and eyes and skin were dark. His nose was thin, high-bridged, and twisted slightly to the right. The ridge above his right eye socket was disfigured with a peculiar dent. Heavy lines ran upward from his mouth. The skin hung loose and wrinkled on his neck. An artist, to whom he went with a friend to have a miniature painted, remarked that he could easily depict the outline of Weld's face, but the expression would be difficult to reproduce. "Its SEVERITY," he said, "is like a streak of lightning." Once as Weld sat on a platform waiting to speak, a woman in the audience whispered to her neighbor: "Mercy, I hope that young man never gets married. I should pity his wife. He'll break her heart." [7]

But it was only in repose that his face repelled. Let it assume expression, and at once the beauty of the soul within shone through. To know him was to feel the warmth of his benignity, to sense his charm, to yield to his persuasiveness. His voice was rich, full, mellow; his presence breathed an almost godlike power. When Weld visited John Greenleaf Whittier, it seemed to the poet's shy maiden sister, Elizabeth, "as if an archangel had visited our home," and to her diary she confided: "His smile has been haunting me . . . ever since he left us." [8]

Scion of Puritan forebears, Weld grew up under the rigorous Puritan discipline which relied on Biblical precepts and a stern, dogmatic theology to thwart the ever-present beguilements of sin. From his boyhood he was infused with an unwavering sense of right and wrong, and with that inquisitive and intrusive morality which insists that one must not be satisfied to purge oneself of sin, but must also try to ransom others from Satan's clutches. There was the customary reverence for the Bible and the Sabbath, the resolute sense of duty, the mistrust of worldly pleasures and diversions, all intensified in Weld's case by reason of his father's calling and the family's ecclesiastical traditions. But there was also warm parental affection, and the questing intellectuality that characterized the home of the New England clerical scholar.

It was the sort of upbringing that makes for quick maturity, and enables apt youths to assume adult responsibilities. At the age of fourteen, Theodore took full charge of a hundred-acre farm, thereby earning enough money to enter Phillips Academy, now Phillips Andover, in his sixteenth year.[9]

He had a resistless urge to get ahead, and in his second year of residence, aspiring to do two years' work in one, he would toil all day and late into the night, then sprint up Andover Hill and down again to put his blood in circulation before retiring. Even his tough young body was unequal to such a regimen, and suddenly his eyesight failed. He was told he might regain it in seven years if he rested regularly in a dark room, and later his physician advised him to travel. But he had no money of his own, and his father was rearing a family on a salary of three hundred dollars a year. Baffled and discouraged, he pondered what he should do until he remembered a course of lectures on the science of mnemonics, or art of improving the memory, which he had attended at Phillips. All the more impressed by reason of his own strange mental lapses, he had pursued the "science" further on his own, until now he believed he was sufficiently well versed to teach it.

His father doubted that a boy of seventeen could command an audience, but Weld mastered the nomenclature of mnemonics, prepared a lecture, and, borrowing the family horse and chaise, set out to try the experiment at Colchester, some fifteen miles from home. His face was preternaturally hairy for a youth's and he left off shaving until his bearded visage looked mature beyond his years. At his father's suggestion he wrote out his talk. But it would seem strange for one supposedly adept in memory training to read his message, so at the last minute he left his manuscript at home and spoke without even a note. His success was greater than he hoped, for after paying all expenses he returned with twenty dollars in his pocket.[10]

Soon he was off to try his luck at Hartford, where Dr. Thomas Gallaudet, principal of the American Asylum and later to be famous for his work in behalf of the deaf, was so impressed that he gave Weld letters of recommendation to leading New England clergymen, among them Lyman Beecher, then pastor at Litchfield, Connecticut. Scanning Gallaudet's testimonial, Beecher told young Weld, "Go ahead. I'll risk you," and was astonished at the young man's platform presence and power with words. Weld's father now consented to allow Theodore to set out on his own, and he lectured at Miss Emma Willard's Female Seminary at Troy, New York, and at Albany, Monticello, Niagara, Utica, and Poughkeepsie.[11] From New York his route led through Ohio, then back across Pennsylvania and Maryland to Washington, D. C., where he visited the Capitol, gazed in youthful awe at Henry Clay, and listened to a thundering speech by Daniel Webster. Turning south, he ranged through Virginia and North Carolina.[12]

Weld's practice was to post an advance announcement of his lectures signed by respected local citizens who had been persuaded to vouch for him by the testimonials he sent ahead. His terms were twelve shillings for a course of four lectures, and subscribers were requested to affix their names to his announcement. If as many as forty subscribed, Weld gave a fifth lecture free. No payment was required until the course was finished. Sometimes he found it necessary to give the first lecture without charge in order to draw a crowd.

Weld was gone from home three years. And if he brought back little money, he had at least proved himself to be a speaker of uncommon natural talent, adroit with words and phrases, and convincing despite his own traits of forgetfulness that must so often have been in startling contrast with what he taught.

On this tour he had his first contact with slavery. He had always had a kindly feeling for the Negro, ever since the time when, as a seven-year-old boy, he had begged permission to sit in school beside a little colored lad who was mistreated by the teacher and shunned and ridiculed by the other students.[13] A boy must possess unusual moral courage to stand against the crowd and allow his latent sympathies to assert themselves in opposition to juvenile intolerance. But moral courage was Weld's by cultural inheritance, and the human sympathy that he displayed so early was enlivened by a firsthand view of slavery. During his sojourn in the South he was convinced of the wrongfulness of holding fellow human creatures in bondage.

His eyes were much improved by the time he arrived back home, and in 1825, when his family moved to Fabius, New York, he entered Hamilton College, located at Clinton, about forty miles away. Having demonstrated his speaking talents, he now tried his hand with the pen. Attending the commencement exercises at Hamilton, he wrote an account for a newspaper, signing his effort with a Latin pseudonym, "Sylvaticus," in keeping with a custom of the time. He hated "puffing," he declared. Every new book, every speech, every anniversary celebration was launched with a puff. "Puffing is the rage of the time." His account would not be dulcified by flummery, he warned. One speech was plain and chaste, he said, but pitched in a harsh key. Another speaker displayed energy but chose a hackneyed subject. A third man showed insufferable conceit. The gestures of a fourth orator were almost spasms. A colloquy on steam was so forced that it burst the boiler.[14]

Weld's comments manifest no little adolescent cynicism and conceit. No doubt the stripling master of the art of mnemonics could have outdone them all.

Weld had been at Hamilton only a few weeks when his life's course was altered by a turn of fate that brought him under the spell of Charles Grandison Finney, the moving spirit in a great revival that was sweeping upstate New York. Trained to be a lawyer, Finney had been converted by George Washington Gale, a Presbyterian minister, who founded Oneida Institute and Knox College. Joining the church and attaining ordination as a preacher, Finney soon earned fame as an itinerant evangelist. He was a tall, grave man, dressed in a natty unclerical gray suit, with a mop of light hair hanging over his forehead and great staring eyes through which his very soul seemed to peer forth. His mien was dignified, his voice loud yet melodious, and to the usual histrionic talents of the frontier preacher he added the lawyer's logic.

Finney's sermons never lasted less than an hour, and he could hold his audience spellbound for two or three times that long when the spirit was upon him. Depicting the glory or the terrors of the world to come, he strummed his auditors' emotions with a voice that ranged from pathos to denunciation. As he faced the side gallery and suddenly wheeled around with outflung arm, the audience on the side toward which he whirled would duck involuntarily; and as he pointed his long forefinger at the ceiling and slowly brought it down, tracing the descent of a sinner to perdition, his hearers in the rear of the building would rise unconsciously to their feet, the better to see the lost soul descend into the imaginary hell in front of the pulpit.[15]

"Ye generation of vipers, how can ye escape the damnation of hell?" would be his challenge; and as he warmed to his work he would address himself to individual members of his congregation, calling upon the Lord to "smite that wicked man, that hardened sinner," to send "trouble, anguish and affliction into his bed chamber this night," or to "shake him over hell." Only the most callous reprobate could resist this personal assault, and as Finney laid about him, the "anxious seat" in front of the pulpit would gradually fill with sinners who were ready to give up. The more conservative clergy of the East deplored Finney's radical methods, charging that a minister had no right to shake his fist in people's faces and shout "You lie! You are going to hell!" [16] Finney denied that he ever used such threats, and claimed he was blamed for the practices of preachers who tried to ape him. But he did put awful emphasis on "hell," "damnation," and "devil," and even years later, when he had given up evangelism and accepted a regular pastorate, he rebuked his congregation one hot Sabbath afternoon by calling out in chiding tones: "Now brethren, how can I preach the gospel to you, how can the Holy Spirit work in your hearts when you come here at half past 2 o'clock and nod over your pudding and milk?"[17]

In his agonizing earnestness of prayer, Finney often spoke to God with a familiarity that seemed to conservative clergymen to border on irreverence. The Reverend Asahel Nettleton was moved to lament: "Seven years ago about two thousand souls were hopefully born into the Kingdom, in this vicinity, with comparative stillness. But the times have altered. The Kingdom of God now cometh with great observation." [18] It was surely true that Finney did not capture souls with guile and snares; he rode them down with irresistible charges.

Finney's meetings usually lasted three or four days, but sometimes he protracted them for weeks. New converts were enlisted in his "Holy Band," and sent forth into the audience to assist him by personal intercession. Although a cynic once said that Finney's converts were more anxious to escape hell than to serve God,[19] yet the essence of his message was that true holiness demands unselfish benevolence and that salvation comes not merely by faith and divine grace but also through good works. In every community where Finney labored he left behind groups of young men, "overflowing with benevolence for unsaved mankind," obsessed with a duty to reform the world.

Beginning his revivals in Oneida County, not far from Weld's new home, Finney soon set the region ablaze. The lowest grogshop in Evans' Mills became a place of regular prayer meetings. At Rome a prominent merchant, coming under Finney's spell, fell out of his seat as though shot. At "Sodom," a crossroads hamlet so called because it was deemed hopelessly degenerate, Finney felt "the Lord let me loose on them in a wonderful manner." At a schoolhouse in the neighborhood he tried to lead his congregation in a hymn; but the people were so unused to spiritual exercises that their discords almost drove the valiant Finney from the meetinghouse. He clasped both hands to his ears and stuck it out, and when the horrible dissonance had stopped, he knelt in prayer, interceding with such effect that people fell off the seats and howled and shrieked for mercy in the aisles. So terrific was the bedlam that Finney had to scream as he adjured them: "You are not in hell yet; and now let me direct you to Christ." The meeting lasted through the night, and in the morning several converts, still too weak to walk alone, were carried home to clear the room for school. "Wonderful outpourings of the Holy Spirit" were reported everywhere. Whole towns were converted. Courts adjourned for lack of business. Jails stood with open doors. Convictions were "very pungent and deep." The Albany Synod reported that "the theatre has been deserted, the tavern sanctified; blasphemy has been silenced, and infidelity confounded." Six years after Finney's visit it was still impossible to organize a dancing party at Gouverneur, and circuses shunned the territory. Ministers from nearby towns came to hear Finney and went home to spread the word. Some three thousand persons were rumored to have experienced conversion. It was as though a reign of terror had seized upon the ungodly.[20]

At nearby Hamilton College, Weld deplored the unseemly excitement. "My father is a real minister of the Gospel," he declared, "grave and courteous, and an honor to his profession. This man is not a minister, and I will never acknowledge him as such." At every chance he warned his fellow students against the impostor Finney.

Pressing north through Antwerp, Gouverneur, DeKalb, and then south again to Westernville and Rome, Finney came at last to Utica, where it chanced that Weld was visiting his aunt. A devout admirer of Finney, she lived next door to the Reverend Samuel Clark Aiken, with whom Finney was staying and at whose church he was holding forth. Distressed at Theodore's recreancy, "Aunt Clark" urged him at least to go and hear Finney, but he spurned her every appeal. Finally she explained that Finney always preached in the afternoon and evening, while Aiken conducted the morning services, and if Theodore would have nothing to do with Finney, he might at least accompany her to Aiken's meeting. Little suspecting duplicity on the part of one as saintly as his aunt, Theodore agreed to go, whereupon she immediately rushed next door to confide the fact of his coming to Aiken and Finney. Weld was a prize well worth the taking, for he was influential with the young men of the county, and his strictures upon Finney had induced a goodly number of them to resist conversion.

As Weld marched down the aisle of the church, his aunt opened the door of the pew and motioned for him to enter first. Then she and several other ladies followed, shutting him in. Aiken opened the meeting. But after the preliminaries, it was

Finney who rose to preach. When he announced as his text "One sinner destroyeth much good," Theodore reached for his hat; but his aunt and the other ladies bowed in prayer with their heads on the pew in front of them, thus rendering escape impossible. "I gave up," Weld recalled, "and resigned myself to my fate; and then for an hour, he just held me up on his toasting fork before that audience."

Weld took it manfully; and he still had no suspicion of Aunt Clark, when she innocently commented on the way home: "Why, Mr. Finney *never* preached in the forenoon before, but *always* in the afternoon."

The next day, however, Weld poured out his indignation to a group of loungers at a store, and when aroused he was "mighty with words." Someone slipped away to tell Finney what was happening, and as Weld's denunciation reached ever more marvelous heights, Finney himself strode in. He tried to interrupt, but Weld shouted him down, abusing him with every epithet to which he could lay tongue. The store filled up with a crowd of shocked or marveling spectators which soon spread into the street, until at last, realizing what a spectacle he was making, Weld desisted and went home.

But Theodore was a kindly man at heart, and, admitting to himself the enormity of his censures, he was overcome with remorse. He resolved to ask Finney's pardon, and went next door to the Aikens' and knocked. The hired girl let him in, and he waited in the hallway for Finney to come downstairs. The light was dim, and Finney did not recognize him till he reached the bottom step. Then he stopped short and exclaimed: "Ah! Is it not enough? Have you followed a minister of the Lord Jesus to his own door to abuse him?"

Weld started to speak. But by this time Finney had seen the expression on his face. Both men went to their knees; and Finney sobbed as he prayed.[21] Thenceforth there was no more devout disciple of Finney than Theodore Weld, who described the evangelist as "that modern Paul" and regarded him as towering

above all other preachers "to an overshadowing height."[22]
For the remainder of the summer Weld worked with Finney as a
member of his "Holy Band," accompanying him to Auburn,
Troy, and numerous other places. Interceding with the waver-
ers, Weld helped in many conversions. And to Finney's innova-
tions he added another when he urged women to speak in
meeting. This was unheard of in that day, except among the
Quakers, and it profaned the Apostle Paul's injunction that
women should be silent in mixed assemblages. Finney was
blamed for flouting the apostolic admonition, and, all unaware of
Weld's complicity, he pleaded that the unseemly boldness of
the women was a spontaneous phenomenon, amazing even to
him.[23] Weld could scarcely suspect that the assertion of
woman's right to speak in public meetings would one day be one
source from which would flower an aggressive demand for female
equality.

Weld worked with such unremitting vigor that his health
became impaired. His brother Charles was unwell, too, so in
the winter of 1827 Theodore left Finney, and the two young
men shipped on a whaling vessel bound for Labrador. Weld
worked before the mast for several months and came back
sinewy and fit.[24]

At Utica, Weld had become acquainted with Charles Stuart, a
retired British army officer. Born in Jamaica, Stuart had served
in the East India Company's forces for thirteen years. He had
risen to the rank of captain, when, according to one story, he
was ordered to make a night attack on a group of unarmed
Indian natives. He refused on the ground that such an assault
would be sheer butchery, whereupon he was court-martialed;
but the court decided he must have had a touch of sun, and sent
him home. Another story has him earning the ill will of his
colonel by rebuking him for breaking the Sabbath, and resigning
when his offended superior dragooned him at every chance.[25]

In 1819 Stuart went to Amherstburg, in Canada, and eventually moved to Utica to be principal of a boys' school. A bachelor, his paternal instincts found expression in good works. During vacations he preached temperance, traveling through the country at his own expense and also distributing Bibles and religious tracts. He was looked upon as "a true man of God"—Weld called him "a perfect being"—but he was also so eccentric that some people thought him crazy. Winter and summer he wore a Scotch plaid frock, with a cape reaching nearly to his elbows. He was as tender-hearted as a woman, and so strongly attracted to children that he often stopped to romp and play with them. Like Weld, he had come under Finney's influence and enlisted in his "Holy Band." Despite the disparity in their ages, Weld and Stuart were mutually attracted from the day they met. Stuart's fondness for the younger man might have struck a casual observer as an unnatural attraction, for, like many religious enthusiasts before and since, Stuart expressed his spiritual yearnings in terms of earthly affection. His advice to Weld was in the style of love letters, and their relationship was almost rapturous. But there was no perversion in it. With Stuart it was a passionate obsession with Weld's spiritual advancement. With Weld it was unbounded admiration for a man of Stuart's character. Stuart also fancied himself to be in love with Weld's sister Cornelia, but his feelings were not reciprocated, and he concluded later that they came merely of "a foolish and romantic attraction."

In the summer of 1829 Stuart returned to England to serve the British antislavery cause, and as the sinfulness of slavery impressed itself on his conscience he wrote to Weld, begging him to enlist in the "sacred cause" of Negro emancipation. Stuart was grateful that God did not treat the white race according to its deserts. He must have exercised great patience, Stuart thought, to restrain Himself from "breaking up the earth beneath our feet, and dashing us all into sudden hell," for what had been done to the Negro. Stuart sent Weld copies of British antislavery pamphlets, several of which he wrote himself, imploring his "prayerful perusal" of them. And as Weld followed his admonition, his mind and heart were won.[26] His reforming bent took more positive antislavery direction.

At Stuart's instigation Weld left Hamilton and enrolled at Oneida Institute at Whitesboro, New York, his mind made up to be a preacher. Stuart sent him money for expenses from time to time, requiring in return only a quarterly report of Weld's spiritual progress.

Oneida was a "manual labor institution," where each student paid part of his expenses by working on the school farm. It had originated through the efforts of the Reverend George W. Gale, who, having impaired his own health through hard study, had regained it through farm work. He began to instruct students on his farm, keeping them fit by farm labor; and noting his achievements, the Oneida Presbytery took over his project with its 114-acre farm, and installed him as president of its school. By the time that Weld enrolled at the academy it had sixty students, the limit of its capacity, and so popular was the new idea of manual labor education that some six hundred applicants were being turned away.[27]

Oneida was not the first school of its sort; the system of manual labor education had originated in Switzerland and was tried in other European countries before being introduced in the United States. Here its supposed benefits—improvement of student health and reduction of the cost of education—were especially needed in theological seminaries, and following Oneida's lead, many of these institutions adopted the idea. At Andover Theological Seminary the trustees built a workshop to accommodate seventy-five students. Maine Wesleyan Seminary had a farm of 140 acres as well as a shop. Theological schools at Auburn, New York; Wilmington, Delaware; Maryville, Tennessee; and Danville, Kentucky, fell in with the plan, as did also colleges such as Bowdoin, Waterville (now Colby) and Middlebury, and academies like the Woodbridge School at South Hadley, Massachusetts, and Phillips at Andover. In all these

schools, however, manual labor was optional; at Oneida it was compulsory.[28]

Tuition at Oneida was $5.50 per quarter, payable in cash, but for twenty-one hours' labor per week a student could earn his board. "My sons are at a school where all the students work on a farm three hours every day, & nearly support themselves by their labor," wrote an observing parent, the rich New York merchant Lewis Tappan, describing Oneida Institute to his brother. "They live very simply and happily. I attended the annual exercises & the students acquitted themselves well. These institutions are multiplying, & the time is not far distant I hope when physical and intellectual education will go on together & be considered inseparable. It has been the disgrace of this country that education has made most men ashamed of manual labor. I was delighted to see young men, who a few hours previously were reaping, mowing, milking etc come onto the platform before a large assembly & deliver their compositions in latin and English—orations, poems, colloquys etc with ease and dignity." With evident pride, Tappan told his brother how his older boy, William, had charge of fourteen pigs and must feed them at four o'clock every morning, carrying their swill in pails hung from a yoke on his shoulders.[29]

All the Oneida students began their labors at 4 A.M. It was no place for sluggards. The rising hour, meals, classes, and work periods were announced by sounding a horn. The day opened with devotions, and some classes met at five o'clock, an hour before breakfast. The diet was frugal. "We have griddle cakes and molasses once a week," a student wrote, "rice and molasses once—hasty pudding once. These we have in the morning. Twice in the week we have codfish and potatoes for dinner. For the remainder we have bread and butter and bread and milk." A student was delegated to read aloud at mealtime while the others ate. Business was also transacted at table. Declamations and formal debates were held each week. Not a moment was lost from rising until bedtime.[30]

As one of the older students—he was now twenty-five—Weld was monitor of the milking class and had charge of some thirty cows. Each morning he must be up in time to have the milk loaded on the wagons, ready to start for Utica, by daybreak. At first the institution had no barn, and Weld asked a neighboring farmer to allow the students to cut some timber from his woodlot. Cynical of the boys' capacity for work, the farmer agreed to give them all the timber they could cut, whereupon Weld organized his milking crew with saws and axes and descended upon the woodlot like a holocaust. Lashing their logs together to form a great raft, the students floated them downstream to the Institute, where they built not only a barn but also several sheds.[31]

Even more basic to Oneida than the manual labor principle were piety and service to mankind. The school was surcharged with high moral purpose, and every Sunday the older students fanned out through the surrounding countryside, often walking several miles, to preach or teach Sunday School. Weld was not only ardent in this sort of work, in addition he was often away for weeks at a time delivering temperance lectures. As a matter of fact, he was so useful he had little time for his books. Oneida was in critical need of money, and President Gale, well aware of Weld's persuasive oratory, sent him forth on frequent money-raising tours.[32] "The Lord has given Brother Weld and this Institution great favor among the people at Rochester," wrote Gale to Finney when Weld returned from one of these campaigns.[32] But Weld's mother and Charles Stuart both warned that he was occupied with "too much serving," and his father implored him to renounce extracurricular activities and complete his ministerial course.[34]

Already, however, Weld was caught in the reform whirl. Causes of every sort decoyed him. A controversial moral issue of the times was the conveyance of mail on Sunday, and one day when Weld returned to Whitesboro from a two-weeks' temperance trip he learned that the local advocates of Sunday mail

had called a meeting at the courthouse that night. Weld inquired if it was open to all, and finding that it was, he and a few students of kindred mind attended. Weld asked permission to speak. He was allowed the floor. But when he spoke for strict Sabbath observance, and it was ascertained that he was a ministerial student, a hostile clamor broke out. Someone shouted, "We did not come here to discuss priestcraft, but to put it down!" Another cried, "I motion that priests work on highways and do military duties"— a protest against the practice of exempting ministers from such unpopular tasks. "I motion they stop preaching," a third man shouted. "I motion someone knock him down," cried another. Weld and his reform neophytes stirred up such hot resentment that they were chased back to the Institute and obliged to hide in a woodhouse.[35]

Weld was a convincing temperance speaker.[36] Fortified with statistics of crime, poverty, and lunacy, sometimes he directed his appeal to drunkards, urging them to reform. On other occasions, abstainers would be his target as he encouraged them to be steadfast and to join temperance societies as a means of concentrating the force of public opinion behind the temperance movement. Again, he spoke to vendors, challenging them to answer if their product had ever made a community more peaceful or happy. Against this group a favorite technique of Weld's was to pose rhetorical objections to their renouncing the liquor business. Did the dealer argue that he must support his family? Weld reminded him of his paramount duty to God. Did he plead that he never sold to drunkards? Weld compared him to a man who owned a collection of poisonous snakes. This man was careful to keep his serpents from biting anyone already infected with their venom, but he flung them with indifference into a throng of persons who had never suffered their bite.

If anyone reasoned that liquor was not altogether harmful, Weld retorted that neither was an eruption of Mt. Aetna. Its lava replenished the soil. But at what an inordinate cost in life and property! Sometimes Weld supplicated the women, ap-

pealing to their pity for the victims of hard drink and beseeching them to bring their subtle influence to bear in the cause of
reform.[37] At Rochester, where he spoke in December, 1830, a
group of eight or ten liquor dealers were persuaded to renounce
the liquor business; and at the Oriskany Woolen Manufactory his
lectures were productive of so much good that the manager and
a number of the employees presented him with a broadcloth
suit.[38] Weld's suggested solution of the liquor problem contemplated no compulsion other than the force of public opinion
and personal influence. It was merely for persons to abstain from
the use of alcoholic beverages themselves and to convince others
of the virtues of abstemiousness. And if it seemed overly simple,
experience has demonstrated that these may well be the only
sanctions that will work.

On March 22, 1831, the *Western Recorder* noted that Weld
was at Utica, where his temperance speeches were drawing
"throngs" to the First Presbyterian Church. A Baptist editor
was so impressed by Weld's forensics that he wrote a summary
of what he heard. He wished the whole population of the Union
might have been there. Not that Weld presented any new facts.
He used the same stale facts the public had heard for years. His
genius lay in his technique—his skill with words and power of
imagery.

"All have read again and again of the 30,000 drunkards which
annually fall victims, in the United States, to intemperance,"
Weld's clerical admirer observed, "of the 200,000 paupers, the
inmates of the alms-houses and poorhouses from this vice; of
the 20,000 convicts, secured in the cells and dungeons of our
prisons; and of the 1500 maniacs, chained in our asylums; but
comparatively few have seen this army mustered, and marched in
regular review. This was done by Mr. W. The mighty host, more
than 200,000 strong, was picked from the gutters and sewers,
the groceries and grog-shops, poor houses, prisons and asylums,
and marshalled with their bloated and shocking visages, their
staggering gait, their filthy and tattered habiliments, their fettered

limbs, and their clanking chains. The first grand division was 150,000 paupers; next in order came the 20,000 convicts, hand-cuffed, from the dungeons and cells of our prisons; then 1500 raving maniacs brought up the rear; and besides the whole, on the field of review, were piled up 30,000 dead men, to complete the horrid assemblage.

"This made up one part of the picture.—Another no less startling succeeded. The extended grave of 30,000 drunkards, annual victims, was then opened before us, and they arrayed on its verge; and immediately behind them, the whole army of the intemperate and temperate, rank after rank, was arranged in accurate gradation, on to the merest sippers. At the close of the year, those in front were tumbled into the grave before them; and the next rank behind were marched up to take their places; and each posterior rank compelled to make the like advance. The next year, another 30,000 were swept into the tomb, and the host was seen in regular advance; and so on, year after year, until the self-secure sippers were beheld occupying the rank in front, on the verge of the drunkard's grave." [39]

It must have been a fearsome and macabre scene, and the man who could conjure up such grisly spectacles found his services in constant demand. Weld's reputation had already reached the point that he was urged to take a church at Troy, to help with a revival at Homer, and to accept a pastorate at New Orleans.[40] But he felt himself deficient in theology, and he held the pastoral office in such high honor that he would accept no permanent appointment until sure that he was adequately prepared.

Charles Grandison Finney, Weld's patron during these early years, was proud of Weld's success; but at the same time he had some misgivings. Weld showed an inclination to conceit, and his personal habits left much to be desired. "If you don't take care I fear you will be spoiled by an idea of your own importance," Finney warned, at the same time admonishing Weld that cleanliness and attention to "the decencies of life" were virtues that ministerial students must not ignore. "You know I am not recommending the stiffness of Scholastic manners," Finney explained; "from such buckram refinement the Lord deliver ministers. Nor am I in favor of those pretty dandy airs which' are sometimes affected by clowns who set up as gentlemen. But when a man appears in good company let him see that his boots & clothes are clean so as not to create disgust by his inattention to what *they will insist upon as decorous*. A word to the wise. Some of your friends have given a hint upon this subject. Your own example must teach upon this subject. I am more afraid that you will be spoiled with pride than I used to be." Conceit was the curse of the ministerial profession, Finney cautioned. "We & all our friends are, if we are not aware, going to be shorn of all our strength by this insidious Delila." [41]

Reformers held it a duty to point out each other's faults, so Weld was not offended. Indeed, the result of Finney's admonition shows the measure of his influence on Weld. For if Weld still remained untidy in his dress, every day thereafter he took a bath, fearful that if he passed a single day, winter or summer, without washing himself from head to foot, he would lose his self-respect.[42] And he recoiled with shuddering loathing from anything that savored of conceit.

Finney was now located temporarily in New York City, where he was preaching in a "free" Presbyterian church. This innovation, a church that, contrary to the then prevailing custom, charged no rent for pews, and where the poor were welcome to worship on an equality with the rich, had been instituted by the philanthropic brothers, Arthur and Lewis Tappan. When Finney advised Weld of his intention to go to New York, he confided that he would live in Arthur Tappan's house and would try to direct the brothers' benevolence toward Oneida Institute.[43] Thus it came about that Lewis Tappan enrolled his two sons at Oneida, and that Lewis, visiting the school, was won to the idea of manual labor education.

Indeed, the new departure in education, of which Oneida was

the prototype, showed such promise that in July, 1831, the Tappan brothers, ever eager to foster benevolent enterprise, organized a Society for Promoting Manual Labor in Literary Institutions. Lewis Tappan had met Weld on one of his visits to Oneida, and from their first acquaintance the brothers had regarded the young man as a potential leader of one or another of their manifold reforms. Manual labor education was second only to temperance in Weld's esteem, but the Tappans had something else in mind for him at first. Finney's "free church" had become so popular that they planned to establish others, and it seemed to them that Weld would be a superb pastor.[44] So Lewis Tappan brought him to New York for a conference about this and another matter that had come to the fore of late.

In England there was tremendous agitation for the abolition of slavery in the British colonies; and the Tappans and other New York philanthropists, stirred by the British excitement, wondered if the time had come to assail American slavery. Weld was well posted on the English situation by reason of his regular correspondence with Charles Stuart, and the Tappans called upon him to explain the status of the British movement to a number of men of antislavery sympathies whom they had summoned to New York.[45] Out of this meeting came a recommendation to organize an American National Antislavery Society. But the idea seemed somewhat premature, and the conferees eventually decided to allow it to lie over pending the outcome in England.[46]

Weld made a number of temperance speeches in New York and was well received. But he refused to accept a pastorate, insisting that he was not ready for the ministry. Whereupon the Tappans, disappointed in their original intention, but resolved to bring him within their reform orbit in any event, offered him the job of heading up the manual labor education movement. This he could scarcely refuse. To bring education to the masses and develop strong minds in healthy bodies would be a boon to mankind, and the job was all the more alluring in that it would afford time for temperance lectures as a sideline. It meant renunciation of his studies for a season; but Weld, having savored the gusty relish of good works, could not resist such an opportunity to serve. At the age of twenty-eight he became general agent of the Society for Promoting Manual Labor in Literary Institutions.

2

THEY WOULD

PERFECT MANKIND

The early decades of the nineteenth century were a millennial age. A surprising number of persons became followers of William Miller, who set a date for the second coming of Christ on earth, and when disappointed, prophesied again and again. Some of his disciples vouchsafed such faith in his predictions that they prepared ascension robes and kept them ready at hand, while a few, fearful that they might die before the great day came, stipulated to be interred on some high place, where they might be off in the van whenever the Angel Gabriel saw fit to sound his horn.[1]

Not many went to these extremes, to be sure, and yet there was a multitude of people who accepted the idea of human perfectibility and foresaw the triumph of holiness and the establishment of the Kingdom of Heaven on earth at no far distant time. The reforming impulse of the period stemmed largely from this hope. Weld himself was a millennialist, and so was Finney. A product of evangelical religion, the millennial fantasy sometimes took weird and unusual forms under the stimulus of American exuberance. The Shakers sought salvation in prudent rhythm. Brook Farm, New Harmony, Hopedale, and other private ventures offering the chance of human improvement in a sequestered communal environment sprang up in such profusion that Ralph Waldo Emerson remarked that there was scarcely a reading man "but has a draft of some community in his waistcoat pocket." [2] Reforms of every sort proliferated, with the "benevolent society" as a favored medium of reformist expression.

There were societies for home and foreign missions, societies for the distribution of Bibles and tracts, a society to encourage the establishment of Sunday Schools, another to reform sailors —a craft held to be especially susceptible to Satan's blandishments—still others to espouse world peace, promote prison reform, abolish imprisonment for debt, and to promote a multitude of other causes. The American Temperance Society and the American Colonization Society were among the largest, and among the more idiosyncratic were those which, under the name of "Female Retrenchment Societies," would persuade the weaker sex to eschew "tea, coffee, rich cake, pastry, preserves, snuff and tobacco, as well as wine and cordials." [3]

Many of these societies held annual spring conventions in New York City. In that adolescent metropolis a group of well-meaning rich men had banded together as the "New York Association of Gentlemen." Consecrated to the perfection of mankind through philanthropy, they pledged themselves to forego the unrestricted accumulation of wealth and to devote their surplus gains to good works. Inasmuch as nearly every one of them was active in a number of benevolent causes and served on the boards of several different philanthropic societies, they constituted a sort of interlocking directorate at the core of the benevolent movement. [4]

Arthur and Lewis Tappan, the charitable New York merchants with whom Weld was now to be associated, were leaders of this group. Arthur was the more prominent of the brothers, not because he was abler or more philanthropic, but because of Lewis' abnegation; for Lewis often relieved his brother of the tedium of business affairs in order that Arthur might spare more time for good works.

A heavy-bearded man with hollow, wrinkled cheeks, and shaggy eyebrows shading his sharp, penetrating eyes, a straight nose, firm lips, and rumpled hair, Arthur no longer had the spruceness of his youth, when, with his handsome face, his tidy clothes, and jaunty air, he seemed destined to become a man of the world. But his father had admonished him to associate only with the virtuous and the good, "if it be possible to find any such," and Arthur had taken his counsel to heart. Toward sin he came to feel "as you would if, putting your hand in your pocket, you touched a toad." His personal cleanliness made him shrink from those whose breath or apparel was tainted with tobacco, which he accounted harmful to the stomach and nervous system. He also suspected an affinity between tobacco and strong drink, doubting that addicts of the weed could "content themselves with washing out their throats with cold water."[5]

Arthur was a small man, never robust, and his migraine headaches made him irritable and abrupt. Entirely lacking in humor, he was as stern with himself as with others. As his philanthropies extended and he was importuned for money, he devised the expedient of removing the extra chair from his office so that those who "came not for goods but their proceeds" would tire sooner, being obliged to stand.

Although more self-effacing than Arthur, Lewis was akin to him in temperament. In some respects more zealous in reform, he was also more impetuous and tenacious. When Arthur became discouraged, Lewis often took over. When Arthur hesitated, Lewis plunged in. But impetuosity sometimes forced him to reconsider, so that he was thought to vacillate.[6]

Much of the Tappans' business success derived from their inauguration of the one-price system, a revolutionary practice in merchandising. Customers at their store soon came to realize the futility of haggling. The Tappans sold at an established price, and it was the same for all.

In the minds of the brothers, however, a more potent factor making for their success was careful supervision of the morals of their clerks. Every morning before the opening hour Arthur or Lewis led devotions in the store. No Tappan employee might drink or smoke, attend the theater, or own acquaintance with an actress. Every clerk must attend devotions twice on Sunday and be prepared on Monday to announce the name of the church, the clergyman, and his text. Prayer meeting twice a week was also prescribed, and at ten o'clock each evening every Tappan employee must be home.[7]

Lewis' letters of his brother Ben, who lived in Steubenville, Ohio, and was something of a freethinker, reflect the reformer's mind. "You ask why I cannot keep my religion to myself," wrote Lewis, when Ben, provoked by Lewis' efforts to reform him, responded with testy bluntness. "I will tell you my dear brother," Lewis explained. "Because I see you are in danger of eternal damnation. Your soul, with its powers & capacity of continual enlargment thro' all eternity, is in peril of being lost! As I love you then, and desire your happiness & usefulness, I urge upon you the obligation of faith in the Son of God. Were I not to do so your blood would be found on my skirts at the Judgment Day." [8]

The assertion is significant to our understanding of the reform impulse of which abolition was one manifestation. As we have noted specifically in the case of Theodore Weld, the nineteenth-century reformers were heirs to the Puritan doctrine of community responsibility for sin.[9] To assure one's own salvation, one must save others, too. A man could not ignore an erring brother and still hope to win salvation for himself. When Ben Tappan was elected to the United States Senate, Lewis wrote: "To tell you the honest truth I should have preferred to have heard that you had become a sincere deacon of a church." [10]

The Tappans' benefactions included the American Tract Society, the American Bible Society, Auburn Theological Seminary, Kenyon College, Weld's own school, the Oneida Institute, the American Education Society, various home and foreign missionary endeavors, sundry temperance organizations, and the General Union for the Observance of the Christian Sabbath; at one time or another the brothers gave financial aid to more than one hundred divinity students at Yale. In the late twenties Arthur founded the *Journal of Commerce* with the aim of bringing a wholesome moral influence to the newspaper field. His paper accepted no "immoral" advertisement, among which he classed those of spirituous liquors, circuses, and theaters. No issue of his sheet appeared on Sunday, and in order that his printers might keep the Sabbath holy, Monday's issue must be ready for distribution by twelve o'clock Saturday night.[11] After losing thirty thousand dollars on this venture, Arthur turned it over to Lewis, a transfer which involved no change of policy. For Lewis, besides sharing Arthur's views on advertising, was even stricter about Sabbath observance, being corresponding secretary of a society to prevent the Sunday conveyance of mail as well as a promoter of a society to oppose the use of illuminating gas in churches in order that gas workers might be free to worship on the Lord's Day.[12]

Weld entered upon his association with the Tappans in the autumn of 1831 and immediately set out to visit schools and colleges throughout the country. His instructions from the trustees of the Society for Promoting Manual Labor in Literary Institutions directed him to collect data from which might be deduced guiding principles for the most successful union of manual labor with study; to ascertain to what extent the manual labor system was suited to conditions in the West; and to compile a journal of his findings.[13] Weld, Lewis Tappan and a few others even cherished the notion of establishing a great national manual labor institution to serve as a pattern, and Weld planned to be on the lookout for the most advantageous site for it.[14]

Almost at the outset of his journey he was laid up with a

sprained arm, a bruised head, and an almost dislocated neck, when a drunken driver ran his stagecoach off the road and down an eight-foot bank near Hartford, Connecticut. The coach turned almost completely over, and the driver and all ten passengers were more or less battered and bruised. "The horses were going at a rapid rate," Weld wrote to Lewis Tappan, "—had just descended a hill, when without the warning of an instant, we found ourselves, en masse, with broken fragments of the stage, hats and bonnets in a jam, cloaks, coats and pantaloons, fit furniture for a rag-shop—men groaning—women in hysterics—tears running, and blood too. . . . I was thrown violently against one of the top beams, head first; and but for my thick fur cap and a large pocket handkerchief which I providentially put in it, have little doubt that the blow would have been very serious." As it was, he was laid up for several days and was obliged to visit a doctor twice. "So much for RUM," he moralized.[15]

Weld had scarcely recovered from this mishap when he had his misadventure and miraculous escape in fording Alum Creek, near Columbus, Ohio. Here, along with the rest of his baggage, he lost his journal, and for some reason never resumed it. As a matter of fact, he thought of himself more as a missionary of manual labor education than as an investigator. To be sure, he interviewed educators and collected facts, but his chief activity was speechmaking.

The disaster at Alum Creek forced him into four weeks of inactivity at Cincinnati. Before he was really able to be up and about, he consented to deliver a temperance speech. His hands were still so benumbed that he could not button his clothes, and it was agreed that he should talk no longer than half an hour. But once he had begun he spoke three times that long, following his initial effort with seven more lectures on seven consecutive nights, then continuing to speak for several evenings more on manual labor. There were times when he could scarcely mount the platform without help, and he clutched the desk for support until, under the stimulus of speaking, his strength seemed to return.[16]

From Cincinnati Weld made his way across Ohio, Indiana, and Illinois to St. Louis, still giddy, but scorning to give way to physical weakness. It was a foolhardy stubbornness and he was to pay dearly for it later. Julia Tappan, who remembered his once ruddy and animated countenance, was surprised when next she saw him a few months afterward. For his "fine healthy color" had given place to pallor, his once abundant hair had thinned perceptibly, and his voice was rasping and raw.[17]

After touring the Middle West, Weld headed into the South, where, in his intervals of lecturing, he studied slavery. At Nashville, Tennessee, he had a long discussion about it with Marius Robinson, an able young student at the University of Nashville. Striking ever deeper south, he spent a month at Huntsville, Alabama, as the guest of Dr. William Allan, a slaveholding Presbyterian minister. Here again he discussed the slavery problem with Doctor Allan, his two sons, and their neighbor, James G. Birney.[18] As yet, Weld favored merely the program of the American Colonization Society—gradual emancipation with transportation of free Negroes to Africa. Throughout the South he found intelligent Southerners quite willing to talk about their "peculiar institution," provided the conversation was out of hearing of the slaves.

Slavery interested him increasingly, but temperance and manual labor education were still his primary concerns. He had expected that manual labor principles might not take too well in the South; they did not accord with planter tradition. Some Southerners did object that they wished their sons to be gentlemen, "not stiffened and spavined, like the slaves, by work." Yet on the whole, Weld thought he encountered no more objections of this sort in the South than he did in the North. And his retort, when anyone raised the point that aristocratic youths might be above a little honest sweat, was to advise them to take a lesson from the apostle Paul, a tentmaker, from Moses, a shepherd, Cincinnatus, a farmer, the disciple John, a fisherman, or Ben Franklin, a printer.

So Weld traveled through the South, talking temperance and manual labor at every opportunity. Food and accommodations were often poor. More than once he put up at rude cabins and even slept under the stars. But he gloried in such hardships as tests of his mettle.

Lewis Tappan still hoped to make him pastor of a "free church," and corresponded with him regularly. Indeed, there was a sharp tug between Weld on the one hand, arguing the importance of the West, and Tappan on the other, urging the claims of the East. While Weld was in Cincinnati, Asa Mahan, a Cincinnati Presbyterian pastor, drew up a petition urging Finney to come to Cincinnati, which twelve ministers and fifteen laymen, including Weld, endorsed. Shortly thereafter, both Mahan and Weld sent Finney personal appeals, Weld pleading that the Ohio Valley could never be moved from Boston, New York, or Philadelphia, and that Cincinnati was the spot for Finney. "Here is to be the battle field of the world," he wrote; "here Satan's seat is. A mighty effort must be made to dislodge him *soon* or the West is undone." [19]

On July 28, 1832, Weld wrote to Tappan from Princeton, Kentucky: "You make certain inquiries about my health. In reply I will give you a sketch of my doings for the last 30 days, & leave you to infer whether I am sick or well. . . . Since the 28th June I have been on the road traveling 5 days & nights. This subtracted from 30 leaves 25. During these twenty five days I have spoken in public 32 times—viz. 15 on Man. Lab. 13 on Temperance & 4 times on *female* Education by special request. Besides this, frequently during the same time [I] spoke *every evening* in Columbia, Tenn. and in the morning rode into the country 9 miles & spoke *every day* at 11 o'clock to the Students and Teachers of the M. L. Seminary & citizens of the vicinity; and on the Sabbath, A M & P.M. on another subject—Temperance. So besides riding 18 miles *every day* under a July sun I was enabled to speak twice, & probably on an average of [an hour and] a half each time for the week. The Lord has seen fit to bless me with great power of physical endurance—a principle of *last*, little affected by wear and tare, and enabling me to do & endure more than most men. And yet you and brother Finney . . . think I should *settle in a city!!* Nay—nay— brother—God has marked out for me a station of another sort. The highways & hedges of the west." [20]

Tappan was provoked at Weld's perversity. The trouble with a man like Weld, he wrote to Finney, is that he thinks the center of the universe is wherever he acts. The Mississippi Valley was important, to be sure, but the railroads, extending ever farther westward, would soon bring every Western businessman to New York twice a year, and if converted in New York, these business leaders would become effective workers at home. "Do what may be done elsewhere, and leave this city the headquarters of Satan, and the nation is not saved," Tappan declared. " . . . A blow struck here reverberates to the extremities of the republic." Tappan could not understand Weld's attitude. Weld could exert a mighty influence if he would listen to reason. [21]

Weld, on his part, thought Tappan was deluded by New York provincialism. The Western merchants who would visit that expanding business center were merely an insignificant fraction of the vast Western population, and their minds would be on everything else but religion while they were "whirling in all the hustle and bustle and chaffering of purchasing, confused and perplexed with the details and statistics of filthy lucre, in the unfittest mood for receiving a healthful moral influence." [22] Both Weld and Tappan were stubborn men, and each was convinced he was right.

Meanwhile, after a swing back to St. Louis and a six-hundred-mile trip on horseback through Missouri, Weld returned to the North, and on October 12, 1832, arrived at Hudson, Ohio, near Cleveland, where he lectured four times on manual labor education and five times on temperance.[23] But far greater than his effect on Hudson was its impact on him, for this backwoods village was the seat of Western Reserve College, and there Charles B. Storrs, the college president, Elizur Wright, professor of mathematics, and Beriah Green, another faculty member, were preaching a new type of abolitionism. It was the aggressive abolitionism of William Lloyd Garrison, who branded slavery as a sin and slaveholders as criminals. It was radical and militant and brooked no temporizing. If slavery was a sin, as assuredly it was, then it must go, and at once. The gradual, careful policy of the American Colonization Society was a compromise with sin.

One able student of the abolition movement would have it that Weld converted Storrs, Wright, and Green to this immediate type of abolitionism,[24] but the evidence indicates that they fired Weld to action. Storrs had been receiving Garrison's paper, the *Liberator*, since February, 1831, and was won to immediatism several months before Weld's visit.[25] Already he was preaching abolition sermons at and near the college, while Wright proclaimed the iniquities of slavery and urged its immediate extinction in a series of articles that appeared periodically in the *Hudson Observer and Telegraph* from August to November, 1832. In the fall term of that year, Storrs, Wright, and Green discussed colonization versus immediatism with the students in a college lecture hall. By the time of Weld's arrival there was turmoil and contention in the college and the town, and the trustees were voicing displeasure.[26]

Storrs was destined to die within a year, but Wright and Green would become spearheads of abolition. Wright was a sanguine, self-reliant Connecticut Yankee aged twenty-eight, slight of build but wiry and tough. Able, even if insufferably headstrong, he could wield a pen "keen as a Damascus blade." A mathematical wizard, he first manifested his reform proclivities at Yale, where he led a successful movement to banish liquor from Phi Beta Kappa banquets. Green, too, was a native of Connecticut. Now a man of forty, unprepossessing but reliable and devout, he had graduated from Middlebury College, studied for the ministry at Andover Theological Seminary and turned to teaching when his health began to fail.

Interplay of influence is difficult to gauge, and there was unquestionably a mutual freshening of spirit between Weld and these men. The whole tone of their subsequent correspondence, however, makes it evident that the antislavery impulse came from them, with Weld ripe for conversion by reason of his recent sojourn in the South.

After delivering another series of temperance lectures at Cleveland, Weld went on to New York, where Wright sent him a letter to bring him up to date on events at Hudson. Green had preached a series of abolition sermons in the college chapel.[27] Twenty students had professed abolition convictions and a number of others were wavering. The trustees were becoming increasingly restive, and Wright suspected they would be glad to rid the college of the agitators. It might bolster some of the weaker spirits among the converts to know how the New York philanthropists regarded the matter, and Wright requested Weld to sound them out. If Providence had blessed him with Weld's talents, Wright avowed, he would devote himself to the cause of the colored race—the "great trial cause of human rights." "Immediate emancipation is the Saviour's doctrine," he declared, "and must be preached though it shake the stars of heaven." [28]

Weld replied that abolition, immediate and universal, was his "desire and prayer to God." Since his visit to Hudson his soul had been in travail on the subject, and if he had finished his education he would make it his life's work. Since arriving in the East he had had "many pitched battles" with persons who favored caution in dealing with the slavery problem, two of them with agents of the American Colonization Society. The idea of immediate emancipation was unpopular in New York and New England, he reported, but the next few years would mark a change in sentiment.

Since the antislavery meeting that Weld attended in New York in the spring of 1831, the benevolent Tappan brothers had pushed their abolition plan aside. Now, under Wright's prompting, Weld brought it to their attention again, and tried to reinvigorate their interest. Arthur Tappan was ready for action at once, Weld informed Wright, and was delighted that Wright,

Storrs, and Green were "scattering light over the Reserve." Lewis Tappan was "offish" when Weld first broached the matter to him, "but I see by a talk of a few minutes with him just now that he's going the whole. . . . If he gets thoroughly abolitionized he will bear all before him." There were other New York philanthropists with secret antislavery leanings, Weld discovered, but they lacked the fortitude to declare themselves.[29]

The Tappan brothers, however, were not of this timorous type. Once aroused, they did not quail. Inspired by Weld, from this time forth they worked unceasingly to organize the antislavery forces, first bringing together a "New York Committee," then elaborating their designs until they reached fulfillment in the formation of the American Anti-Slavery Society in December, 1833.

As for Weld, his manual labor job was not yet finished, and he busied himself with his report. It must have been refreshing to settle down for a while, for in the year of his agency he had traveled a total of 4,575 miles: 2,630 miles by boat and stagecoach, 1,800 miles on horseback, and 145 miles on foot. En route he made 236 public addresses.

His report to the Society for Promoting Manual Labor in Literary Institutions, while not altogether in line with his instructions, was a masterpiece of its kind. Beginning with a history of the society and a brief account of his own labors, Weld presented voluminous testimony of physicians and educators to prove that study unaccompanied by exercise was detrimental to health, morals, and intellect. Adducing the arguments he had developed in his speeches, Weld cited Demosthenes, Pericles, Sophocles, Xenophon, and Caesar as examples of *active* thinkers. Aristotle, Socrates, and Plato walked while they lectured. Robert Burns felt the power of the Muse most poignantly while in rapid motion. Franklin, Fulton, Whitney, Paul the Apostle, Peter the Hermit, John Knox, and Patrick Henry were all men "of active bodily habits."

Look at your typical college student, adjured Weld, and you

will note "a listless inactivity, a reluctance to locomotion, an aversion to all vigorous, protracted effort, a timid shrinking from all high attempt." A full-length portrait would depict the typical collegian "with his feet elevated upon a mantelpiece as high as his head, body bent like a half-moon or a horse-shoe, lolling, stretching, yawning, smoking, snoring," or, if he were represented in motion, it would be with a lounging air, arms dangling, and a loose-jointed gait. That was what came of neglecting the body while trying to train the mind. A judicious admixture of manual labor was the proper remedy; for it would tone the body, stimulate the intellect, safeguard the student's morals by occupying his spare time, teach him useful skills, promote industry, temperance, originality, and manliness. By cheapening the cost of education it would broaden the country's intellectual base, and by demonstrating the compatibility of physical and intellectual endeavor it would do away with absurd social distinctions between those who work with their brains and those who produce with their hands.

Weld saw the chief danger to the manual labor program in injudicious multiplication of schools. A few strong manual labor schools were what was wanted to begin with, to serve as models for others. "One deep respiration gives more vigor than a thousand gaspings," was the way Weld put it. "Arm ten full grown men, rather than a myriad of Lilliputians," he advised.

Many of Weld's conclusions seem obvious today. But this was not so in his time. His study was regarded as so significant and advanced that it was printed in a pamphlet of 120 pages and widely disseminated.[30]

Indeed, for a few years it seemed that Weld's efforts in behalf of the manual labor principle might give a new direction to education. The idea was well adapted to the country at that time, especially to the West, where land and building materials, particularly lumber, were abundant and cheap, but where labor was a scarce commodity. On the frontier there was need of unskilled labor to clear forests, erect school buildings, and raise food for the students; and the new system offered means whereby the students could perform these tasks themselves. In 1832, a committee of the Pennsylvania legislature reported favorably on a project to establish a manual labor academy for training the state's teachers. In 1836, a resolution was introduced in the United States Senate directing the committee on public lands to inquire into the feasibility of making a grant of land to each new state for the establishment of colleges designed to educate the poor under a manual labor plan. A number of schools and colleges contemplated conversion to the new scheme.[31]

With Weld's resignation as agent, the Society for Promoting Manual Labor in Literary Institutions ceased to function, but Weld's labors had some permanent results. The idea of manual labor education, exerting a strong appeal for many years, was not only a factor in the establishment of land grant colleges later in the century[32] but also provided the impetus for the foundation of a number of other colleges, some of them of unquestioned standing and proved accomplishment, which still operate upon a self-help manual labor plan today. And rare indeed nowadays is the educational institution that makes no provision for the student's physical welfare.

At the time that Weld rendered his report to the trustees of the Society for Promoting Manual Labor in Literary Institutions he was twenty-nine years old and had had a varied experience. He could have continued as the society's agent had he so desired, but he had never given up his aspiration to the ministry. At the conclusion of his report he announced his resignation. "Gentlemen of the Committee," he declared, "the experience of a year has convinced me that the agency to which I was called by your appointment furnishes a field of usefulness wide as human interests. Nothing could induce me to leave it but the most settled convictions of duty. My heart cleaves to the manual labor system; and though I can no longer *publicly* advocate it as an agent of your society, I hope soon to plead its cause in the humbler sphere of *personal example,* while pursuing my professional studies, in a rising institution at the West, in which *manual labor is a* DAILY REQUISITION."

Weld's valedictory was a rousing manual labor speech in New York City. Marshaling his favorite arguments, he pleaded for the training of vigorous, self-reliant men to work in the West. The great valley of the Mississippi was like a sleeping giant. Soon it would wake and sway the world. And it would need a host of lusty leaders.[33]

With Weld's convictions of the future greatness of the West, it was natural that he should choose a western school to complete his training. With opportunity to study all the manual labor colleges, the one he settled upon was Lane Seminary, at Cincinnati. Weld had visited it twice on his lecture tour, the first time in February or March, 1832, when he spoke at Cincinnati, then again in September; and while Weld made no specific recommendations regarding the establishment of a model national institution, his letters make it evident that he hoped Lane would assume that role.[34] Already a number of his former classmates at Oneida had enrolled at Lane upon his recommendation and had been urging him to join them. Several young men with whom he had become acquainted in the South also planned to matriculate, among them Marius Robinson and the two sons of Doctor Allan. A new college, unencumbered by tradition and located in the thriving Ohio valley, it impressed Weld as a place where he might make his influence effectual.

Indeed, he had already counseled with the trustees regarding faculty appointments,[35] and might even have had a teaching position himself had he so desired; for when Weld became agent for the Manual Labor Society, F. Y. Vail, Lane's financial agent, knowing that Weld would be influential in directing the flow of Tappan money, had turned his blandishments upon him, pleading that "we only need your plan and efforts identified with our own in order to make it strictly a national, model institution. . . . We want now, my dear brother, just such a man as you are (I do not flatter you) to be the mainspring in the whole concern. We want the funds promised you exceedingly for buildings for 500 or 600 students, for more land if necessary, for workshops, tools, etc." [36] Importuning him again, Vail wrote: "And remember that, by God's blessing, you are yet to bear one of the four corners of our institution by occupying the chair of Sacred Rhetoric and Oratory." [37] But with his usual self-abasement Weld declined the offer. He still had much to learn, and chose to enroll as a student.

After a brief visit with his family in New York state, Weld and three other prospective Lane students traveled overland to the headwaters of French Creek where they bought a boat for six dollars and floated down to the Allegheny River, then down that stream to Pittsburgh. "We had good times," Weld remembered, "discussing antislavery, and stopping occasionally to get supplies, hold prayer-meetings, or find a place to sleep; if we could not, we got along on the boat." From Pittsburgh they took passage on a river steamer to Cincinnati, sleeping on deck and earning their way by helping to load wood. "I believe there were some other of the Oneida boys that hired on flat-boats," Weld recalled, "and earned some money to begin their studies." [38]

3

LANE SEMINARY

Lane Seminary had its origin in a
donation of five thousand dollars by two brothers whose name it
bore, followed by a grant of sixty acres of land by Elnathan Kemper.[1] Fifteen thousand dollars came from other citizens of Cincinnati, and efforts were made to raise more money in the East. Several persons suggested Lyman Beecher for Lane's president, and
Arthur Tappan promised the income from twenty thousand dollars for a professorship of theology if Beecher would accept the
presidency. Another thirty thousand dollars was pledged on like
condition, and in the fall of 1830 the trustees elected Beecher
president.[2] Weld and the Tappan brothers had great hopes for
Lane, and as slavery became uppermost in their thoughts they
designed to make it not only the prototype of manual labor colleges but a center of antislavery activity as well.

Lane's location was ideal, for Cincinnati, standing at the gateway to the West and Southwest, was destined to phenomenal
growth as settlers in ever increasing numbers pressed toward the

western country. Already the city's population numbered some thirty thousand. Its waterfront was thronged with puffing river steamers, long-oared flatboats, and rafts. Two steamers plied constantly to Covington on the Kentucky side, for no bridge spanned the river at that point as yet. Cotton, lumber, and manufactured goods of all descriptions piled up on the city's wharves. Cattle and hogs bellowed and grunted in its stock pens. In the teeming business district, which ranged along the low-lying waterfront against the backdrop of limestone hills where the residential area was steadily expanding, punctilious bankers and merchants and aristocratic planters of genteel dress and tastes rubbed elbows with Yankee drummers, the proud pilots and crewmen of the river steamers, rough-clad herdsmen and drovers, tough stevedores, hustling artisans, and hard-bitten keelboat men.

The city had wide streets and modern buildings, mostly of pale brick or native gray stone. Swine roamed the streets with impunity, however, and one visitor noted an inordinate amount of mud, filth, and stagnant water, which would "set them a scrubbing" if the ever-threatening cholera should break out.

Cincinnati was a Southern city on free soil. A majority of the residents were Southerners. A good part of the city's merchandise went South, and much of its market produce was Southern-grown. Southern planters with their families took the best hotel rooms. The soft, slurred Southern speech was heard more often than the Yankee twang. Family servants were often slaves, hired from masters across the river, and there was a large section, known as Green Town, where some twenty-five hundred free blacks had congregated. The tone and culture of the town were Southern, notwithstanding the numerous and pushing Northern element.[3]

Lane Seminary was situated two miles north of the city proper in a high, secluded area known as Walnut Hills. Lyman Beecher's daughter Catherine thought she had never seen a place so capable of being made a paradise, although she was disappointed to find that both the city and the river were hidden by the intervening hills.

When Weld arrived the main brick building was already up, and other smaller structures were under construction. President Beecher's house was a solid, two-story brick with a long L running back into a grove which often served as a picnic ground for the students and the young people of Beecher's congregation; for the doctor, besides being president of the college, was also pastor of Cincinnati's Second Presbyterian Church. The whole campus was embowered in gigantic beeches, tulip trees, and black oaks, "a genuine noble old forest," a visitor observed, "which they are improving to the best advantage." Where the trees had been cleared, stumps still dotted the landscape.[4]

In Beecher, Lane had acquired a man accounted the foremost preacher of his day. A graduate of Yale, he had begun his ministry at East Hampton, on Long Island, at a salary of three hundred dollars a year and firewood. From there he had gone to Litchfield, Connecticut, where Weld first met him, thence to Boston, where he took over a new church with thirty-seven members and soon made it one of the largest and most influential in the city. He was a strong temperance and missionary man, intensely anti-Catholic, and he had accepted the presidency of Lane because, like Weld, he saw the future of the country in the West.

Both his father and his grandfather were blacksmiths, and much of their physical vigor was handed down to him. Short and square-built, he was so intensely energetic that he kept a sand pile in his cellar and went down from time to time to shovel it from one side to the other. He would put his numerous children to work at chopping and carrying wood, inspiring them to mighty efforts by his example, for like Weld he had unbounded faith in exercise. He thought his powers sufficient for any task. In Boston he had made it his mission to combat Unitarianism, and when asked how long he thought it would take him to extirpate it, he replied: "Humph! Several years I suppose—roots and all." [5]

Beecher was always too busy to spend much time on sermons. Usually he would begin his preparation only an hour or so before the service, retiring to his study, throwing off his coat, and taking a few swings with the dumbbells to loosen up, then working feverishly until the first bell rang. With that he would rush down the stairs, herd his wife and children out the door and down the street, and be mounting to the pulpit as the last peal of the final bell died out.[6]

At night he was so taut from the labors of the day that he must "run down" and "let off steam" before he could sleep. Surrounded by his children, he would bring out his fiddle and saw away on "Auld Lang Syne," "Bonnie Doon," or "Mary's Dream." He aspired to render more complicated melodies arranged in difficult keys, but, according to his daughter, "he invariably broke down, and ended the performance with a pshaw!" In moments of extreme exuberance, Beecher sometimes let out with "Go to the devil and shake yourself," and, if Mrs. Beecher had retired, he might lay aside the fiddle and break into a double-shuffle or jig.[7]

Beecher was in his middle fifties when he came to Lane, and his energy was somewhat abated. But he still chopped wood and dug stumps from his garden and lawn while wrestling with administrative or theological problems. One Lane student, a friend of Weld's named George Clark, remembered that one day when Beecher failed to appear for a lecture, the class appointed Clark to look him up. Calling at the Beecher house, he was told that the doctor was shooting squirrels. Finally Clark found him in the woods a mile away, chasing a black squirrel around a tree. "That rascal hides from me on the other side so that I can't get a fair shot," complained Beecher as Clark came up. Clark reminded him of his class, whereupon the doctor gasped: "What! Is it lecture time? Well! well! I must go." And he set out for the campus at a lope. He came by his absent-mindedness as he did his physical vigor; for his blacksmith father, when sent to the henhouse to gather eggs, was wont to stuff his trousers pockets with them, then, coming into the house, he would forget them and sit down, only to rise quickly and cry out in stricken tones, "Oh, wife!" [8]

The Beechers were to be a distinguished family, so much so that critics of Lyman Beecher maintained that his loins were wiser than his head. Two of the Beecher boys, George and William, were already in the ministry. Edward, who was also an ordained clergyman, had gone to Jacksonville, Illinois, as the first president of Illinois College. As the abolition movement gained headway, he would be the first of the Beechers to plunge into it. Henry Ward was attending Amherst and Charles was at Bowdoin, but they were home at Walnut Hills during vacations. They, too, were planning to enter the ministry. Catherine, the oldest girl, was in her middle thirties, and had left the successful girls' school she had founded at Hartford, Connecticut, to come to Cincinnati with her father. Eager to continue her pioneer work in female education, she organized "The Western Female Institute" in Cincinnati. James and Thomas, who were also destined for the ministry, were mere boys. Harriet, who would be the most famous of them all, was in her early twenties. Already she had made some tentative gestures with her pen. In 1833 she wrote and published a geography. She contributed to the local newspapers, and in 1834 her first magazine article would be published. She was a diffident girl, and no one realized how tremendous an impression had been made upon her sensitive nature by a visit to a slave plantation across the river in Kentucky.

Two members of Lane's faculty were noteworthy. John Morgan, a young Irishman, a graduate of Williams College, was a peerless expositor of Scripture and an excellent reader of hymns. A huge man, he walked with a rolling gait that reminded one student of "a dutch scupper careening at its moorings." [9] He was the sort of man Weld liked—rough, virile, tough-minded—and his influence on Weld was lasting.

Weld left no recorded impression of another professor, Calvin Stowe, a young widower who was to marry Harriet Beecher. A graduate of Bowdoin and Andover Theological Seminary, Stowe came to Lane from Dartmouth, where the students had dubbed him "Old Snyder." He dressed shabbily and had an air of stuffy stiffness. "Not exactly a stiffness, either," an acquaintance remarked, "a sort of tare and fret." [10]

For the rest, Lane's faculty was commonplace; but this was not so of its students. Of the forty members of the first theological class, thirty, including Weld, were over twenty-six years old, and nine of these were in their thirties. All were college graduates or had finished the equivalent of a college course. One had practiced medicine for ten years. Twelve had served as agents of benevolent societies. Six were married, and three had been so for at least ten years.[11] A few were Southerners, but the great majority—thirty-one of the forty—were natives of New England or upstate New York, a number having come from that region around Auburn, Rochester, and Utica where the embers of Finney's great revival still glowed hot. Several of this contingent had been members of Finney's "Holy Band," and with them, as well as with the twenty-four students who came to Lane from Oneida Institute, Weld's influence was paramount.[12]

In the literary department, eighteen of the fifty-six students were over twenty-five. And Lane was probably the first institution in America to waive the color line, for James Bradley, a member of Lane's first class, was a Guinea Negro who had bought his freedom. When the pious and free-handed Arthur Tappan asked Beecher what action Lane's trustees had taken toward admitting Negro students, Beecher replied that no action was needed and he hoped none ever would be. "Our only qualifications for admission to the seminary are qualifications intellectual, moral, and religious, without reference to color," he asserted, "which I have no reason to think would have any influence here, certainly never with my consent." [13] It was a most advanced position for the time and place.

Beecher remarked the students' piety, maturity, and all-round excellence, and young Charles Beecher recalled that they were an unusual group—a little uncivilized, he thought, entirely radical, and terribly in earnest.[14]

From the first there were problems of discipline. The students were too mature and independent to accept the customary restrictions of college life. They had such intense dislike for Thomas J. Biggs, professor of church history and church polity, that it came to the point where they refused to attend his lectures; and to keep the peace, Beecher prevailed upon them to listen to the unpopular professor once a week if he and Stowe would take his other classes. The students also claimed a voice in the selection of the faculty. Those who enrolled before Weld's arrival kept him apprised of proposed faculty appointments and solicited his opinions and suggestions, and the trustees did so, too. The students made it clear to Beecher and the trustees that they wanted a faculty of men "who must teach or starve"—men who could make men. They would tolerate no professors like one who had taught languages at Oneida Institute, who walked among the students like a speechless ghost, gave no composition or declamation assignments, lay abed late of mornings, and profaned his body with tea and coffee.[15]

Beecher was well aware of Weld's influence. "In the estimate of the class," said Beecher, "he was president. He took the lead of the whole institution. The young men had, many of them, been under his care, and they thought he was a god." Beecher rated Weld a man of unusual natural capacity whose education needed broadening.[16] Notwithstanding the students' disposition to encroach on faculty and trustee functions, and to look to Weld for leadership, both Weld and Beecher were too high-minded for jealousy. Had the troublesome slavery question not intruded, friendly relations between them would probably have been sustained.

For Weld made himself invaluable. Besides setting a high example by his diligence in theological studies, he taught one class and helped supervise the manual labor department, which consisted of the school farm together with printing, coopering, and cabinet-making shops. Weld exulted and expanded under the inspiriting life. When Harriet Beecher attended the examination of her brother George in Presbytery, she noted that "over in the pew opposite to us are the students of Lane Seminary, with attentive eyes. There is Theodore Weld, all awake, nodding from side to side and scarce keeping still a minute together." [17] Weld wrote home that he had "never been placed in circumstances so imposing." Weld and Beecher shared the platform as speakers at the anniversary exercises of the Cincinnati Temperance Society in 1833.[18]

Hardly was Lane Seminary in operation when an epidemic of the ever-menacing cholera threatened to wipe it out. Within three days of the outbreak, thirty students were down. The steward and his family fell ill, and those students who were still able to be up and about were obliged not only to nurse their disabled fellows but also to take over the kitchen. Three students died. Weld took the lead in combating the epidemic. "For ten days I did not go to my room but once to change my clothes," he wrote to his family, "but cannot particularize. The Lord sustained me throughout. I never seemed to myself to possess more energy of body or mind. I had not during the whole time, scarcely a single sensation of fatigue, or the least disposition to sleep, though in more than one instance I was without sleep forty-eight hours in succession. . . . Extraordinary providence provides *extraordinary* supplies always adequate to the demand." [19] Oblivious of danger or fatigue, Weld emerged from the ordeal a greater hero than ever in the eyes of his fellow students.

As Lane Seminary suffered its birth pangs, events of moment were happening in the East, and Weld's numerous friends and acquaintances kept him informed about them. In England, the movement for emancipation in the British West Indies was reaching crescendo, and the susceptible ears of Arthur and Lewis Tappan and other members of the New York Association of Gentlemen were vibrant with anticipation. Since the time Weld talked with the Tappans after his antislavery awakening by the Western Reserve professors, Wright, Green, and Storrs, the large-hearted New Yorkers had been eager to make a move for freedom. Now the time for action seemed close at hand, and the "New York Committee," which had been organized some time before, perfected its plans.

In the autumn of 1833, Elizur Wright wrote Weld that he was leaving Western Reserve to head up the "New York Committee's" work. He would correspond with persons of known abolition sympathies, edit pamphlets and tracts, and try to enlist agents, all with a purpose to encourage the formation of local groups from which the projected national society might draw delegates. Before resigning his college job to go to New York, Wright was pleased to witness the formation of the "Western Reserve Anti-Slavery Society" out of the " 'Bone and Sinew' of our community—yes the *heart* and *soul* of it," he wrote. And Beriah Green, who had also resigned from Western Reserve to assume the presidency of Oneida Institute, had accepted his new post on express condition that he was to be in no wise trammeled in expression of his abolition convictions.[20]

A short time after the receipt of Wright's first letter, Weld received a formal invitation to the organization meeting of the American Antislavery Society, which was to be held at Philadelphia on December 4, 1833. Accompanying the invitation was a personal letter from Wright, beseeching him to come. "My whole heart is with you," Weld replied, "but a physical impossibility prevents my personal attendance." [21]

Shortly after the meeting, Wright wrote to Weld that the national society was now in being and "the question is whether it shall *live*. The infant is sound in its limbs, but its breathing is the problem." [22] He did not supply details about the Philadelphia meeting, but the omens had been both good and bad. The delegates had assembled at the appointed time. Many of them were delegates only in name, however, since they came on their own initiative. Most of them were young. A dozen were ministers. But it was the Quaker element that predominated; even a few Quaker ladies had taken seats in the audience. The sittings were guarded, but no one was refused admittance. A group of Southern medical students, gathering in the gallery, had threatened to become obstreperous at times. No Philadelphian had dared court local displeasure by agreeing to preside, so Beriah Green had taken the chair.[23]

The burghers of Philadelphia watched proceedings with suppressed malevolence. Crowds gathered in the streets around the meeting place, drifted off in groups, then reassembled. Young toughs loitered on the corners, hopeful of encouragement to do violence. One noon the crowd became so ugly that the delegates dared not go out for lunch. But Josiah Coffin rounded up a quantity of cheese which was washed down with pitchers of cold water.

William Lloyd Garrison, the fiery young apostle of freedom from Massachusetts, had drawn up the Declaration of Sentiments. Basing the antislavery movement on the spirit of the Declaration of Independence and the revealed will of God, this document declared the society's purpose to organize auxiliary societies in every city, town, and village; to send out agents to remonstrate, entreat, and rebuke; to circulate periodicals and tracts, to enlist the pulpit and press, to purify the churches of the guilt of complicity with slavery, to improve the condition of the free Negroes, and to bring the entire nation to speedy repentance.

Furnished by Wright with a copy of this Declaration, Weld noted that it admitted that each state had a constitutional right to legislate upon slavery within its own limits, and that Congress had no power to interfere. But Congress did have power to prohibit slavery in the District of Columbia, to abolish the interstate slave trade, and to prevent the spread of slavery to national Territories. The fathers of the American Republic had waged a war for freedom. The abolitionists were about to declare another. "*Their* weapons were physical," the Declaration asserted. " . . . *Ours* shall be such only as the opposition of moral purity to moral corruption, the destruction of error by the potency of truth, the overthrow of prejudice by the power of love, the abolition of slavery by the spirit of repentance." [24]

Wright informed Weld that Arthur Tappan had been elected president, although he was unable to attend the meeting, and that young Garrison was secretary of foreign correspondence. But it was upon Wright himself, as secretary of domestic correspondence, that the major duties would devolve.

Wright must have regretted that Weld was not on hand to hear Beriah Green's inspiriting appeal as he brought the three-day session to a close. "But now we must retire from these balmy influences and breathe another atmosphere," Green warned. "The chill hoar frost will be upon us. The storm and tempest will rise, and the waves of persecution will dash against our souls. Let us be prepared for the worst. Let us fasten ourselves to the throne of God as with hooks of steel. If we cling not to Him, our names . . . will be as dust. Let us court no applause; indulge in no spirit of vain boasting. Let us be assured that our only hope in grappling with the bony monster is in an Arm which is stronger than ours. Let us fix our gaze on God, and walk in the light of his countenance. If our cause is just—and we know it is—His omnipotence is pledged to its triumph. Let this cause be entwined around our very hearts. Let our hearts grow to it, so that nothing but death can sunder the bond." [25]

In informing Weld of the successful outcome of the meeting, Wright explained the pressing need for "a number of faithful mighty agents, in whose persons the Society shall live and breathe and wax strong before the public. We must have men who will electrify the mass wherever they move,—and they must move on no small scale." Weld, Garrison, the Reverend Samuel May of Connecticut, and the Reverend Amos A. Phelps of Massachusetts were the men they wanted. Would Weld devote himself to the work? The Society would pay the same salary as that paid by the Bible and Tract societies—eight dollars a week and traveling expenses.[26]

When Weld felt constrained to refuse, due to his determination to complete his education, Wright sent him a commission and instructions anyway, with a plea that he give whatever time he could to antislavery work. The *sin* of slavery was the idea to be stressed, the instructions explained; the force of truth would be the weapon. Compensation to masters was reprobated: first, because it would imply the rightfulness of slavery; second, because it was unnecessary, inasmuch as the masters would find free labor to be more profitable than that of slaves. Schemes of expatriation contemplating the removal of the blacks from the country were also disapproved, for they all originated in prejudice against color, and this prejudice must not be indulged but suppressed.[27]

Within a month of his receipt of this commission Weld was offered the position of corresponding secretary and general agent of the American Society for the Observance of the Seventh Commandment, whose purpose was to redeem females who had "deviated from the path of virtue."[28] But this he also refused. For meanwhile there had come a powerful awakening at Lane, manifesting itself in a frontal assault on slavery and an effort to improve the condition of the free blacks in Cincinnati. Weld was the prime mover and had enlisted heart and soul. There would be momentous consequences, not the least of which was that Weld, almost unwittingly, would soon find himself in the forefront of the antislavery movement. To understand the full significance of the happenings, however, we should first know something about the prevailing attitude toward slavery in that day.

4

A SYSTEM

SANCTIONED

BY TIME

The *abolitionists insisted there was* nothing to be said in slavery's favor. Yet, at its theoretical best, it was a system that assured the Negro worker food, clothing, shelter, fair working conditions, care in sickness and old age —a system that brought security from the cradle to the grave, a boon for which free labor is still striving. Its defenders claimed that it brought the benefits of Christian civilization to a benighted race and provided the master race with wealth and leisure for attainment of the highest culture.

At its worst, however, it was a horror, for it gave one man unmitigated authority over another, even to the power of life and death. To be sure, there were laws to restrain brutality and sadism, but their enforcement was altogether in the hands of the master race. No Negro could bear witness against a white man, and white men were reluctant to take the part of the Negro where the master-slave relation was involved. Public opinion was a more powerful deterrent to brutish practices than law, and even stronger was self-interest, inasmuch as slaves were valuable property. Nor were the practices of slavery as revolting to the conscience of that time as they would be today. The favorite disciplinary instrument was the lash; but flogging was still a legal and customary punishment in the American navy. Many an American jack-tar bore the welts of the cat-o'-nine-tails on his back, and when flogging was outlawed in 1850, high naval officers predicted a breakdown of discipline on shipboard.[1]

It is futile to indulge in generalizations about slavery. Even today historians disagree, and their conclusions are still too often colored by sectional bias. One of the ablest modern studies by a Southerner seems to a Northern student to be no more than "a latter-day phase of the pro-slavery argument," [2] and Northern treatments are apt to seem obfuscated and prejudiced to Southerners. As a matter of fact, the source materials on slavery are so varied and voluminous that one is all too prone to see in them what his subconscious bias makes him wish to see.

For the slave's condition varied with the sort of work he did: whether he was a liveried flunky in a pretentious mansion, or a drudging field hand. It varied with his location: be it the tobacco and cotton region of the border and middle states, the Black Belt, the miasmatic rice swamps of South Carolina, or the sugar plantations of Louisiana. It was also conditioned by the size of the economic unit to which the slave belonged: whether it was a small farm where he came under the direct supervision of the master, or a far-flung plantation where the Negroes worked in gangs under bosses and overseers. Primarily, and in every case, however, it depended upon personal characteristics and temperament, on the whims and traits and differences of human nature.[3]

The food of the slave was plain. His house was usually little more than a rude shelter. He worked long hours. But so did the Northern farmer and mill hand, and so did the frontiersman who was seeking to hew out a future with ax or plow. Defenders of slavery seldom failed to contrast the lot of the Northern worker, laboring until age or ill health brought him down and then thrown on his own resources, with that of the slave, who was supposedly assured of care when he fell ill or could work no longer.[4] But the slave was in a fixed condition for life, whereas the Northern laborer was never denied the chance to better his lot, and often did. Abraham Lincoln summed it up succinctly when he said: "I never knew a man who wished to be himself a slave. Consider if you know any *good* thing, that no man desires for himself."

The most vicious maxim of the system and the prop on which it was sustained was its denial of human attributes to the Negro—the insistence upon his innate moral and intellectual inferiority to the white man, and his assignment to a position in the order of nature only a little more exalted than that of a brute. With few exceptions this notion found favor both North and South. It was the crux of the slave system, the keystone of the arch, the shoring strut that held the structure up. Once grant that the Negro was a man like other men, and the prime justification for slavery fell to the ground.

Slavery had always had its critics, South as well as North. The Quakers had early taken the view that it was wrong and had forbidden members of their congregations to own slaves. For the rest, Southerners, being more closely involved with the system, were naturally more concerned about it than Northerners. Washington, Jefferson, Patrick Henry, Madison, Monroe, John Randolph of Roanoke had all opposed it, and in Colonial and Revolutionary times, and even as late as the early years of the nineteenth century, most thinking Southerners conceded it to be an evil. But they refused to take responsibility for it, accounting themselves victims of an inherited system. And if their forebears were culpable for fostering it, they were no more to be blamed than the British government, which had encouraged the bringing of slaves to the colonies in the face of Colonial protests, nor than the Yankee shipmasters, who had grown rich from the slave traffic. As a matter of fact, the slaveowner saw himself as worthy of some sympathy by reason of his being obliged to live encompassed by a host of ignorant and brutal savages who would probably welcome a chance to murder him and his kin. In 1791 the blacks of Santo Domingo had revolted and slaked their blood lust with a horrible massacre of the whites, and who could tell when the Southern slaves might take it into their heads to do the same? Not a few people, both North and South, were convinced that to agitate the slave question was to invite a bloody revolt. Fear was to be a strong factor in popular detestation of the abolitionists.

Negroes were originally held in bondage in the North as well as in the South; but as climatic and economic conditions proved unfavorable, slavery was proscribed in one Northern state after another. During the period of the Revolutionary War it seemed to be waning even in the South; and many Southerners, perhaps even a majority in the border states, were willing to see it go. But there was one insuperable difficulty. What should be done with the blacks if they were freed?

In many sections of the South the blacks had come to outnumber the whites; elsewhere they were a numerous minority. To the Southern mind it was unthinkable that a million or more freed Negroes should remain in the South unless they were subjected to white control. But how to control them if they were freed? Many of the slaves were but a step or two removed from barbarism and the memory of the Santo Domingo slaughter still burned vividly in Southern minds. A latter-day Southern historian has seen the "central theme of Southern history" as a determination on the part of the Caucasian element to keep the South a white man's country.[5] Another historian sees the key to the Southern attitude in the determination of the planter class to retain control. Well aware of the threat to his own dominance in the potential political power of the Southern mudsill, especially if he should seek alliance with the working masses of the North, the planter sought to smother the poor white's incipient class consciousness by rousing his race prejudice and sectional pride. [6]

Whichever thesis one accepts, it is still true that the race problem transcended the problem of slavery, and it was as difficult of solution then as it continues to be today.

Colonization of the Negroes in some foreign land seemed to offer the only solution, and in 1817 the American Colonization Society was organized to encourage manumission accompanied by transportation of freed colored persons to Liberia. Southern legislatures gave official endorsement to the project and sometimes granted funds to further it.

But even while slavery was being decried, it was slowly, almost imperceptibly, reaching out its tentacles to encompass the nation. The system underwent great changes during the first years of the nineteenth century, changes that were analogous to those accompanying the industrial development in the North. As a result of the invention of the cotton gin in 1793, the profits of cotton culture increased enormously. Until this new development, most slaveholders owned only a few slaves. In Southern towns and villages, doctors, lawyers, and prominent businessmen might hold one or two household servants. On the smaller farms the owner and his sons often worked in the fields side by side with their slaves. Old ladies and elderly gentlemen might own three or four Negroes whom they hired out, taking their wages for support. In 1790 it was estimated that there were twenty thousand families owning one slave apiece, slightly more than fifteen thousand families that owned from five to nine slaves each, and not more than two hundred and forty-three families in the entire nation who could boast of a hundred or more.

But the cotton gin, together with the exploitation of the rich soil of the Old Southwest and the insatiable demands of the English cotton mills with their improved machinery, brought agricultural capitalism to the South, just as other inventions were bringing industrial capitalism to the North. In some regions farms gave way to plantations, where slaves were worked in gangs. As the demand for slaves increased, slave breeding became a lucrative business in the border slave states, where slavery as an agricultural system was becoming unprofitable. With employment of overseers on the expanding plantations, the planter lost his personal contact with his slaves, just as the New England mill owner lost his personal relationship with his employees. Profits became enormous, and with increased profits came a change in Southern sentiment.

Nor was this change confined to the South. The slave economy meshed with the economic life of the whole nation and brought profits to the North as well as to the South. Northern manufacturers found raw material and mass markets below the Mason-Dixon line, and Northern merchants welcomed the trade of Southern planters. Northern ships carried lucrative cargoes of slave products—cotton, rice, sugar, tobacco; and Northern banks held loans secured by Southern land and Southern crops and Southern "chattels." The Northern aristocrat was as fearful of an awakening of the masses as was the Southern planter, and quite as willing to resort to racial prejudice to lull class consciousness. Northern laborers had no desire to compete with a host of freed black workers. To the great majority of people it seemed best to leave the South and its "peculiar institution" alone.[7] The tentacles of slavery curled ever more tightly about the economic, social, and political life of the entire nation, squeezing and enmeshing, warping the country's thinking.

The attitude of the country was reflected by the church, whose membership was a cross-section of the population, and whose dominant elements were the elder clergy and the munificent contributors, both naturally inclined to conservatism. Slaveholding communicants and Southern clergymen were no less pious than their Northern brethren, and to the latter it was unthinkable to adjudge them sinful. Then, too, there was the matter of church unity. The Northern clergy were well enough acquainted with the sentiment of church members to foresee that slavery agitation would not only sunder the national denominational organizations, but would also foment bitter quarrels within individual congregations. Rufus Choate expressed the general feeling against agitation of the subject in a speech to a group of Harvard divinity students when he declared: "I go to my pew as I go to my bed, for repose." [8]

But if this was the prevailing attitude, it was not universal. Abolition was a religious movement, and the churches would provide it with leadership and recruits. "The largest part of abolitionists are Christians," wrote Lewis Tappan on November 13, 1835, "men devotedly pious. . . . I rely chiefly upon pious men & women in this matter. They will be meek & prayerful; & God will prosper them." [9] Harriet Beecher Stowe summed up the church's position when she explained that it was responsible for the continued existence of slavery, inasmuch as it had the power to put it down but would not do so. On the other hand, a majority of the abolitionists were church members, and many of the most influential antislavery workers were ministers.

But the antislavery element was insignificant at first. Slavery could boast of many friends at the North, and those who were not friendly were generally acquiescent. Hostile to scolds and troublemakers, most persons wanted well enough let alone. Still, there was a latent dislike of slavery that became manifest whenever the institution showed a disposition to spread, and coupled with this was a sectional jealousy of the power of the "slaveocracy" in national affairs, a power which would be augmented if the balance of slave and free-state representation in the United States Senate should be upset.

In 1820, when Missouri applied for admission to the Union with a constitution sanctioning slavery, Congressman Tallmadge of New York had moved to amend the enabling act with a prohibition of slavery. But Southern representatives sprang sturdily to slavery's defense. As the debate waxed acrimonious, Northern congressmen, while disclaiming any intention of molesting slavery in the states where it existed, denounced it as a social anachronism, a transgression of God's will, and a mockery of the American ideal of democracy as proclaimed in the Declaration of Independence. Southern congressmen preferred not to discuss the ethics of slavery; their defense was based on strict construction of the

Constitution and the right of each new state to determine its own internal policies.[10] But a few days after the passage of the compromise measure, which admitted Maine as a free state as an offset to Missouri, and prohibited the introduction of slavery into any other part of the Louisiana Purchase north of the parallel of 36° 30', John Quincy Adams, who had followed the development of the Southern argument with deep misgivings, asserted: "The discussion of this Missouri question has betrayed the secret of their souls. In the abstract they admit that slavery is an evil, they disclaim all participation in the introduction of it, and cast all upon the shoulders of our grandam Britain. But when probed to the quick upon it, they show at the bottom of their souls pride and vainglory in their condition of masterdom."

Jefferson likened the debates over the Missouri Compromise to a firebell in the night, and as the fearsome tolling sounded over the South, the more radical proslavery leaders began to develop the argument that slavery was a positive good, a blessing to master and slave alike. This theory was accepted more readily in the deep South than in the border states, where criticism of slavery could still frequently be heard. As late as 1831 Weld found no hindrance to fair-minded discussion in Kentucky and even as far south as northern Alabama. Less than two years after Weld's visit, however, it had come to be that antislavery discussion even in Virginia, Maryland, Delaware, and Kentucky must be of local origin and tactful in tone. No longer was it safe for an outsider to voice objections. In the deep South there was no longer toleration of criticism from any source, and this taboo would soon embrace the border states as well.[11] Freedom of speech and of the press were passing in the South. "We are sorry to see the Southern people running headlong into a fanaticism as hateful as that of the abolitionists," a Northern friend of Southern rights lamented.[12] For decades there had been a movement of antislavery Southerners to the free Northwest; now in the eighteen-thirties a number of potential liberal leaders who would not be throttled in the expression of their antislavery sentiments joined the northward trek, thus depriving the South of that very influence that might have effected an amelioration of the harsher features of slavery and given Southern thought a liberal leavening.[13]

The changing Southern attitude toward slavery became manifest and vocal when young Garrison, founding his antislavery newspaper, the *Liberator*, in Boston, on January 1, 1831, brought slavery under a galling attack. For Garrison was purposely provocative, his target the nation's conscience. "I am accused of harsh language," he observed. "I admit the charge. I have not been able to find a soft word to describe villainy, or to identify the perpetrator of it. The man who makes a chattel of his brother—what is he? The man who keeps back the hire of his laborers by fraud—what is he? They who prohibit the circulation of the Bible—what are they? They who compel three millions of men and women to herd together, like brute beasts—what are they? They who sell mothers by the pound, and children in lots to suit purchasers—what are they? I care not what terms are applied to them, provided they do apply. If they are not thieves, if they are not tyrants, if they are not men-stealers, I should like to know what is their true character, and by what names they may be called. It is as mild an epithet to say that a thief is a thief, as it is to say that a spade is a spade.

"The anti-slavery cause is beset with many dangers; but there is one which we have special reason to apprehend. It is that this hollow cant about hard language will insensibly check the free utterance of thought and close application of truth. . . . The whole scope of the English language is inadequate to describe the horrors and impurities of slavery. Instead, therefore, of repudiating any of its strong terms, we rather need a new and stronger dialect."

Cloaked in a hidebound righteousness, Garrison was incapable of entertaining the thought that he might be unfair. Nor could he understand why men should hate him when he merely meant to scourge away their sins.

Although he was soon to come to symbolize fanaticism in the

minds of his enemies, Garrison's appearance and manners were those of the urbane gentleman. A native of Newburyport, Massachusetts, two years younger than Weld, he was only twenty-six when he founded the *Liberator*. While serving his apprenticeship on sundry New England newspapers, he had denounced war, intemperance, lotteries, imprisonment for debt, infidelity and irreligion, and transportation of mail on Sunday. He had edited the *Genius of Emancipation* in Baltimore in partnership with the pioneer abolitionist, Benjamin Lundy, and had served a jail term there for libeling a slave-carrying shipowner. His benevolence, like that of most reformers of his day, was all-embracing. The whole sum of the world's evils must be eradicated that man might be brought to perfection. Even for a millennialist his thinking was uncommonly advanced. "In attempting to put away the evil that is in the world," he wrote, "we must forget all national distinctions and geographical boundaries, and remember that we are indeed members of one family, to whom there is nothing foreign, nothing remote." As motto for the *Liberator* he proclaimed: "Our Country is the World—Our Countrymen are all Mankind." With the passing years he would mark the presence of evil behind every bush, and his sharp but scattering volleys would draw heavy counterfire.

Within eight months of the founding of the *Liberator* there was bloodshed in the South. The slave Nat Turner led a Negro insurrection in Virginia that resulted in the murder of several whites. The rising was speedily put down, and the participants were punished ruthlessly, a number of them with death; but many a Southern family wondered if other would-be Nat Turners might be lurking in the darkness which enshrouded the Negro shanties behind the big house. Southerners recalled the incendiary Yankee paper that had been coming in the mails. Was this abolition editor inciting the slaves?

As a matter of fact, Garrison deplored violence and had never sent a copy of his paper to a slave. There was really no connection between the founding of the *Liberator* and Nat Turner's gamble with fate. But how could the South know that? A Washington editor denounced the man whose fanaticism had "caused the plains of the South to be manured with human blood." Georgetown, D. C., prescribed a fine of twenty-five dollars or thirty days in jail for any free colored person who took a copy of the *Liberator* from the post office; and if the fine and jail fees were not paid, the offender was to be sold into slavery for four months.

A "Vigilance Association" in Columbia, South Carolina, offered fifteen hundred dollars reward for the arrest and conviction of any person circulating the *Liberator* or any other paper of "Seditious tendencies." At Raleigh, North Carolina, Garrison and his partner, Isaac Knapp, were indicted for felony under a newly enacted law which prescribed whipping and imprisonment for inciting slaves to revolt, and death if the offense should be repeated. The Georgia legislature offered five thousand dollars reward to anyone who would bring Garrison into the state for arrest and conviction.[14] As Garrison looked out on Boston Harbor and saw ships taking cargo for the South, he must have wondered if he might be dragged from his bed some stormy night and hustled aboard.

The night of January 6, 1832, would have been an ideal time. Pitch black darkness settled over Boston as a shrieking nor'easter drove in from the tumbling North Atlantic bringing rain and sleet and snow. The streets were deep in slush. But if any of slavery's hirelings had come for Garrison that night they would not have found him at home. Early in the evening he had set out for the African Baptist Church on "Nigger Hill." Toward this humble meeting house other men from various parts of Boston were also picking their way. They came in secret, for if their purpose had been known the public temper would have raged more fiercely than the elements.

In the basement of the little colored church they organized the New England Antislavery Society. This was to be the fulcrum of Garrison's power within the antislavery movement. Antedating the American Antislavery Society, it eventually became auxiliary to it. Garrison played only a minor part in the organization of the national society and held only a minor office until years later.[15] As late as January, 1833, Weld knew little about him. On December 31, 1832, Garrison invited Weld to speak at the anniversary meeting of the New England Society. Replying on January 2, Weld declined because of prior engagements. "Besides, Sir," he added, "I am ignorant of the history, specific plans, modes of operation, present position and ultimate aims of the N.E. Anti Slavery Society. . . . I have been quite out of the range of its publications, have never seen any of them or indeed *any* expose of its operations, and all the definite knowledge of its plans and principles which I possess has been filtrated thro the perversions and distortions of its avowed opposers." [16]

Weld's assertion is significant. First, it shows that the New York group of antislavery leaders with whom he was associated were working independently of Garrison. Second, it substantiates the assertion of a modern student of the antislavery movement that it was really Garrison's enemies who gave him fame. Except for a small group of radicals, mostly in New England, Garrison had little following. The *Liberator's* circulation was never large; indeed, it was sustained in large degree by the subscriptions of free Negroes. Northern papers would probably have paid little attention to it had the Southern press also ignored it. But to the South it gave examples of what Southerners took for typical abolitionist pronouncements. Southern papers clipped Garrison's articles and editorialized about them. In this way they were brought to the attention of Northern editors. Thus Garrison came to symbolize the abolition movement. An elementary principle of propaganda is that it is more effective against a man than against an idea. In Garrison the proslavery element found just the sort of target it wanted, and proceeded to make him notorious.[17] Garrison's primacy in bringing the slavery issue into prominence cannot be denied. But modern historical research has demonstrated that it was the New York group of abolitionists, abetted by the Westerners whom Weld would bring into the movement, that gave antislavery its most effective impulse. As the South closed ranks against antislavery argument, the American Colonization Society was the only emancipationist organization that was tolerated in the South, and with the changing attitude toward slavery its program also changed. In the face of Southern opinion it was useless to urge general manumission, even if the leaders of the Colonization Society had not already realized that such a goal was beyond their means in any event. For even to transport the annual increase in the slave population to Liberia would take more ships than were available. So the colonizationists worked with individual masters who showed a disposition to emancipate their slaves provided they could be taken out of the country and given a start on their own. Removal of Negroes already free was also a prime objective and one with which both North and South were sympathetic, inasmuch as free Negroes were regarded as a nuisance everywhere. Despised as little better than animals, living apart in poverty and filth, denied opportunity for education and self-betterment, these unfortunate victims of race prejudice were for the most part ignorant, diseased, and often criminal. And in the South they were deemed a dangerous element whose presence incited discontent among the slaves.

Prior to the abolition movement, the American Colonization Society was accepted everywhere as "a most glorious Christian enterprise." Every church in the land set apart one Sunday every year for a colonization sermon and offering. The society published a monthly magazine and employed a number of agents.[18] It won a large following of intelligent liberals both North and South, and many persons—among them Abraham Lincoln until late in his career—thought that colonization offered the most practical solution of the race problem. But the abolitionists claimed that the society subscribed to the "degraded race" belief and held the slaveholder blameless. They thought it lulled the public conscience, for wherever its doctrines had permeated, abolitionism met apathy or hostility. Once when Lewis Tappan had listened for an hour to a colonization sermon, he vented his displeasure by dropping two copies of an abolition pamphlet, *The Slave's Friend,*—and nothing more—into the collection box.[19] Colonization was the major hindrance to the beginnings of the abolition movement. In order to obtain a hearing, the abolitionists discovered that they must first discredit it.

Garrison had directed his guns upon it in the early issues of the *Liberator*, and in 1832 he not only stepped up his fire but took to the lecture platform. More effective, however, was his treatise, *Thoughts on African Colonization*, in which he accused the Colonization Society of deceiving and misleading the nation. It was not truly opposed to slavery, he contended, it was really an apologist for slaveholders. The patrons of this society "content themselves with representing slavery as an evil," he complained, "a misfortune,—a calamity which has been entailed upon us by former generations,—*and not as an individual* CRIME, embracing in its folds robbery, cruelty, oppression and piracy. *They do not identify the criminals*; they make no direct, pungent, earnest appeal to the consciences of men-stealers." [20] In July, 1833, a group of New York abolitionists wrote a challenging letter to the Colonization Society asking if its aim was to effect the "complete extinction of slavery in the United States." Weld, Arthur and Lewis Tappan, and Charles G. Finney were included among the signers.[21] The next month Weld's name appeared again, along with those of Asa Mahan, John Morgan, Green, Storrs, and more than a hundred others, most of whom were ministers, on "A Declaration of Sentiment" favoring immediate abolition, which had been drawn up by the Reverend Amos A. Phelps.[22] Abolitionists were convinced that colonizationists were much more interested in removing the free blacks to Africa than in giving the slaves their freedom.

Thus, by the time of Weld's matriculation at Lane Seminary, abolition had had two manifestations, one centering in Boston, the other in New York. The New York group was just now organized and under way. The Boston movement, headed up by Garrison, had already engendered disapprobation so emphatic as to make it evident that the great majority of people were content with the *status quo*. "Away with these dangerous agitators!" was the prevailing sentiment, both North and South.

5

THE LANE DEBATES

W*hen Weld enrolled at Lane Seminary*
he was the only student with forthright abolitionist convictions. Some others had antislavery leanings, but they favored the gradual methods of the colonizationists. As one student, Huntington Lyman, put it: "I suppose there was a general consent in the institution that slavery was somehow wrong and to be got rid of. There was not a readiness to pronounce it a sin." [1] A student colonization society had a large and active membership.

Weld not only held aloof from the society but determined to undermine it. Working quietly but persistently, he concentrated his efforts on William T. Allan, the Alabamian, and won him over. [2] Born and reared in the midst of slavery and a prospective heir to slaves himself, Allan was a powerful ally. Working together, he and Weld soon enlisted so many students that they challenged the colonizationists to a public discussion. The faculty were invited to attend and take part, if they wished, and Beecher favored doing so at first. He would propound his notion that abolition and colonization were not antagonistic and should move concomitantly. But some faculty members, and especially the unpopular Professor Biggs, foresaw unpleasant divisions within the student body and public indignation inimical to the welfare of the seminary. In the end the faculty advised postponement. Their action was merely admonitory, however, and the students decided to go ahead.[3]

This public discussion of slavery—known to history as the Lane Debates—continued for eighteen nights. Despite the inflammatory nature of the subject, good temper ruled throughout. The spirit of the meetings was prayerful and inquisitive, with no invective or denunciation, even though eighteen of the participants came of slaveholding families and one owned slaves himself.[4] The first nine nights were devoted to the question whether it was the duty of the slaveholding states to abolish slavery immediately. Weld opened the inquiry and held forth for two whole evenings. Then William Allan told about the slaves' condition in Alabama. Asa Stone, who had been teaching in Mississippi, described what he had seen there. James Bradley, the colored man, had the audience in tears as he related how he was brought to the United States on a slave ship as a child, and sold to a South Carolina planter, who, moving to Arkansas, had allowed Bradley to work out his freedom. James A. Thome, a Kentuckian, told how slavery demoralized the planters' sons and degraded society generally. Huntington Lyman described slave life in Louisiana. At the conclusion, all except four or five students, who had not yet formed an opinion, voted for immediate abolition.[5] It is noteworthy, however, that under the phraseology of the question under discussion it was the people of the slave states who were to act.

The remaining nine nights were devoted to consideration of the American Colonization Society, the question being whether the doctrines, tendencies, and spirit of the society were such as to render it worthy of the patronage of Christian people. There were several able discourses, but Weld's surpassed them all. One student,

John P. Pierce, recalled that he was a staunch colonizationist when the inquiry began, and would not even attend at first. "I have no precise recollection of the Debates, saving bro. Weld," he wrote years later, "who was the means of opening my blind eyes." [6] At the end the students voted down colonization almost unanimously and proceeded to organize an abolition society.

It would seem that Weld and the Northern students were content to remain in the background and give the prominent positions to Southerners so that the movement might appear to be of Southern origin, for every one of the officers of the society was from the South: William T. Allan of Alabama, president; Marius R. Robinson of Tennessee, vice-president; Andrew Benton of Missouri, recording secretary; James A. Thome of Kentucky, treasurer; and C. S. Hodges of Virginia, auditor. On the board of managers, besides Weld, were James Bradley of Guinea, Abner S. Ross of New Jersey, James M. Allan of Alabama, Huntington Lyman, George Whipple, Henry B. Stanton, and James Steele, the last four being from New York.[7]

And the students had been aroused to more than mere lip service. "We believe that faith without *works* is dead," wrote Weld to Lewis Tappan. "We have formed a large and efficient organization for elevating the colored people of Cincinnati."

Among the students' projects were a lyceum, at which they lectured to the free Negroes of Cincinnati three or four times a week on grammar, arithmetic, geography, and kindred elementary subjects; a school held every week-day evening, where Negroes were taught to read; three Sunday Schools, and several Bible classes. Augustus Wattles obtained leave of absence from the seminary in order to devote his entire time to teaching the colored people. His school became so crowded that for several days he had to turn ten to twenty persons away; but soon he was joined by the Tennesseean Marius Robinson, who also obtained leave of absence from the seminary. Other students gave part-time help, sharing the teaching burden in order not to hinder their own studies.[8]

Weld took time off whenever possible to teach grammar. The evening schools often ended in prayer-meetings, and Weld, listening to the sad, sweet lilt of Negro voices raised in a hymn, is reported to have exclaimed: "Bless the Lord they can sing." In response to an appeal from Weld, Arthur Tappan paid the expenses of sending four young ladies from New York to take over the burden of teaching the colored women and children.

Weld undertook a study of the local Negro problem. "Of the almost 3000 blacks in Cincinnati more than three-fourths of the adults are emancipated slaves who worked out their own freedom," he reported to Lewis Tappan. ". . . I visited this week about 30 families, and found that some members of more than half these families were still in bondage, and the father, mother and children were struggling to lay up money enough to purchase their freedom. I found one man who had just finished paying for his wife and five children. Another man and wife who bought themselves some years ago, and have been working day and night to purchase their children; they had just redeemed the last! and had paid for themselves and children 1400 dollars! Another woman who recently paid the last instalment of the purchase money for her husband. She had purchased him by taking in washing, and working late at night, after going out and performing as help at hard work. But I cannot tell half, and must stop. After spending three or four hours, and getting facts, I was forced to stop from sheer heartache and agony." [9]

Weld's concern for the blacks became so poignant that every minute he could spare from his studies was devoted to them. "If I ate in the City it was at their Tables," he recalled. "If I slept in the City it was in their homes. If I attended parties, it was *theirs— weddings—theirs—Funerals—theirs—Religious meetings—theirs—* Sabbath schools—Bible classes—theirs. During the 18 months that I spent at Lane Seminary *I did not attend Dr. Beechers Church once.* Nor did I ever attend any other of the Presbyterian Churches in the City except brother Mahans, and did not attend there more than half a dozen times. . . . The white methodist I attended once only. . . . I was with the colored people in their meetings by day and by night."[10]

Still Weld could not forego his exercise. To keep fit he went into the deep woods late at night and climbed young trees, working his way up until they bent down under his weight and then dropping off fourteen feet or more to the ground.

Weld foresaw far-reaching consequences from this work among the Negroes, because here was a group who were "their own letters of introduction on the score of energy, decision, perseverence and high attempt—an excellent material to work upon." Here the Lane students, at their own doorstep, had a chance to explode the racial inferiority myth. Augustus Wattles was enthusiastic. "Everything goes on here as we could wish," he wrote to the editor of the *Emancipator*, the organ of the American Antislavery Society. "Our colored brethren are animated with hope. A calm determination to alter their condition is firmly fixed in every breast. Elevation, moral, political, and religious, fires their mind. . . . Frequently, in passing their houses, old women will stop me, and ask if I think they are too old to learn. On receiving for answer, You are never too old to learn, they brighten up, and commonly add, 'We have been slaves and never seen such times as these. We have most done paying for ourselves (or our children, as the case may be,) then we shall come to school.' There has been no opposition to our schools and I am induced to believe the citizens generally approve them." [11]

But Wattles did not know the citizens. Already a strong groundswell of opposition was spreading rapidly, just as it had done in New England whenever attempts at Negro education had been made.

A short time before the Lane experiment, Simeon Jocelyn, a minister of New Haven, Connecticut, and one of those who attended the New York antislavery meeting with Weld in 1831, had planned a Negro college in the shadow of Yale. Arthur Tappan backed him. But when Jocelyn announced his project, New

Haven voiced its anguish with a vigor that bent its elms. Jocelyn bowed to public prejudice; but Prudence Crandall, a pretty young Quakeress whose limpid eyes, soft smile, and boyish-bobbed hair belied her consecrated stubbornness, was less discreet. She had established a girls' school at Canterbury, Connecticut, and accepted a young colored girl as one of her pupils. When the outraged parents of her other pupils withdrew their girls from school and the townspeople insulted Miss Crandall on the street, she flouted their intolerance by opening a school for colored girls.

Local indignation broke with a roar and a shriek. "Once open the door," warned that local dignitary, Canterbury's town clerk, "and New England will become the Liberia of America." Merchants refused to sell Miss Crandall their produce. Physicians would not call at her school. An old vagrancy law was invoked against her pupils. Public conveyances refused to carry them. Offal was thrown in her well. And an attempt to burn the dwelling which housed her school miscarried only because the sills of the antiquated building were too rotten to ignite. The Connecticut legislature came to the aid of the townsmen with a law prohibiting the establishment of Negro schools without permission from the local selectmen.[12]

Lyman Beecher was in Boston when this trouble began, and was well acquainted with New England feeling. But he thought the situation in Cincinnati was different. The Yankees objected to projects calculated to draw Negroes to communities hitherto unblemished by their presence, whereas in Cincinnati the blacks were already numerous. When the students undertook their Negro education project, Beecher anticipated no trouble from the schools as such. The danger, as he saw it, came from the students' insistence upon treating the colored folk as social equals. Wattles boarded with a colored family. Sometimes the student teachers stayed overnight in the city in colored homes. A number of colored girls came out to the seminary in a carriage to interview their instructors, and a student was seen on the street with a colored girl.[13]

With this, resentful rumblings broke out in the city, and the Lane faculty convened the student body to warn them of the dangerous consequences of "carrying the doctrine of intercourse into practical effect." Beecher called Weld into conference to urge him to persuade the students to defer to public sentiment. "Said I," the doctor recalled, "you are taking just the course to defeat your own object, and prevent yourself from doing good. If you want to teach colored schools, I can fill your pockets with money; but if you will visit in colored families, and walk with them in the streets, you will be overwhelmed." [14] Surely it was not necessary to treat the Negroes as social equals in order to succor them, Beecher implored.

But Weld retorted that the students must live with the colored folk to win their confidence, that to make any distinction in social intercourse because of color was an odious and sinful prejudice, and that someone must move in advance of public sentiment if anything were ever to be done. One night Weld and Beecher were closeted in impassioned argument until two o'clock.

Beecher's forebodings were to be abundantly justified, however, for in May, 1834, some three months after the Lane debates, the *Western Monthly Magazine*, published in Cincinnati, criticized the Lane students as "precocious undergraduates" and "embryo clergymen" whose "sophomoric declamations" were raising malignant passions and rancorous party spirit, and whose social radicalism deserved the prompt rebuke of public sentiment. As Cincinnati rallied to the battle cry, Weld justified the students in the columns of the *Cincinnati Journal*. Why should students not examine the subject of slavery, he challenged, and especially ministerial students? Was it not the province of theological seminaries to educate the heart as well as the mind? "Whom does it behoove to keep his heart in contact with the woes and guilt of a perishing world, if not the student who is preparing for the ministry?" It was the duty of theological seminaries to acquaint their students with the moral problems of the age, and free discussion was the way to truth. The editor was ill-advised if he thought to stifle the antislavery impulse by appeals to public prejudice. "Sir," warned Weld, "you have mistaken alike the cause, the age, and the men, if you think to intimidate by threats, or to silence by clamors, or shame by sneers, or put down by authority . . . those who have put their hands to this work. Through the grace of God, the history of the next five years will teach this lesson to the most reluctant learner." [15]

Weld forcefully expressed the spirit of his antislavery band, but it was evident that they were facing trouble. Cincinnati seethed with pent-up prejudice, and there was talk of organizing a march upon the college. Beecher and the faculty took alarm, and, again calling the students together, urged them to bide their time. They were right in their designs, Beecher admitted, but they were too far in advance of public sentiment.[16] "The young men . . . were not guilty of doing wrong," sneered Elizur Wright at Beecher's opposition, "but of doing *right* TOO SOON." [17]

The students appointed a committee with William T. Allan as chairman to consider the faculty plea, but their conclusion was that they could not modify their stand. The cause of the trouble was malicious gossip about the real character of the students' relations with the Negroes, they contended, and the actions which were scandalizing Cincinnati were exactly the same as those which were commended in missionaries who worked among the blacks in Africa. The students would not renounce the basic tenet of their enterprise—equal treatment of all men according to their character, and regardless of color.[18]

The twelve-weeks' summer vacation was now at hand and with the departure of the students the excitement was expected to die down, so the faculty did not attempt to refute the students' argument. Beecher went East on a money-raising tour; Stowe left on a vacation. James A. Thome and Henry B. Stanton attended the anniversary exercises of the American Antislavery Society in New York City, where their account of the students' activities electrified the meeting.

Weld and a number of other students remained at the seminary, preparing abolition pamphlets and compiling a mailing list of persons to whom to send them.[19] The students continued with their work in the colored schools, and on several occasions colored persons, coming out from the city for consultations with their student instructors, were seen on the college grounds.

It may be that Lane was a way station on the Underground Railroad and that Weld sometimes served as conductor. The evidence—inconclusive to be sure—is in a letter from Huntington Lyman to Weld, written when both of them were old men. "In conclusion," Lyman wrote, after congratulating Weld on his eighty-eighth birthday, "I want to know if you ever used my horse without first asking me. You remember I owned the only horse that was owned in Lane Seminary by a man of my grade. It was understood that that horse might be taken without question by any brother who had on hand 'Business of Egypt.' There was between the Ohio River and the south end of the 'Underground Rail Road' a space over which it behooved us to transmit our commodities with dispatch. We regarded as advisable to send across that stretch not only with great speed, but not even to tell each other when we had in hand such 'Business of Egypt.'

"I want you should signalize this your birthday by frank confession," demanded Lyman. "Did you ever use my horse as aforesaid on errand as aforesaid? Don't be afraid. All action for trespass is outlawed. Sometimes I found that my horse had had a sweat. The cause I did not at that day inquire after. It might have been belly ache or it might have been 'Business of Egypt.' We in that day were 'Willingly ignorant.' "[20]

It is regrettable that we do not have Weld's answer respecting this "Business of Egypt."

At any rate, with the faculty dispersed in that summer of 1834, the Lane students could do pretty much as they pleased. In Cincinnati, however, a number of Lane's conservative trustees, hearing rumors of what was taking place, became restive about these dangerous goings on. But in the absence of the faculty they were reluctant to act, and the students continued their propaganda work throughout the summer.

In addition, Weld performed one of his most notable achievements when he enlisted the young Kentuckian, James G. Birney. Weld and Birney had met in Huntsville, Alabama, two years before. Since then their antislavery thinking had diverged. While Weld became a proselytizing abolitionist, Birney had become an active worker for colonization.

Weld's senior by eleven years, Birney was born in Danville, Kentucky, the son of a Scotch-Irish immigrant who had won wealth and social station in Kentucky. The Birneys' winter residence was a brick mansion in Danville, while Woodlawn, their summer home, located half a mile from town, was accounted a bluegrass showplace. Reared in these luxurious surroundings, Birney enjoyed the advantages of wealth. Private tutors and local academies prepared him for Princeton, where he graduated in 1810, going from there to Philadelphia to study law. Generously supplied with money, he lived as became a young blood of the bluegrass, mingling in the best Philadelphia society, wearing the latest fashions, indulging his fondness for fine furniture and table service, and driving a pair of blooded bays sent from the Woodlawn pastures.

Returning to Danville at the age of twenty-three, he opened his own law office, married Agatha McDowell, daughter of a Federal judge and niece of a Kentucky governor, and won election to the Kentucky legislature. The young couple acquired several slaves.

Kentucky was overrun with young political aspirants, and, to better his chances for preferment, Birney bought a plantation near Huntsville, Alabama. Here the Birneys' bountiful hospitality, combined with the extravagance of fine saddle and driving horses and Birney's propensity to bet on cards and horse races, soon put them in debt. Compelled to mortgage the plantation, Birney moved into Huntsville to practice law in earnest. Here he recouped his fortunes, built a large home, became a respected citizen, and was elected mayor. Forswearing gambling forever, Birney spent his evenings in his garden, pruning his bushes and young trees, hoeing his vegetables, and tying up his vines.[21]

It was here that he became acquainted with Weld, when the young apostle of manual labor visited Doctor Allan. The two men had some ardent discussions of slavery; and Birney may have told Weld how he had been obliged to leave his plantation in charge of an overseer, how he disliked the overseer system, and, indeed, the whole philosophy of slavery.[22]

Soon after Weld's visit Birney sold his plantation, freed his field hands, moved back to Danville, and became an agent of the American Colonization Society. An agent's life was rigorous at best, and for a man of Birney's position to forego the settled comforts of home to perform the duties of a peripatetic agency showed consecration and idealism beyond the ordinary. But Birney took up his duties with zestful relish, traveling through the South to solicit funds and organize auxiliary societies. Yet the more he saw of slavery the more he doubted. Like Weld, he came to see the gradual approach of the colonizationist as ineffective. "If *gradual* emancipation be insisted on," he wrote, "the conscience of the slave-holder is left undisturbed, and you gain nothing." [23] In the early summer of 1834, Birney visited Lane Seminary to talk over his perplexities with Weld.[24] It was a momentous meeting. On June 10, 1834, Elizur Wright wrote to Beriah Green from the antislavery headquarters office in New York: "It seems that our Dear Br. Weld has had a long confab with Birney, & by the blessing of God, he has renounced his colonization." [25]

It was true. Birney was ready to admit that "colonization has done more to rock the conscience of the Slaveholder into slumber, and to make his slumber soft and peaceful, than all other causes united." [26] He gave up his agency, resigned as vice-president of the Kentucky Colonization Society, and came out four-square for abolition.

During the remainder of the summer he and Weld were in frequent correspondence. Birney prepared a statement of his views on colonization and brought it to Lane Seminary for Weld's and Professor Morgan's suggestions, for Morgan was working hand in glove with the students.[27] The students raised one hundred dollars to have Birney's article published, and Henry B. Stanton took the money to Lexington, where the article was printed as a pamphlet, and remained there to supervise packing and shipping. Weld ordered a thousand copies sent to Cincinnati as soon as possible so that the students who were going home might distribute them during vacation.[28]

On July 21, Birney sent Weld a list of persons in middle and lower Alabama, Louisiana, and Mississippi who might be persuaded to distribute antislavery tracts. The opposition was in full cry in Danville, he reported, and his abolition views had cost him a chance to teach at Centre College where he had planned to try to win some of the students.[29] Weld was delighted with Birney's spirit, and reported to anti-slavery headquarters that he "throws his whole soul into the cause." [30]

Meanwhile, Weld had troubles of his own, for the executive committee of Lane's board of trustees had cracked down. The moving spirit behind their action was the unloved Professor Biggs, who thought the seminary had become "a reproach and a loathing in the land." [31] Moreover, fifteen of the twenty-six trustees were business or professional men with dealings in the South (seven others were ministers), and if pressure had not already been brought upon them, they were well aware that it soon would be, and that to have the abolition label pasted onto Lane would be disastrous for them.[32] At a special meeting on August 20 the executive committee declared that slavery was no subject for immature minds. It must be approached with "diffidence and discretion," for it had baffled the wisdom of the country's ablest men. No seminary of learning, especially no theological college, should take sides where Christians differed; for such a course would not only lessen the institution's influence and discredit Christian education, but would also warp the students' judgment and unfit their minds for "genial and useful intercourse with mankind." Party spirit, generated too early in life and blended with the acquisition of knowledge, might become a "constitutional disease of the mind extremely difficult of cure and destructive of its future usefulness."

Thus, for the protection of the institution and the good of the student body, the executive committee decreed a ban on all student societies except those designed to further the course of study. Public statements or communication on the part of students in meetings or at meals were prohibited unless prior approval was obtained. Measures would be taken to discourage even private discussion of distracting subjects, and offenders would be punished with expulsion.[33] In order that old students as well as those contemplating entrance might be informed of these rules, the committee had them printed in the *Cincinnati Daily Gazette*.[34]

Weld risked expulsion by continuing his antislavery labors. Birney was pondering what he was best fitted to do. Each wished to counsel with the other, so they arranged a rendezvous.[35]

It was mid-afternoon of a September day when Weld reined up his mount in a forest glade some twenty miles north of the village of Georgetown, Kentucky. He had scarcely halted when, above the murmurs of the forest breeze, he heard the hoofbeats of Birney's horse approaching from the South. As Birney cantered into the clearing and the two men wheeled their horses side by side, the contrast in their persons and accoutrements was striking. Weld's clothes were in their usual disarray, and the submissive cob that carried him had the mark of the livery stable. Birney, on the other hand, was clearly the Southern gentleman. His ruddy cheeks betokened outdoor exercise; his blue eyes, warm, but with a hint of chill, suggested a man of friendly disposition accustomed to use authority. His brows were wide, his nose and chin sharp-cut and regular. Lush sideburns fringed his cheeks. A habit of compressing his straight lips made his expression stern, but it was softened by the delicate lines that crinkled from the corners of his mouth. Although he was only five feet nine inches in height, he was tough-knit; and he bore himself with dignity and self-possession.

Near the meeting place was "a quiet house of entertainment" to which the two men repaired and where they remained until late the following afternoon, discussing the antislavery movement in all its aspects. Weld was resolved to persevere in antislavery work, and advised Birney to begin work in Kentucky, either as an agent or an antislavery editor, for hostility to abolition seemed less intense in Kentucky than elsewhere in the slave states. "We parted much refreshed," wrote Birney in his diary, "as I trust on both sides. I have seen in no man such a rare combination of great intellectual powers with Christian simplicity. He must make a powerful impression on the public mind of the country, if he lives ten years." [36]

Returning to Lane Seminary, Weld counseled the students to ignore the new rules. They would not become effective until ratified by the whole board in any event, and it would not meet until October. Much could be done before then.

Besides his "Letter on Colonization," Birney had prepared a "Letter to the Ministerial Elders of the Presbyterian Church in Kentucky," which he sent to Weld to be printed, inasmuch as his Lexington printer had been threatened with violence if he should ever use his press for antislavery purposes again. James Allan came down from Lane to bring Birney three hundred copies, and reported that the Lane students, well supplied with ammunition, were mailing out their tracts with intensified zeal.[37]

Antislavery circles were agog at what Weld had done in bringing Birney into the movement. Elizur Wright wrote to an antislavery agent, Amos A. Phelps, that Birney was "a chosen vessel." He was ready "to embark his all, indeed he has done it already. He will labor in Kentucky and the whole of that region, either as our agent, or as an individual, as upon a little experience of the effect of his *debut* will be thought best. But he must be supported. In taking the stand he does, he alienates a rich Father, gives up a lucrative profession, sacrifices a large property which *was considered his.*" Birney had a large family and Weld had recommended that his salary be no less than fifteen hundred dollars a year. In the present state of the national society's finances, this sum must be raised by private subscription. The ever-generous Arthur Tappan had promised a contribution, and Wright was confident he could raise the rest of it.[38]

Meanwhile, things went on as before at Lane. President Beecher and Professor Stowe were still in the East, and Professor Morgan, who was friendly to the students' enterprise, was also away now. Indeed, the only professor on the grounds was Biggs. Dismayed by the prospect of being throttled in his antislavery efforts, Weld wrote to Beecher to hurry home. The Reverend Asa Mahan, the only trustee friendly to the students' cause, added his entreaty to Weld's. Beecher did start west, but at Columbus he turned northeast to Granville, then went back East to renew his money-raising efforts. He could do but one work at a time, he explained in answer to Weld's plea, and he hoped the students would do nothing rash until he returned.[39] He claimed later that he could have composed the difficulties, had he been on the ground; yet he seems deliberately to have stayed away, adhering perhaps to the belief he had expressed when the students first began their antislavery agitation, that "if we and our friends do not amplify the evil by too much alarm. . . . the evil will subside and pass away."

But the situation had passed beyond all hope of self-solution. On October 6, the trustees met, ratified the action of the executive committee by a vote of fourteen to three, and instructed the faculty to enforce the new rules.[40] Professor Morgan was dismissed, thereby raising the issue of academic freedom, and Weld and William Allan were threatened with expulsion.[41]

At the opening of the fall term the students assembled in the chapel and sent a committee to ask the faculty to meet with the student body and interpret the new code. Beecher, Stowe, and Biggs undertook to do so,[42] whereupon another committee was sent to ask if students were to be allowed to discuss the new rules among themselves. They were not, was the reply; so a third committee asked if students might discuss the propriety of remaining in the seminary. This also was declared to be under the ban. According to Asa Mahan's account: "One of the leading students now arose, and remarked, that one privilege remained to them, namely, to say, by rising to their feet, whether they would, or would not, continue members of the Institution under existing circumstances. For himself, . . . the most solemn convictions of duty to his God, his conscience, his country, and the race, constrained him to say, that he could no longer continue a student of Lane Seminary." [43]

Weld was probably the student incendiary. At any rate he was the author of a statement of the students' position, which fifty-one of them signed.[44] Then all the protestants withdrew from school. Two went to Auburn Seminary, four to the Yale Divinity School, two to Western Theological Seminary at Allegheny Town, near Pittsburgh, and one to Miami College. Four "confessed their error" and requested reinstatement.[45] The remainder set up a school of their own at nearby Cumminsville and undertook to teach one another while they continued their efforts with the Cincinnati Negroes. Weld drew drafts on Arthur Tappan for their support, and Salmon P. Chase, a young Cincinnati attorney who had been stirred by the students' antislavery endeavors, persuaded his brother-in-law, James Ludlow, to allow the students the use of a large house.[46] Beecher eventually persuaded the trustees to withdraw their resolutions against Weld and Allan and to modify their regulations in some degree.[47] Then he pleaded with the students to return, arguing that they had played into the hands of Professor Biggs, who wished to be rid of them.

A justification of the trustees' action, signed by Beecher, Biggs, and Stowe, placed the blame for all the trouble upon Weld, whose abolition obsession had made him reckless of all consequences, "even though it were the prosperity of the seminary

itself." "But while we feel called upon to say this," Weld's ac-
cusers continued, "justice and affection require us to render at
the same time, a willing and melancholy homage to the talents,
and piety, and moral courage, and energy of the individual,
while we lament that want of early guidance and subordination
which might have qualified his mind to act safely by con-
sultation in alliance with other minds, instead of relying with a
perilous confidence in his own sufficiency. We regard it as an em-
inent instance of the monomania, which not unfrequently is the
result of the concentration of a powerful intellect and burning
zeal upon any one momentous subject to the exclusion of others;
and while our high expectations and warm affections have been
disappointed in him and others of our young men, it is not
without hope and daily prayer, that the past may suffice,
and that wiser counsels and more auspicious movements may
characterize their future course." 48

Weld no longer faced the threat of expulsion, but he had
been soundly spanked, and it was clear that his antislavery usefulness at Lane was at an end. On October 7, 1834, he resigned, and
at once enlisted as a full-time agent of the American Antislavery
Society.49 Elizur Wright wrote to the Reverend Amos A. Phelps
that in Cincinnati Weld was now accused of going to Lane de-
signedly to stir up trouble. "Horrible crime!" Wright hooted.
"Marvellous foreknowledge! They think the rest of the 'boys'
now Weld has left them, as soon as cold weather comes, 'will be
glad to get back.' " 50

But the students were a stubborn, hard-set lot. And to make
them even more steadfast, now, in the very hour of their ex-
tremity, they were about to be offered a chance to enter a new
college on their own terms.

Thus, at Lane, as would so often be the case, efforts at repres-
sion merely served to feed the antislavery fires. The Lane rebels
were more resolved than ever to persevere in antislavery work.
The Lane troubles publicized the abolition cause throughout
the West. Indeed, the repercussions echoed all over the North.

The president of Amherst College, learning that an abolition society had been organized on his campus, challenged the members to declare themselves, and was startled when fifty of his "very best young men" came forward. He advised them to disband their organization and hinted at punitive measures if they refused.[51] In 1835 some fifty students left Phillips Andover Seminary when they were refused permission to organize an antislavery society. A student society at Hamilton College was dissolved by the faculty. Some students left Marietta College when expression of antislavery sentiment was suppressed. At Hanover College in Indiana the faculty tried to discourage antislavery expression without prohibiting it. A student abolitionist was dismissed from Granville, the present Denison. The president of Miami was compelled to resign by antiabolition trustees.[52] Charles Follen, professor of German literature at Harvard, was not reappointed because of his abolitionist activities.

The student secession cost Lane Seminary dearly. The Tappans fulfilled their commitments but would give the institution no further aid. On January 20, 1838, Arthur Tappan wrote to Beecher: "I thank you for the particulars respecting your Seminary and regret that I cannot feel any sympathy in the happiness you express in its present and anticipated prosperity." [53]

As was to be the case in every attempt to quiet antislavery agitation, the controversy raised the issue of free speech. The Lane students justified their defiance of the faculty on that ground, and antislavery papers made it their rallying cry. The New York Evangelist asked: "In what age do we live? and in what country?" The Liberator declared that Lane Seminary must now be looked upon "as strictly a Bastile of oppression—a spiritual Inquisition." With the Lane debates and the ensuing troubles, what in the West up to this time had been merely a harmless, drifting cloud, now began to assume the forbidding aspect of a thunderhead.

6

O B E R L I N

I*n the autumn of 1834, John J. Ship-*
herd set out from Oberlin, Ohio, for the East. He was agent for
a new colony of which he was a cofounder, and his purpose was to
raise money and discover a president for the manual labor college
which was a part of his project.

Established by a group of New England emigrants on a tract
of uninviting hardpan thirty-three miles southwest of Cleveland, Oberlin combined the fad of communal living with an educational ideal. The idea was to found a colony devoted to the
upbuilding of a Christian educational institution with a purpose to "concentrate Christian forces, and train Christian character, for effective operation upon the world without." The
lands were not held in common, but each colonist agreed to manage his holdings for the common good. In order to have time
and health for God's service the colonists covenanted to re-
strict their acquisitions of land, to eat only plain and wholesome foods, to renounce all bad habits, especially the smoking

88

or chewing of tobacco, unless it was deemed necessary as a medicine, and even to give up drinks like tea and coffee, or any other food or beverage that was expensive and calculated merely to gratify the palate.

They forswore expensive and unwholesome fashions in dress, especially tight lacing. Their houses would be plain, their furnishings purely utilitarian. They would give their children the best of Christian education. And they would care for the widows, the orphans, and the needy as for themselves. No student would be admitted "who while on his way journeyed on the Sabbath." [1]

Their ardor would be tempered somewhat with time and the advent of new settlers whose sanctity fell short of that of the founders; but the original settlers were inordinately devout, even if the general level of consecration did not match that of one brother who bought a barrel of Graham crackers upon which he proposed to subsist for a whole year, and which, by the end of that time, had become so hard that he must needs crack them with a hammer, as he would a hickory nut. [2]

When Shipherd set out on his mission the colony had survived its birth-pangs, and primary and secondary schools as well as a college department had been established; but the theological seminary, which was to be the capstone of the whole concern, was still merely an idea, and the institution had dire need of money. Shipherd struck south from Oberlin to take the National Road, and at Columbus he fell in with Theodore J. Keep, son of the Reverend John Keep, president of Oberlin's board of trustees. Young Keep had gone to Lane Seminary to matriculate, but before he could do so the trouble had broken out, and without enrolling at the seminary he had signed the students' protest and was now on his way home. Shipherd already knew something of the situation at Lane and had planned to stop at Cincinnati. Now, after learning further details from Keep, he began to see the Lane imbroglio as a possible godsend to Oberlin. For the Reverend Asa Mahan, the only Lane trustee who had

espoused the students' cause, would make Oberlin an ideal president; and at Cumminsville the nucleus of a theological student
body might be had by judicious persuasion.[3]

Never a man to ignore what seemed to be the beckoning of
Providence, Shipherd made all haste to Cincinnati, taking the
first conveyance he could find, a two-wheeled mail cart. Jounc-
ing into Cincinnati on this bruising vehicle, Shipherd sought out
Mahan, an imperious, highhanded individual, argumentative but
uncompromisingly righteous, and rated by Weld "the best man
west of the mountains." For several days Shipherd said nothing
to Mahan about his mission, although he talked at length about
his college. Several students from Cumminsville called at Mahan's
residence, and Shipherd confided in them. Then he journeyed to
Cumminsville to confer with all the students. To a man they
endorsed Mahan and also recommended Morgan as a professor. As
for their own future, they agreed to counsel with Weld, but
they seemed disposed to come to Oberlin provided they were
guaranteed full freedom of speech on all reform issues and if the
trustees would agree to admit colored students on equal terms
with whites.[4]

Shipherd hastened back to Cincinnati and broached his proposal to Mahan. The latter was willing to accept the presidency
on the students' terms, and recommended Weld as professor of
theology. Weld would not only be a superlative teacher, he explained, but his influence with the students would be decisive.
So Mahan and Shipherd started after Weld, who had begun his
antislavery labors at Ripley, some fifty miles up the Ohio River.

Arriving by steamboat, Shipherd and Mahan learned that
Weld, after speaking in Ripley for eleven consecutive nights,
had now gone on to Hillsborough. So they spent the night with
the veteran abolitionist John Rankin, from whose home, high
on a bluff above the river, a lamp shone in a window every night
to serve as a beacon for any fugitive slave who might be making
his furtive way to freedom. The next morning Rankin hitched
up his horse and buggy and drove his visitors to Hillsborough.

But Weld was now committed to the antislavery cause. It was clear to him, he told the emissaries, that the abolition of slavery and the elevation of the colored race had demands upon him superior to those of any other cause.[5] Finney would be an ideal professor of theology, however, and would probably be willing to come to Oberlin, inasmuch as his labors at the Broadway Tabernacle in New York, where he had been installed by the Tappans, were proving too onerous for his health. As for the Lane students, Weld would use his influence to induce them to go to Oberlin, provided the trustees met their stipulations.[6]

So Shipherd and Mahan went on to New York, where they found the Tappan brothers much pleased with the Oberlin project, and with Weld's suggestion of a professorship for Finney. Arthur Tappan promised ten thousand dollars for a building to house the theological students and guaranteed a loan of ten thousand more, while Lewis Tappan and a group of philanthropists agreed to pay the salaries of eight professors at six hundred dollars per year, all on condition that Finney accept the appointment.[7] And when Finney still seemed skeptical of Oberlin's financial stability, it is said that Arthur Tappan confided that if necessary he would back the enterprise to the full extent of his income, which was then about a hundred thousand dollars a year, reserving only enough for a modest living for himself and his family.[8]

On December 15, 1834, Shipherd wrote to the Oberlin trustees recommending Mahan and Morgan, urging the passage of a resolution that students would be admitted irrespective of color, and explaining the great good fortune that such a resolve would ensure. On January 1, 1835, the board elected Mahan and Morgan, but on the matter of colored admissions it was not so easily moved.[9] Oberlin had already made a radical departure in accepting women on the same terms as men,[10] and several of the girls in the academy declared they would leave, even if they must "wade Lake Erie," sooner than risk living in an institution that also housed colored men.[11] A poll of the student body showed twenty-six in favor of colored admissions and thirty-two opposed; of the girls, six voted for Negro admission with fifteen against it.[12] Some of the Oberlin townsmen also feared a black influx; so the trustees turned the proposition down. Shipherd implored them to reconsider, reminding them that Western Reserve, the Princeton Theological Seminary, and even Lane, admitted Negroes.

The basic point at Oberlin was the question of trustee versus faculty control of the internal affairs of the college, with control of admission of students an important corollary. On February 10, 1835, the trustees agreed to give the faculty jurisdiction over these matters, and, the faculty being what it was, free discussion of moral issues and admission of qualified Negroes was assured.[13] Soon after this momentous decision a lone Negro was seen approaching the village, and a small boy, son of one of the trustees, who had overheard his parents talking about a Negro inundation, dashed home shouting, "They're coming, father! They're coming!"

While these events were taking place at Oberlin, Weld continued his trek through Ohio, lecturing five times at Concord, seven times at Oldtown where he debated with a physician and a Baptist deacon, nine times at Bloomingsburg, and fourteen times at Circleville where the Presbyterian minister denounced him as a rebel and mischief maker.[14] "Birney is pouring the *whole truth* into the ears of the Pharaohs of Kentucky in open and public assembly. Weld is fast abolitionizing Ohio," wrote Elizur Wright to Amos Phelps from antislavery headquarters. The colonizationists were on the run, Wright exulted. "They throw up bile as if they had swallowed an ocean of Ipecac." [15] By April, 1835, Weld had visited some forty towns and villages, and abolition societies were sprouting everywhere he went.[16]

Whenever he had time to write, Weld sent encouragement to the students at Cumminsville; and they in their turn sent him long, round-robin letters, each man relating what news he could remember. They had been fearful of Weld's safety when he opened his campaign at Ripley, for they had heard rumors that the Kentuckians planned to cross the river en masse to silence him. The Alabamian William Allan confided that his father was provoked at William's conduct and was urging him to return to Lane. "They blow away against abolitionists down there at a terrible rate," Allan reported, "—say they'll cut my throat, that I'm afraid to come home, etc." But the Kentuckian James A. Thome was overjoyed that his father was so moved by reports of the students' consecration that he had given one of his slaves his freedom as a Christmas present.[17]

With Oberlin committed to racial tolerance, Weld urged the Cumminsville group to enroll there. The students were ready to go if provision could be made for their Negro schools, and it was finally agreed that Augustus Wattles and three others, together with the young ladies Arthur Tappan had sent from New York, would remain in Cincinnati. Some help could also be expected from a group of Cincinnati ladies who had been assisting part-time. They meant well and were faithful workers, wrote Phoebe Mathews, one of Tappan's protégées, to Weld, "but they do wish us to stoop so often to prejudice. . . . And they feel so bad if perchance we lay our hands on a curly head, or kiss a colored face."[18] But at least this arrangement would assure the schools' survival, so in May, 1835, some twenty of the Lane rebels left Cumminsville to enroll at Oberlin.[19]

Already consecrated to religious purposes, with the accession of these young zealots Oberlin became a center of Christian idealism. Ever in the vanguard of reform, whenever workers were needed in a righteous enterprise Oberlin could offer recruits. Later, when the American Antislavery Society appealed to Weld to enlist additional agents, he could turn with confidence to Oberlin.

Meanwhile, Weld had called a convention to meet at Zanesville on April 22, 1835, to organize an Ohio State Abolition Society, and had proceeded to Zanesville to put the local citizenry in friendly mood.[20] But Zanesville locked its doors, and he could find no place to lecture—"not a shanty even," he reported. Across the Muskingum River in Putnam the situation was scarcely better, but he finally obtained the use of a public room. At his first lecture, however, he was greeted by a mob that broke the windows, battered down the door, and met him with stones and clubs when he came out. The village trustees forbade further use of the room, but a daring householder permitted Weld to use his parlor.

Weld had planned to have a large representation of colored persons at the state convention. But the people of Zanesville and Putnam were so incensed at the prospect that they vented their malice against the local black folk. Several were discharged from their employment. Other employers were threatened with prosecution under a state law which prescribed a fine for employing a colored person from another state who had not given bond for good behavior. A colored man who attended one of Weld's lectures was knocked down on a bridge going home. In a panic the Negroes called a meeting of their own and resolved to boycott Weld's lectures and to stay away from the convention. They appointed a committee to meet Weld privately and explain the reasons for their decision. If they attended, they would induce many prejudiced white persons to stay away, and the prejudiced ones were just the class who should come. They would also subject themselves to mob violence to no good purpose, besides imperiling their white friends as well. "We will stay at home and pray," they said. And Weld agreed they were right.

When the convention met, rumor reached Lewis Tappan in New York that colored delegates had been excluded, and he wrote Weld a chiding letter which roused the latter's ire. Weld had thought his reputation was sufficient to refute any suspicion of race prejudice, he retorted. Treatment of every man according to his intrinsic worth was his inflexible maxim. But he saw nothing to be gained by mere "ostentatious display of superiority to prejudice," or by "blustering bravado defiance" of custom and public sentiment. His principles were unreservedly equalitarian, but it was folly to flaunt them before a bigoted populace when to do so would endanger the colored folk.[21]

Despite the hostility of the townsmen, the state society was organized at Zanesville. Birney came up from Kentucky. Rankin was there from Ripley. The Lane rebels were represented by delegations from Oberlin and Cincinnati. A number of Quakers attended and promised support. Twenty local societies were represented out of thirty-eight already functioning within the state.[22]

In May, 1835, Elizur Wright, at New York headquarters, informed Weld that his salary had been assumed by the Young Men's Antislavery Society of New York City and was forthwith increased to eight hundred dollars a year. The increase was probably of no consequence to Weld except as it signified satisfaction with his work and provided more money for him to give away. He never desired more money than his simple needs required, and once when Charles Stuart sent him fifty dollars at Lane he immediately turned the whole sum over to the colored schools. Huntington Lyman told Weld's brother Charles about this, and Charles Weld, knowing Theodore's habits full well, had remarked: "Oh, yes, and the next day he very probably wrote to me to borrow money for shirts." [23]

Weld received the news of his increased salary at Pittsburgh, where he was attending the General Assembly of the Presbyterian Church. Of all the sects in the Western country the Presbyterians seemed most amenable to abolition doctrine, and Weld wanted to learn the sentiments of ministers and elders. He hoped to hold one or two public meetings and win the open support of some church leaders, if that were possible.

Elizur Wright and Lewis Tappan urged Weld to force the slavery issue onto the floor, even at the risk of splitting the Assembly asunder, for they were tired of having the question approached in the manner of the old minister who was wont to ask: "Now brethren, how near can we come to doing what is *right*, and keep together?" [24] But Weld was never a deliberate troublemaker, and he preferred to work backstage.

For two weeks he buttonholed delegates in personal conferences, and he was pleased to report a gratifying awakening of conscience. The year before, only two members of the Assembly had been forthright abolitionists; now forty-eight persons, a fourth of the delegates, were favorably disposed. Twenty-seven of these men were ministers, six of them from slave states. "Our principles are perforating the torpid conscience of the church with tremendous power," Weld exulted. The primary opposition now came from "the *aristocracy* and fashionable worldliness of the church—those who are never found in *advance* of public sentiment—those who oppose entire abstenance from *all* alcoholic drinks and stickle greatly for wine and beer, in short, those Christians who join actively in a moral enterprize *only when it begins to become popular*." [25] But among the more lowly church folk abolition was making impressive gains.

When Weld returned to Ohio at the conclusion of the conference, Elizur Wright pressed him to furnish him with something he might publish. Weld's reports were inspiriting and vivid, but he was so modest about his work that he insisted they be considered confidential, for his fear of seeming vain or egotistical had become a haunting obsession. But if every agent took that attitude, Wright pointed out, the society must be mute about its work. People were contributing money and wanted to know to what use it was put. "Suppose now our agents write us not a word but under seal of secrecy," Wright asked; "what shall we answer? Shall not *we* judge of the 'egotism,' the 'vanity,' etc? Has an agent a right to be more 'egotistical' to one of us than to the public? Why should not an agent write just as he *thinks* and *feels*, and why should not his letters be published when they will encourage all real friends and throw dismay into the ranks of the enemy?" [26] But this was a sore point with Weld. It touched his modesty, which he called "pride"; and he was steadfast.

It was only in matters of self-glorification, however, that he was uncoöperative. More agents were urgently needed by the national society and Weld knew where to get them. In those days it was customary for colleges to hold their long vacation in the wintertime, when students could earn money by teaching. As the autumn term of 1835 drew to a close, Weld headed for Oberlin. The place was hard to find, the roads were little more than forest trails, and the buildings and equipment were still rudimentary. As Weld passed through the town he noted that most of the houses were painted red, the cheapest and most durable color. The village square was so studded with stumps that an agile boy could cross it by leaping from one to another. Approaching the campus, Weld saw the log cabin that had first served President Mahan as a residence, although he had a brick house now, as did Finney. And Weld scrutinized with special interest the long, low building, battened with slabs still covered with their pristine bark, that housed the theological students. One other frame building, two stories in height, with a chapel on the first floor and a dormitory above, had been completed. Tappan Hall, the gift of Arthur Tappan, and two other structures were in process of erection.

The Lane rebels greeted Weld with affectionate delight. They recounted their tribulations at Cincinnati since he had left them. They acclaimed the virtues and stimulus of Oberlin. True, they had a lean and hungry look, induced by the school's stern vegetarian diet, and their quarters in "Slab Hall," where they slept two in a room, were little more than cells, each with a stovepipe through the roof, and one window and a door to the outside, with no communication within the building. The floors had developed eccentric dips since the blocks supporting the building had sunk and twisted when the first frost left the ground. The chapel was neither plastered nor lathed and had no heat, and the seats were rough boards placed on blocks. But these were trivialities to be passed off without a second thought, just as Mrs. Shipherd made light of the fetid milk, which always tasted of wild garlic, by observing that at least they had no longing for the leeks and onions of Egypt.[27]

For twenty-one nights Weld lectured on abolition in the cold and dingy chapel. "You may judge something of the interest," he reported to Lewis Tappan, ". . . when I tell you that from five to six hundred males and females attend every night, and sit shivering . . . without anything to lean back against, and this too until nine o'clock." [28] James H. Fairchild, then a sophomore student who would later be a professor and then president of Oberlin, recalled the marvelous power with which Weld spoke. To listen to such an excoriation of slavery was an experience he never forgot. Fairchild doubted if any community was ever more profoundly moved by the eloquence of a single man. College students and bearded men alike sat spellbound. Studies suffered some interruption, but Fairchild thought Weld's lectures were an education in themselves.[29] Weld gave Oberlin such an antislavery baptism that it was ever after an abolition citadel.

Before Weld was half finished with his lectures, six students volunteered to accept antislavery agencies. All of them had come from Lane: Samuel Gould, who would earn fame as an abolition money raiser, William T. Allan, James A. Thome, John W. Alvord, Huntington Lyman, and Sereno W. Streeter. All were destined to begin their work in Ohio or western Pennsylvania except Lyman, who would go to western New York, where he had lived and was well known. Every day Weld spent an hour or more indoctrinating them with facts and arguments.[30]

Of the remaining Lane rebels, Henry B. Stanton had already accepted an agency and was working in Rhode Island with astonishing success. Augustus Wattles, Marius Robinson, Edward Weed, and Augustus Hopkins were still in Cincinnati, teaching the blacks. Others were completing their course at Oberlin. Hiram Wilson, a Lane rebel who would graduate in 1836, served a year as abolition agent in southern Ohio, then labored with the twenty thousand fugitive slaves who had found a haven in Upper Canada; and there twelve other students from Oberlin soon joined him. David S. Ingraham would go to Jamaica to work as a missionary among the recently emancipated Negroes, and seven other students would follow him. Some of them died in the field, and Ingraham himself, after four years of exhausting labor, came back to his native land just in time to die. By 1840, thirty-nine former Oberlin students, half of whom were women, were teaching colored schools in the West. Twenty students had by that time served as agents of the American Antislavery Society in Ohio, Michigan, Indiana, and parts of western Pennsylvania and western New York. Six had gone as missionaries to the Indians.[31]

At first the West had lagged behind the East in antislavery enterprise. But now the thunderhead was rumbling west of the mountains, and Theodore Weld, the man whose face was fearsome as a lightning stroke, was aiming the bolts.

7

A YEAR

TO ABOLITIONIZE

OHIO

When *Weld departed from Oberlin*
he took his six recruits to Cleveland. "There," one of them recalled, "was opened a school of abolition, where, copying documents, with hints, discourses, and suggestions, we spent two
weeks in earnest and most profitable drill." [1]

But if Weld excelled as an organizer, he was no mere closet
strategist. Having put his young men into action, he returned
to the firing line, inspiring them by his example. He had learned
his methods from Finney, and his tactics were to speak for two
hours or more, night after night, until he brought conviction
to his listeners. Joseph Tuttle, later to be president of Wabash
College, hearing Weld speak at St. Albans, in Licking County,
Ohio, testified that he was stirred more powerfully than at any
other time in his life. "Never have I seen an audience more excited," he declared. ". . . The speaker was a very manly, noble

looking man. . . . He used no notes, but spoke with the utmost precision and fluency. . . . His imagination was brilliant, his humor, at times, overpowering, and his invective in all respects the most terrible I ever heard. His voice was wonderful in its compass and power." ² James G. Birney recorded in his diary that he had never known such "a rare combination of talents." "I give him one year to abolitionize Ohio," was his prediction.³

But the opposition was girding for defense. A meeting in Cleveland denounced abolitionists as "unwise, dangerous, and deserving the emphatic reprehension and zealous opposition of every friend of peace." Other gatherings branded Weld and men of his type as "traveling disseminators of treason and discord," and reprobated their doctrines as "tending directly to a civil war and a dissolution of the Union by breaking up the original pact." ⁴ Birney reported that he thought it best to leave Kentucky and wanted Weld's advice about setting up an abolition paper in Cincinnati.⁵ Weld found himself beset by risks and difficulties.

Arriving in town in his shag overcoat, his linsey-woolsey suit and cowhide boots, Weld usually sought out the local Presbyterian minister and obtained permission to hold a meeting in his church. More often than not, however, his first meeting incited a riot. After the first night, use of the church would be denied, and his subsequent meetings were held in a store, a warehouse, a private home, or a barn. Usually Weld's persistence wore down the indignation of the mobs, and after the first two or three nights he suffered no further molestation. Then it was that Weld got down to work, becoming, in Lyman Beecher's words, "logic on fire. . . . As eloquent as an angel and powerful as thunder!" Local celebrities who heckled him—especially clergymen or lawyers—were challenged to debate; and many of them were finally induced to make public admission of error. Although Weld and Lyman Beecher had never got along too well, Weld had profited from one of Beecher's lessons. "Young gentlemen," the doctor had admonished the Lane students, "don't stand before a looking glass and make gestures. Pump yourselves brim full of your subject till you can't hold another drop, and then knock out the bung and let nature caper." 6

Weld regarded slavery solely as a moral issue, a question of right versus wrong. "As a question of politics and national economy, I have passed it with scarce a look or word," he declared, "believing that the business of abolitionists is with the heart of the nation, rather than with its purse strings." It was to conscience that he directed his appeal, trying to bring to bear "the accumulated pressure of myriad wrongs and woes and hoarded guilt." 7

Like Finney, from whom he learned the tactics of evangelism, Weld used his abolition converts as co-laborers, sending them among the audience to urge others to repentance. At the last of his series of meetings he asked all believers to rise; sometimes the whole audience stood up. At Steubenville, when Weld made this appeal, a young lawyer, Edwin M. Stanton, rose from the front row and, turning to the audience with uplifted arms, encouraged them all to rise.8 At Jefferson, Joshua R. Giddings and his law partner, Ben Wade, were moved by Weld's eloquence to take the lead in organizing a local society, and Giddings entertained Weld at his house.9 In Steubenville, the pacific Weld must have been startled by what his oratory had wrought when Ben Tappan, brother of Arthur and Lewis, offered "in sober earnest" to subscribe five hundred dollars for powder and ball to set the Negro free.10 At North Bend, near Cincinnati, William Henry Harrison heard Weld lecture and defended his right to voice his views without disturbance.11 But Ben Tappan backslid quickly when he ran for the United States Senate, a retrogression for which his brother Lewis did not fail to chide him; and Harrison trod warily around the slavery issue when he was nominated for president in 1840. Abolition inclinations were no boon to those who sought political office.

Weld and other pioneer speakers encountered mobs so frequently that they came to consider a riot as part of their introduction. Often the disturbers were merely exuberant youths, who cropped the manes and tails of horses tethered outside the meetinghouse, and confined their assaults to a few barrages of eggs—preferably those of an advanced maturity. All too frequently, however, there were more vicious participants, who, fired with liquor, might become extremely dangerous. At a Presbyterian church in Circleville, Weld was struck on the head with a stone thrown through a window. While he stopped his discourse momentarily to allow his head to clear, some of the men in the audience hung their cloaks in the windows, and Weld, recovering his senses, went on to finish his address. The next night the use of the church was denied him; but he held forth to a capacity audience in a store room, while stones and clubs showered against the shutters.

As Weld left the building, he was greeted by an angry crowd outside the door. Many of the disturbers had disguised their faces with lampblack, and all were armed with stones and eggs and nails. "But the Lord restrained them," Weld reported, " . . . and not a hair of my head was injured. Next evening, same state of things, with increase of violent demonstrations. The next, such was the uproar that a number of gentlemen insisted upon forming an escort and seeing me safely to my lodgings, which they did. This state of things lasted till I had spoken six or seven times, then hushed down and for the latter course [I] had a smooth sea. I lectured fourteen times . . . and now Circleville may be set down as a strong abolition center." [12]

Often these mobs were instigated by the "respectable" element in a town; occasionally the "better element" participated in the rioting. This may have been the case at Chardon, where Weld fell victim to an extraordinary technique. Speaking on the second floor of the courthouse, he had scarcely taken his place behind the judge's bench when he heard a rhythmic tramp, tramp, tramp, ascending the stairs. The door of the courtroom was flung open and a body of men in regular formation, four abreast, came marching up the aisle. Ascending the platform, they crowded Weld to the aisle, down the aisle to the door, on down the steps, and out into the street; then, returning to the courtroom, they used the same technique to disperse the crowd.

On another occasion Weld reported: "I had hardly begun to speak again when a mob gathered with tin horns, sleigh bells, drums, etc., and ding dong'd like bedlam broke loose; valorously pelted the *ladies* with rotten *eggs*, and performed divers other feats all strictly in keeping." Still Weld persisted, and by the close of the meeting he had gained thirty or forty converts.[13]

He seemed almost irresistible if folk would only listen. At Painesville, where a mob invaded his meeting with a bass drum, one of the assailants became so interested in the few words he was able to catch above the thumping of the drum that he begged the drummer to desist, and when that worthy paid no heed to his entreaties he silenced him by kicking in the drumhead.

Weld found that his greatest danger came when he emerged from the meetinghouse and had to confront the mob. Sometimes, as was the case at Circleville, his sympathizers formed a bodyguard to see him to his lodgings; but more often Weld simply drew himself up to his full height, folded his arms, and stood surveying his tormentors. He had learned that such is the psychology of mobs that they were reluctant to assault a man with folded arms.

Weld's co-workers, meeting the same sort of hostility that he encountered, were not always so fortunate as he was. In Nashville, Amos Dresser received twenty lashes on his bare back when abolition pamphlets were discovered in his luggage.[14] Weld's friend Charles Stuart was driven out of Plainfield, Connecticut, by a crowd of angry farmers armed with buggy whips.[15] At Berlin, in Trumbull County, Ohio, Marius Robinson was dragged from a store where he was sleeping at ten o'clock one Saturday night, taken down the road about a mile, stripped naked, tarred and feathered, and driven in a wagon about ten miles farther from town. Set down at daybreak on Sunday morning, he was taken in by a farmer and his wife, who gave him clothing. He had a deep gash in his hip, inflicted when he was dragged over a rack of scythes in the store, and a piece of flesh came off his arm with the tar. But he would only rest until evening, when, going on to the next village, he delivered a lecture on "the Bible view of slavery." He was "considerably bruised and sore," he said, making light of his hurts when he wrote to Weld, "but lectured the better for it." [16]

Equally dauntless were James A. Thome and John W. Alvord, both Lane rebels. Alvord was "a joyous warrior" who seemed almost to welcome mob violence and always saw the comic side of his adventures. "Last night Midd[l]ebury puked," he wrote to Weld, recounting an experience in that Ohio village. "Her stomach had evidently been overloaded" with the two abolition repasts he and Thome had given her," he continued. "Spasmodic heavings and retchings were manifest during the whole day. Toward night symptoms more alarming. The com[mittee] of arrangements . . . came to us and affected to be terribly frightened—advised that the meeting be omitted. We told them it was their concern—we had no personal fears—and if the house was unlocked and lighted we should be there. 6 oclock came. . . . A goodly number soon gathered in, and Bro [ther] Thome proceeded to lecture. All still until about 8 [o'clock] when in came a broadside of Eggs. Glass, Egg shells, whites and yolks flew on every side. Br. Thom[e']s Fact Book received an egg just in its bowels and I doubt whether one in the House escaped a spattering. I have been trying to clean off this morning, but cant get off the stink. Thome dodged like a stoned gander. He brought up at length against the side of the desk, cocked his eye and stood gazing upward at the flying missiles as they stream[e]d in ropy masses through the house. I fear he'll never stand the 'Goose Egg' without winking. He apologizes to me this morning by saying he thought the *stove was crackin*!!!! Well to go on. The audience soon got seated again and Br. T. went on. In about 20 minutes, we heard again the yell of the mob outside, and di-

rectly another crash told us that another Egg plaster was on
its way. They now continued the fire some time like scattering
musketry, mingled with their howlings. There was about 40 of
them. A Mr. Kent, a merchant of this place, attempted to go
out, when a volley was discharged at him and one of them hit him
plump in the right Eye. He cam[e] back groaning most pite-
ously. I understand that he says this morning that he is an abolitionist. It being now 9 o'clock, a resolution was passed unanimously to meet in the same place on Friday eve. They then appointed a committee to bring if possible the rioters to justice
and the meeting adjourned. The meeting was composed of some
of the best men of the village and all appeared firm. The Committee appointed are none of them abolitionists, but are well on
the way. I think this will bring the people here to a stand. The
mob threaten today dreadfully. Whether the citizens will cower
before them or not [we] dont know. There are a few determined
men here, but the mob are set on by men of influence most of
whom are church members. Abolitionists heretofore in this place
have always been mobbed out. We must try to carry the day this
time if possible. Have just heard that 26 panes of glass are
broken and many eggs smashed without coming through. . . ."

As a postscript to this letter Thome added his own comment.
"Weld—What I have to say is that this story of Johns about me
'is just as mean as purssly,'" he protested. "I was brave as a warrior; but I did really think the stove was exploding with a tremendous force. So soon as I was undeceived, I was bold as a Lion.
It was a ludicrous scene though after all. Don't you believe me?" [17]

At one place where Thome tried to hold a meeting in a
church, the minister threatened to bar the door with a club.
Thome was often "egged," but he thought the eggs did great
good, hatching abolitionists by bringing public condemnation of
disorder. Edward Weed, another Lane rebel, agreed. "These mob-
ocrats are all great cowards," he mocked, "and seldom do anything but make great swelling threats, curse, swear, blackguard,
throw eggs, snow balls and get drunk. . . . I have been in a great

many mobs but have never apprehended a great deal of danger. They always further the cause." [18] Weld and his young abolitionist lecturers had faith that God would guard them from all harm.

At another village, a few antiabolition emissaries sneaked into a meetinghouse before a scheduled abolition meeting and stopped the stovepipe with rags. But the abolitionists reported scornfully that like most proslavery efforts "it resulted in nothing but *smoke*." When the meeting began, the hostile crowd outside put a large dog through the window. But the antislavery oratory lulled him, and he lay down and slept.[19]

For the most part, abolitionists were pacifists and would not resist attack. But there were exceptions. At the anniversary meeting of the Ohio State Society at Granville, in April, 1836, the beleaguered antislavery men rushed out of their meeting armed with clubs and dispersed a mob. The proslavery element sent to nearby towns for reinforcements and the next night, about eleven o'clock, so Thome reported to Weld, a mob of two hundred with a fiddler making music at their head advanced on the barn where the abolition meeting was in progress. But so many of the abolitionists had provided themselves with cudgels that the mob dared not attack. The barn was some distance outside the village, and at the conclusion of the meeting the abolitionists, men and women, walked back in double file. As they passed the tavern that served as proslavery headquarters, someone shouted, "egg the squaws," and a heavy barrage was let loose. An abolitionist and his lady were jostled into a ditch, and this started a free-for-all. Several abolitionists were knocked down with clubs and one mobster was stabbed with a dirk.[20]

Donn Piatt, attending an abolition meeting in Ohio which was dispersed by rioters, heard more curses from the audience than he would have credited a group of reformers with knowing.[21]

The hostility that Weld and his men encountered was typical of what was happening throughout the country. For the South, buffeted by antislavery blasts, had begun to fight back. Southern mails were closed to antislavery pamphlets. Southern states appealed to Northern legislatures to make abolition agitation a penal offense. Nonimportation agreements were projected against those Northern cities that "show hostility or a criminal indifference to our rights and interests." Meetings were held throughout the North to assure the South of Northern sympathy. The Northern press demanded measures to suppress the agitation, and in Massachusetts and Rhode Island there were legislative hearings to determine what should be done. But Northern legislatures were reluctant to abridge the right of free speech, so self-appointed guardians of tranquillity sometimes took matters in hand.[22]

On October 21, 1835, William Lloyd Garrison was seized by an antiabolition mob in Boston. Led through the streets with a rope around his waist, he was saved from what might have been a severe manhandling by being locked up in protective custody. Prominent among his assailants were men in broadcloth, some even in high hats, and a number of the younger bullies appeared to be merchants' clerks.[23]

Michigan and New Jersey also witnessed rioting. The colored section of Philadelphia was raided, burned, and looted for three days. Tar and feathers were applied to abolitionists in Indiana. George Thompson, an English abolition orator who was imported to serve the cause in America, was turned out of his lodgings in New York City and mobbed in Maine, New Hampshire, and Massachusetts. The wildest rumors circulated. Five thousand dollars were said to have been offered on the New York stock exchange for Arthur Tappan's head. It was rumored that one city in the South had offered three thousand dollars for Tappan's ears, and that New Orleans had raised a purse of twenty thousand dollars for anyone who would kidnap Garrison.[24]

The whole country was in ferment; so much so that the more moderate antislavery sympathizers began to express alarm. Weld's former mentor, Charles Grandison Finney, foresaw the possibility of civil war. "Will not our present movements in abolition result in that?" he protested to Weld. "Have you no fear of this?" he asked. "If not, why have you not? Nothing is more manifest to me than that the present movements will result in this, unless our present mode of abolitionizing the country be greatly modified." Finney's suggested solution was to make the abolition movement subsidiary to a great religious revival. Salvation should be urged upon the nation; and with awareness of sin, abolition would come peaceably and naturally. "I tell you again that unless we have such an extensive Revival of religion as to soften the church and alarm the world we are all among the breakers," Finney warned.[25] But reformers are seldom mindful of alarms. Weld and his men continued their work with undiminished zeal.

One of the strongest prejudices the abolitionists were obliged to combat stemmed from misunderstanding of their purposes. By "immediate" emancipation they had in mind the beginning at once of a project which would reach fulfillment over a period of years; but the ambiguity of this expression induced many persons to believe that their purpose was not only to free the blacks but to grant full social and political rights to all of them at once. Indeed, some of the more radical abolitionists subscribed to this idea, a fact which made it all the more difficult for those whose zeal stopped short of such an unconditional policy to treat it as a misconception.

James A. Thome told Weld how he tried to meet objections founded on this fallacy in a lecture delivered at Akron. "First," he explained, "I was particularly careful to *disclaim* certain things which are confounded with abolitionism; such as social intercourse, amalgamation, etc. I further stated that we did not claim for the slave the right of voting immediately, or eligibility to office. Also that we did not wish them *turned loose,* having the possession of unlicensed liberty; nor even to be governed by the same *code* of Laws which are *adapted* to intelligent citizens. That on the contrary we believed that it would be necessary to form a special code of Laws restricting them in their freedom, upon the same general principles that apply to foreigners, minors, etc."

Thome was challenged by a lawyer who expressed astonishment at such assertions. He would embrace abolitionism himself if those were its doctrines; but he could not believe that Thome had rightly represented it. "He proceeded then to give his view of abolition," recounted Thome, "and after he had dressed it up in a bear-skin, he fell upon it like a whole kennel of hell-hounds, and he tore it to pieces most adroitly. I complimented him for his skill and *voraciousness*, and hoped that he would have a *happy digestion* of his *bear-skin* and *straw*. I then proceeded to state what abolition *was*; and I blazed and threw sky-rockets, and talked of human rights, touched upon the Amer[ican] Revolution and brought heaven and earth together. I did all the speaking on our side—spoke four times—followed each time by some lawyer or other important personage. Each successive opponent emulated the first dog, in barking at a man of straw, and tearing bear-skins." [26]

Weld and his coworkers found their most receptive audiences in the villages and small towns. The cities, where the business interests often had dealings in the South, and where the workingmen feared the economic competition of free Negroes, were almost uniformly hostile. James G. Birney saw little hope of winning "the aristocracy and the thoughtless rabble" of the cities and large towns; the country's hope lay in its "honest yeomanry." "Let the great cities *alone*," Weld adjured Lewis Tappan, "they must be burned down by *back fires*. The springs to touch in order to move them lie in the *country*." "Sometimes in Ohio," Weld later recalled, "I found it utterly impossible to find rest for the sole of my foot in the capital of a county; but spend a few weeks in the towns around it among the yeomanry and instead of being thrust out, I would be invited and importuned to go to the county seat." [27]

"I do hope your Ex[ecutive] Com[mittee] will speedily take up this matter of *City bombardment*," he further wrote to Lewis

Tappan. "I hope in conscience that New York, Philadelphia, Boston, Portland, Providence, Albany, etc will be let alone for the present season. Let them lie fallow. Or better let them hold their own and be satisfied with that and let every thing in the shape of agents, papers, etc., be poured upon the *country*,—the *country* —the villages—and smaller cities in the interior. In that way the city will *feel* the effect of lectures more vastly than [if] they were fulminated in her." [28]

Weld and his coworkers in Ohio found the Western Reserve to be a most fertile ground. Settled by New Englanders, this area in the northeastern section of the state was now more like the New England of the eighteenth century than was New England itself. Yet even here there was hostility at first, and Weld encountered stones and eggs at Ravenna. But appeal to the Puritan conscience was not in vain, and as Weld and his young cohorts worked back and forth across this region it became more nearly unanimous for abolition than any other area in the United States.[29] In December, 1835, the Western Reserve Synod of the Presbyterian Church took an unprecedented step when it passed an antislavery resolution by unanimous vote—the same resolution, incidentally, that it had voted down the year before. "If the pricks we have given the monster do not make him roar this winter in his den, I am mistaken," gloated Elizur Wright.

The effectiveness of Weld and his young colleagues is attested by the annual reports of the American Antislavery Society. When the society held its annual meeting on May 12, 1835, Elizur Wright was proud to announce that 220 local societies were reporting to the national organization. Massachusetts led with forty-seven, followed by New York with forty and Ohio with thirty-eight.[31] But by the time of the next annual meeting, on May 10, 1836, there were 527 societies, and Ohio was far in the lead with 133. Next came New York with 103 and Massachusetts with 87.[32] Garrison may have been much better known, but Weld and his young coworkers were doing stupendous work.

8

A TIME

TO TEST

MEN'S SOULS

With the Ohio sod well broken, Weld
left its further cultivation to his young recruits while he journeyed on to western Pennsylvania. His reputation had preceded
him, and church groups vied for his lectures. Pittsburgh, almost
untouched by abolition influence, gave him a pleasing welcome
and the *Pittsburgh Times* described him as "one of nature's
orators—not a declaimer—but a logician of great tact and power.
His inexhaustible fund of anecdotes and general information—
with the power of being intensely pathetic, enables him to give
the greatest imaginable interest to the subject." [1]

Year after year Elizur Wright urged Weld to speak at the
anniversary exercises of the American Antislavery Society which
were held in New York City. But Weld would not even attend.
"The stateliness and Pomp and Circumstance of an anniversary
I loathe in my inmost soul," he wrote to Lewis Tappan. "It seems

so like ostentatious display, a mere make believe and mouthing, a sham and show off. It is an element I was never made to move in. My heart was never *in* that way of doing things and never can be. . . . I am a Backwoodsman—can grub up stumps and roll logs and burn brush heaps and break green sward. Let me keep about my *own* business and stay in my *own* place."

He saw no good to come of anniversaries. "I fear much lest our antislavery agents get too much in the habit of *gadding*," he explained, "attending anniversaries, sailing around in Cleopatra's barge, clustering together, six, eight, or ten of them in a place at a big meeting, staying a few days and then streaming away some hundred miles to another and another, and lingering round large cities. The great desideratum of our cause is *work, work*, boneing down to it." [2]

Weld never remained long in a community after things were going well. The executive committee of the national society now urged him to go to New York State, Elizur Wright declaring that "As the battle goes in this empire state, it will go elsewhere." Indeed, it seemed that Weld was wanted everywhere, and he was distressed as to where he should go. [3] After some further speeches in Ohio and western Pennsylvania, however, he set his course for New York and began to work his way across the state toward Utica. Here he expected trouble, for on October 21, 1835, about four months prior to his arrival and the same day that Garrison was mobbed in Boston, delegates who assembled in Utica to organize the New York State Antislavery Society had been dispersed by a mob of "very respectable gentlemen" led by a member of Congress and a judge. Some of the abolitionists had shown a disposition to fight back. But they were outnumbered; and yells, catcalls, and swinging fists broke up the meeting. Among the spectators, however, was a rich landowner, Gerrit Smith, a colonizationist who had been wavering toward immediatism. The rowdyism of the anti-abolitionists completed his conversion, and he invited the convention to adjourn to his country estate at nearby Peterboro. Hastening home in a driving rain to make ready for the arrival of his guests, he put his numerous household to work baking bread and rolls, grinding coffee, paring apples for pies, and making other preparations for entertainment.[4] Weld's estimate of the differing attitudes of town and country was given a striking illustration, for as the abolitionists straggled out of Utica before the angry townsmen, the farmers in the neighborhood brought out their teams and wagons and transported the fugitives free of charge to Peterboro.

Had Weld been a less intrepid man, he would have stayed away from Utica, but to him a danger spot was like a magnet. He opened his campaign in Utica as he had planned, and by the eleventh night such throngs were coming to hear him that many persons were turned away.

Indeed, so great was Weld's success in New York State that his fame flashed like a meteor in abolition circles. Garrison rejoiced in his victories and yearned to hear him speak.[5] The ladies of the Massachusetts Female Antislavery Society invited him to accept a three-months' commission to lecture as their agent in Boston and eastern Bay State towns;[6] but Weld replied that he was the sole antislavery agent in New York State where at least a dozen lecturers were needed. He was familiar in upstate New York, he explained, but utterly unknown in Massachusetts. "I am a *Backwoodsman untamed.* My bearish proportions have never been licked into *city shape,* and are quite too uncombed and shaggy for 'Boston notions,' . . . A stump is my throne, my parish, my home; my element the *everydayisms* of plain common life. . . ."[7]

Weld's experience in New York was the same as that in Ohio—hostility or even threatening mobs at first, until he won a hearing; then respectful attention, and finally heavy enlistments in the local antislavery society or the organization of a new one if none already existed. Nor were these converts mere pledge-signers, for Weld had little patience with that sort. "If your hearts ache and bleed we want you," he would plead, "you will help us;

but if you merely adopt our principles as dry theories, do let us alone, we have millstones enough swinging at our necks already. Further, if you join us merely out of a sense of *duty*, we pray you keep aloof, and give place to those who leap into our ranks because they cannot keep themselves out; who, instead of whining *duty*, shout 'privilege,' 'delight' . . . as they give their names to execration and their bodies to buffetings."[8] Weld's progress was a triumph until he came to Troy, but there he was to suffer a dismal defeat.

"Anti Abolition fury, after being pent up for a few months, is breaking out anew, and with deadlier hate than ever," he reported. On two different occasions a mob rushed up the aisle while he was speaking and tried to drag him from the platform. Stones, bricks, eggs, and cudgels were thrown at him while he spoke. When he left the meetinghouse he was a target for missiles all the way to his lodgings, and only the most strenuous efforts of his sympathizers kept him from the clutches of his tormentors. One of the city officials was an open leader of the rabble, and the mayor and city council were less than half-hearted in their efforts to quell the riots.[9]

Had Weld been a man of lesser mettle, he could have availed himself of a valid excuse to give up, for Elizur Wright, acting under instructions from the executive committee of the national society, urged him to leave Troy and go to Newport to speak before the Rhode Island legislature which was considering appeals from Southern states to pass repressive laws against the abolitionists. It is "their own spontaneous offer," Wright explained, referring to the Rhode Island legislators; for they wished to be fair and give the abolitionists a chance to present their case. Newport was a favored vacation spot for aristocratic Southerners and proslavery Northerners, a place where Weld might do incalculable good. And Weld might so arrange his schedule that he could also appear before the Connecticut legislature on the same trip.[10]

Seconding Wright's plea, the New England clergyman Simeon Jocelyn also urged Weld to come. Newport was a very old town, he pointed out, and had been deeply implicated in the slave trade. Weld would have a mighty opposition to combat; but to carry Newport would be equal to a victory in Charleston, South Carolina.[11] Henry B. Stanton had been stoned in Newport the same day that Garrison was mobbed in Boston, and a few weeks later, when William Goodell announced a temperance lecture at Newport, a crier had been employed to go through the streets to warn the citizens that Goodell's real purpose was to speak on abolition. The citizens had manifested their feelings in such unmistakable terms that Goodell's lecture was "deferred." [12]

Weld would have been overjoyed to meet the Newport challenge, but he would not retreat from Troy under fire. Twice he was severely hurt by missiles, but he was resolved to battle it out.[13] Refusing the mission to Rhode Island, and even canceling engagements in nearby towns, he continued to speak at Troy. But local feeling was so intense that he was reconciled to martyrdom. To a sympathetic clergyman he wrote: "Let every abolitionist debate the matter once and for all, and settle it for himself . . . whether he can lie upon the rack—and clasp the faggot—and tread with steady step the scaffold—whether he can stand at the post of duty and having done all and suffered all, stand—and if cloven down, fall and die a martyr 'not accepting deliverance.' "

This was abolition's proving time, he thought, a time to test men's souls and show forth their true qualities. And a great many so-called converts were shrinking from the blast. "Poor outside whitewash!" Weld exclaimed, "the tempest will batter it off the first stroke; and masks and veils, and sheep cloathing gone, gone at the first blast of fire. God gird us to do all valiantly for the helpless and innocent. Blessed are they who die in the harness and are buried on the field or bleach there." [14]

By this time Troy was in such turmoil that the mayor announced publicly that he regretted his lack of legal power to put Weld out of the city; and finally, in desperation, he declared that, law or no law, he would eject him forcibly if he refused to go. For the first time, Weld's persistence had failed to overcome the rancor of a mob. Realizing the futility of further efforts, he departed peaceably. He had suffered his first setback.

Weld labored on in other parts of New York state with great success, especially in Washington County, close by Vermont.[15] But he was a broken man. His health had been uncertain since his adventure in Alum Creek. He had worked unremittingly for two years under severe mental and physical pressure. He had overtaxed his throat and his voice was gone. He must give up public lecturing for a season.

Meanwhile, the executive committee of the American Antislavery Society had determined upon a change in tactics. Weld and his men had demonstrated the effectiveness of antislavery lecturers, and the executive committee now determined to increase the number of its paid agents to seventy, the number of the Biblical apostles, and, in accordance with Weld's suggestion, to send them into the country districts. "The good cause goes steadily on," wrote Elizur Wright to his parents. "What we most want now is a greater number of lecturers. We are striving to get at least 50 into the field as soon as the busy season of the farmers is over. These will operate in the *country* places. Agents never spend their strength in vain in the country. The great cities we cannot expect to carry till the country is won." [16]

Although Weld avoided the antislavery anniversaries and seldom visited the headquarters office, he kept abreast of everything that went on. His opinions were solicited and carried weight. He was prolific with ideas. From Utica he wrote to Lewis Tappan that the national society should turn its attention to the education and elevation of free Negroes, as the students had done in Cincinnati. Such a program would convince the South that abolition was a truly benevolent movement, unconcerned with "politics, sectional feeling, *party*ism, filthy lucre or any other filthy thing. It would win the candid slaveholder and silence the cavils of the uncandid. By developing the potentialities of the free Negroes of the North it would set them off in striking contrast with the slaves and show that it was slavery that kept the Negro brutish. It would shatter the myth of an inferior race, to which at least three-fifths of the Northern people subscribed. It would prepare the blacks for civil rights. And it would give every Northern abolitionist a job to do. "Let them everywhere establish day schools, evening schools, debating societies, Lyceums, Libraries, etc," he suggested, ". . . and make it a business to call out and vivify and combustionize latent mind. Thus Abolitionism will be living abolitionism, all its fluids in brisk circulation."

This work was too important to be left to casual and unorganized benevolence, Weld wrote. It should be a separate, well-organized department of the antislavery effort under a competent head; and Augustus Wattles, who had gained invaluable experience in Cincinnati and was eager to find his proper place in abolitionism, was a man well qualified to undertake it.[17] Weld's proposal was brought before the executive committee, and a few months later Elizur Wright was pleased to inform Weld that Wattles had been appointed "generalissimo of the colored people." [18]

With Weld incapacitated for further public speaking, the executive committee delegated him to enlist the proposed new agents and prepare them for their work, while Henry B. Stanton, Weld's close friend of the Lane days, was sent out to raise money to pay them. During the late summer and early autumn of 1836, Weld toured New England, combing the colleges and seminaries for recruits.[19] Their job would demand consecration and devotion beyond the ordinary, and Weld wanted only men of heroic mold. Among others, he enlisted Ichabod Codding, then a student at Middlebury College, who, with Owen Lovejoy, was destined later to lead the abolition movement in Illinois.[20]

From New England Weld went to the headquarters office in New York City, where he and Wright mapped out the new agents' work. Weld must have enjoyed the respite after years of strenuous endeavor. He was several times a guest of Lewis Tappan at breakfast, luncheon, or tea. Tappan exchanged watches with him, as he had determined to do when next they met. "I wished him to have a better one than the one he wore three years ago," Tappan recorded in his diary. "I gave it to him." Then, with the meticulousness of the business man, he added: "The value was $21. The one I gave him in exchange cost $45." [21]

Weld and Tappan attended church together, and one Sunday Weld risked disaster to his scratchy throat by speaking to the pupils of Tappan's Sunday School. He attended several meetings of the American Antislavery Society's executive committee.[22] Tappan urged him to accept the position of executive secretary of the national society. If he would assume general charge and Stanton would serve as financial agent, Tappan would have the sort of men he wanted at headquarters. But the job did not appeal to Weld. He preferred to work in the ranks.[23]

Weld's vacation was soon interrupted by a mission to the West. The Oberlin students who had labored as antislavery agents in Ohio during the winter had returned to college in the spring. There they came under Finney's influence, and several of them reported that they were undecided whether to reënlist in antislavery work or labor in the field of general reform. So Weld repaired to Oberlin to reinvigorate them, winning back almost all the former agents and adding twelve additional workers to the ranks.[24]

Wright thought all the agents should be summoned to New York for instruction before they were sent out, and Weld was the man to teach them platform technique and fire their zeal. They should be kindled, warmed, and "combustionized" to a "*welding* heat," wrote Wright. They should be apprised of what to expect and how to meet it, for it was wisdom to look before one leaped, "especially if you are going to leap among rattlesnakes or steel traps." [25] Moreover, some members of the executive committee were themselves in need of energizing. Wright thought they were too concerned about money, especially since some of them saw indications of an approaching financial depression. Tappan and Gerrit Smith, both generous contributors, should be disabused of the notion that if they "should fail to pay their notes at *three o'clock* some day, the cause of God's oppressed would fall through!" "The whole big fallow is as mellow as an ash-heap," declared Wright, "and we, forsooth, are too prudent to buy seed more than enough to sow a few patches, for fear we shall not have money enough to pay the harvesters!" Still he did not wish to be too harsh toward the committee. "The noblest horse, you know," said he, "sometimes has a *prudent fit* going up a long hill." [26]

Despite his aversion to conventions of any sort, Weld agreed to take charge of the agents' meeting, and the workers came together on November 8. They were in session until the twenty-seventh. The course was intensive, with daily sessions from nine o'clock to one, from three to five, and from seven to nine.[27] Weld and the other leaders scarcely took time to eat. Garrison, who came down from Boston, thought the meetings were the most important ever held to advance the antislavery cause, with the exception of the one at which the New England Antislavery Society was organized and that which saw the formation of the American Antislavery Society in Philadelphia.[28] Some forty agents attended of the sixty the society had employed. (It eventually obtained ten more.) [29] Garrison, Stanton, Beriah Green, Charles Stuart, Phelps, Wright, Thome, Dresser, and many others spoke. Their subjects were: What is immediate emancipation?—The consequences of emancipation to the South and to the North—Hebrew servitude—Colonization—Compensated emancipation—Prejudice—The treatment and condition of the free colored population—Gradualism.[30]

At one session Weld spoke for two hours on the question, "What is Slavery?" [31] For four straight days he held forth on "The Bible Argument against Slavery." One listener had never heard "so grand and beautiful an exposition of the dignity and nobility of man in my life." Garrison described Weld as "the central luminary around which they all revolved." Another attendant said: "He was the master spirit, the principal speaker in that assembly, his labors were intense—I have heard him speak 8 or 10 hours in a day at three sessions of the Convention, notwithstanding he had a severe cold—human nature could not endure it . . . for besides his speaking he would be up night after night until 2 & 3 o'clock." [32] Every day Weld felt his aching throat becoming worse until he could not speak above a whisper. Still he kept on. At the end he was almost prostrate.

But as the young men left New York to broadcast the anti-slavery message to the country, they carried the teachings of Theodore Weld throughout the North. Indeed, his influence even penetrated into the South, for Marius Robinson, after working in southern Ohio around Salem, Steubenville, and Marietta, ventured across the Ohio River into the Virginia panhandle. Wheeling was receptive, but the region around Parkersburg was "flaming hot." [33] Yet the zeal which Weld inspired took heavy toll. His voice would never be altogether well again.

9

A N T I S L A V E R Y

E D I T O R

H*aving indoctrinated "the Seventy"*
and sent them on their way, Weld remained in New York. His
throat was so aggravated that he resolved to give it a prolonged
rest, and on April 14 he resigned as an agent. But if he could not
speak, there was much he could do at headquarters. He edited
tracts. He counseled with the agency committee regarding the
placement of agents, a matter requiring planning and judgment
if the central office was to use its limited manpower to the best
advantage. If an agent proved unequal to his work, he was shifted
to a less difficult field; men of anti-Masonic convictions were
kept away from territories where Freemasonry was strong; dull
speakers were sent to places where they could do administrative
or organizational work; men who were competent to meet the
colonization argument were deployed in colonizationist strong-
holds. Agents were shifted constantly according to their varying aptitudes.[1]

At first Weld had no title and no specific job at headquarters.

He helped wherever he could. He had thought the dull routine of office work would stifle him, but he found it vastly exciting. Here he was at the very center of the antislavery movement where he could watch the meshing of all the cogs. The office was filled with visitors from morning till night. He was busy without letup, "with a dozen and more stunning me with questions and discussions and a tap on the shoulder at least as often as once in a minute or two." Elizur Wright, Henry B. Stanton, Joshua Leavitt, and John Greenleaf Whittier, who comprised the office staff, were jabbering constantly. "They buzz—hum, hum, buzz, buzz, all the time," Weld reported.[2]

Wright was executive secretary and in general charge. Stanton, who had demonstrated his ability in New England, had been brought to headquarters to supervise a petition campaign. Leavitt was a Yale graduate, forty-three years old, who had begun to practice law, returned to Yale for a divinity degree, but after preaching for three years had become secretary of the Seaman's Friend Society. Ranging wide in the reform arena, he had founded sailors' missions, compiled an evangelical hymnal, combated liquor and vice. An experienced journalist, his special job was to edit the American Antislavery Society's paper, the *Emancipator*. He was fiery, cocky, self-confident; and his Massachusetts origin and powerful physique had earned him the sobriquet, "the sturdy Puritan."

Whittier was a protégé of Garrison's, although he would break with him later. Only thirty years old, he was already widely known as an editor and poet. Tall and slim, with black eyes gleaming in his swarthy face, he relieved the office tedium with his quick wit, and sometimes flashed out with quick temper. Simple and reticent in manner, he was dandified in dress. Inclined to be romantic, he spent many of his evenings with a young poetess, Lucy Hooper, who lived in Brooklyn. While Whittier was working at the headquarters office, Isaac Knapp, the publisher of Garrison's *Liberator,* brought out the first collected edition of Whittier's poems.[3]

Weld worked well with all three of these men. He and Whittier prepared a "library system" of antislavery literature, suitably bound and boxed, and available to local societies at cost. Weld and the young poet were much together and indulged in long discussions. One summer evening about sundown they climbed to a balcony above the entrance to the City Hall and became so engrossed in conversation that they failed to hear the clock boom out the hours overhead, and were surprised when they saw the sun rising.[4]

"Weld, Whittier, Stanton, Wright," wrote Wright to his parents, "—what a pestilent, dangerous clump of fanatics all in one little room plotting freedom for the slaves! We are all busy—of course more than usually so." [5]

Weld became so absorbed in office work that with his usual disregard of health he overtaxed himself. Obliged to take a vacation, he visited his brother Lewis at Hartford, Connecticut, went to Manlius, New York, to see his parents, then spent a week at his native town of Hampton, Connecticut, where he rambled over the nearby hills and revisited the scenes of his early childhood. He had hoped to accompany Charles Stuart on a trip to England, but was afraid to undertake it in his uncertain health. Yet even on vacation he could not put antislavery labors entirely aside. Everywhere he went he talked abolition, not to public audiences, but to lawyers, clergymen, legislators—anyone who would listen.

Visiting Hartford, Connecticut, he learned of a slave girl, Nancy Jackson, twenty-four years old, the property of a Presbyterian elder from Georgia, who had brought the girl to Hartford with his family two years before and was keeping her there in bondage. Weld and a local abolitionist instituted suit to obtain her freedom, and Weld showed remarkable knowledge of the legal aspects of slavery by proffering advice and citations of authorities to his lawyers.[6]

The girl was brought before Justice Thomas Scott Williams on a writ of habeas corpus, and the facts of the case being presented, the judge deferred the arguments of counsel until the sitting of the Court of Errors in order that the decision might be made by a full bench. On June 17, 1837, the court declared the girl free, thus setting a precedent which might liberate every slave brought into Connecticut and would carry weight in other Northern states as well.[7] Weld reported that he was plentifully threatened with mob violence during the course of the trial, but he showed his usual indifference to danger.

By the summer of 1837, Weld was back at headquarters, ready to welcome his old friend, James G. Birney, who, largely through Weld's influence, had been appointed executive secretary during Weld's absence.[8] At Weld's suggestion Wright now took over foreign correspondence and routine editorial work, Stanton was put in charge of finances, Leavitt continued to edit the *Emancipator*, and Birney assumed responsibility for relations with auxiliary societies and agents. Weld himself was editor of special publications.[9]

It was a job for which he was well qualified, for Stanton declared that he "will pick a dry metaphysical bone for a week, with the gusto of an epicure dining on his favorite dish. Long protracted investigation seems to rest, rather than fatigue him. He will dig a month with the patience of a Cornwall miner, into a dusty library for a rare fact to elucidate or fortify a new position." [10]

To the people of that day the divine inspiration of the Bible and its authority over the minds and hearts of men were accepted tenets. There were a few freethinkers, to be sure, but the generality of people took the Bible as infallible. Southerners claimed that slavery was sanctioned by the Old Testament and permitted by the New Testament, while antislavery Northerners insisted that it was in direct violation of God's commands. Each side backed up its assertions with ample citations of scripture; and, in refutation, each reminded the other of the devil's skill in quoting scripture for his purpose. Southerners started with the premise that moral laws never change, that what was right in Biblical times is right today. If God allowed His chosen people to own slaves, as the Old Testament asserted He did, then slavery was sanctioned by God. The argument was elaborated and refined in ultimate degree, and gave the abolitionists no end of trouble.[11]

Early in Weld's antislavery career he had developed a "Bible argument against slavery" for special use on Sundays; and whenever he trained agents he gave them special instruction along this line. It was a feature of the New York agents' convention, and all the Oberlin agents had mastered it. Indeed, Weld's argument was so effective that while he was still an agent Elizur Wright had urged him to write it out for publication, even if to do so required his hiring an amanuensis or taking two or three weeks off from lecturing. Weld finally got around to doing it, and the argument was published anonymously in the *Quarterly Anti-Slavery Magazine* for April, 1837, under the title "Is Slavery from Above or Beneath." Weld's disquisition proved so popular in antislavery circles that one of his first editorial assignments was to prepare it for publication as a pamphlet.[12] In less than a year it had gone through three editions, and the national society continued to bring out new editions for several years. Antislavery papers quoted it extensively, some of them reprinting the whole pamphlet in serial form. The *Philanthropist* rated it "the most comprehensive and condensed, the clearest and most conclusive, of any we have seen on the subject." [13]

Weld began by defining slavery, whose essence, as he saw it, was reducing men to articles of property, converting persons into things. It was not a matter of curtailing rights, but of annihilating them; not of restraining liberty, but of destroying it. This was the nature of American slavery, and there was nothing like it under Mosaic law. All the prescriptions of that code which proslavery men were pleased to quote as defining the relations of masters and slaves were really admonitions to masters and servants. Weld contended that slavery as Americans knew it never existed among the Hebrews. The Jewish system of servitude was contractual. Hence, slavery in the American sense was entirely lacking in Biblical sanction. In explaining the meaning of certain Biblical terms, Weld showed no little learning in philology. His knowledge of the Old Testament was profound. It would be profitless to reconstruct his argument in detail. Suffice it to say that his work was immensely influential. The pamphlet was scattered broadcast through the North in God-fearing homes, and became a textbook for antislavery agents.[14]

A multitude of special publications kept Weld busy. James A. Thome, whose health, like Weld's, had broken down in lecturing, had been sent to the West Indies with J. Horace Kimball, editor of the *Herald of Freedom* at Concord, New Hampshire, to study the results of emancipation in Antigua, Barbados, and Jamaica. In Antigua, abolition was immediate; in Barbados and Jamaica a system of apprenticeship had been interposed between slavery and freedom. Weld and Thome conceived the idea of studying conditions in these islands with a view to disproving the contention of the proslavery press that emancipation had been a failure, and Weld persuaded the executive committee to provide the necessary money.[15] Thome and Kimball spent six months in first-hand study. Kimball had contracted tuberculosis before he undertook the trip, and died soon after his return, at the age of twenty-six; but Thome compiled the results of their investigation in a manuscript of some eleven hundred pages.

Weld thought this much too long; the audience they wished to reach would never read it. So he notified Thome that he would undertake to reduce it by about five hundred pages. Even this drastic revision was not enough for Weld. The book was still too long, and he went over it again, cutting out sentences and paragraphs in an effort to compress it to readable length. Nor was his editing confined to deletions. He verified every statement carefully in order to make the book immune to criticism. "By the way, my dear brother," he chided Thome, "you were exceedingly careless in some little things, which if they had been printed as they were left in the manuscript would have kicked the dish over." [16] Thome was appalled at Weld's dissection of his handiwork, which amounted almost to a rewriting, but he took it in good part.

The book was published early in 1838 in an edition of twenty-five hundred copies under the title *Emancipation in the West Indies*.[17] But the edition was so soon exhausted that the executive committee authorized Weld to make another revision and prepare the book for stereotyping with a purpose to bring out another printing of a hundred thousand copies.[18]

Thome and Kimball's conclusion was that apprenticeship did not work well in Jamaica because of the planters' failure to coöperate. In Barbados it brought marked benefits to whites and blacks alike; but Antigua, where emancipation was complete and unconditional, showed the most striking advance. Instead of the troubles and disruption that had been anticipated by reason of the abrupt change in established social and economic relationships, there had come blessings to all classes, manifesting themselves in increased economic efficiency, elevation of character and moral tone, banishment of fear of Negro insurrection, amelioration of racial prejudice and distrust, and promotion of general tranquillity and well-being.

The case for immediate emancipation presented by Weld, Thome, and Kimball was so convincing that the leaders of the American Antislavery Society abandoned the policy of immediate emancipation gradually accomplished, which few persons could comprehend, and now announced for unconditional freedom without delay. Most persons, including many abolitionists themselves, had believed that was their objective from the first.[19]

Weld wrote several antislavery disquisitions for the *New York Sun*. He also revised a series of articles he had written for the *New York Evening Post*, where they appeared over the signature of "Wythe," in order that the national society might republish them as a pamphlet with the title *The Power of Congress over the District of Columbia.*[20]

Publication of this tract was part of a new strategy which contemplated stepping up the petition campaign, with special emphasis on Congress' power and duty to abolish slavery and the slave trade in the District of Columbia. From the beginning of the antislavery movement abolitionists had sought to influence Congress through petitions. The Quakers had long been active in this line, centering their fire on slavery in the District and the Territories. Whittier initiated a petition movement in New England through the medium of the Essex County Antislavery Society, and in 1835 the New England society began to circularize. In the West, the Lane students sponsored a monster petition, and Weld wrote a section into the constitution of the Ohio Antislavery Society pledging it to make the utmost use of petitions. As early as 1834 the American Antislavery Society had undertaken to encourage these local efforts by sending out printed forms; and so eager was the response that Congress was deluged. Irritated almost beyond endurance, Southern congressmen, abetted by Northern sympathizers, had invoked a "gag" rule prohibiting the reception or discussion of these pleas.

In this they were ill-advised. Petition for redress of grievances was a cherished American right whose abridgment brought a new champion onto the field. Up in the chamber of the House of Representatives rose old John Quincy Adams to excoriate and denounce. Although he had been wary of antislavery agitation, seeing it from its beginnings as a menace to the union of the states, yet he was even more apprehensive of curtailment of constitutional rights. Day after day he shuffled into the chamber laden with petitions subscribed with long lists of names, and day after day he insisted upon presenting them, only to be silenced when the Speaker applied the gag.

An able, learned, testy-tempered man, the Puritan zeal of his forebears coursed in his veins. Obstinate, uncompromising, fearless, stern, he had not thought it beneath his dignity to serve in the lower house of Congress after holding the high office of president as well as serving as secretary of state and at important diplomatic posts. Enfeebled by age, his voice, once rich and resonant, now tremulous and fitful from his years, he tried repeatedly to override the gag, only to see it made a permanent rule of the House. The rank and file of the abolitionists thought he had joined their clan, but actually he held himself aloof, hating slavery, but holding it subordinate to the questions of constitutional privilege and his own right of free speech as a member of the House. If he was not an abolitionist, nevertheless he would use every device or subterfuge to put antislavery petitions before the House. James G. Birney, taking over the direction of the national society, was determined to make the most of this ally.[21] "We wish to remind our friends of what is before them the coming fall and winter," wrote Leavitt in the *Emancipator*. "Petitions are to be circulated and sent to Congress by hundreds and thousands, praying for the abolition of slavery in the District of Columbia. The State Legislatures should also be memorialized." [22]

The attack was well planned. Two persons were appointed in every county to receive petition forms from national headquarters and to see that they were subscribed with signatures and sent to Congress. These persons in turn selected two leaders in each township. "Let petitions be circulated wherever signers can be got," read the instructions. "Neglect no one. Follow the farmer to his field, the wood-chopper to the forest. Hail the shopkeeper behind his counter; call the clerk from his desk; stop the waggoner with his team; forget not the matron, ask for her daughter. Let no frown deter, no repulse baffle. Explain, discuss, argue, persuade." The North was flooded with petitions, which, subscribed with long lists of names, cascaded into Washington upon apprehensive congressmen.

Brief and to the point, most of the petitions protested

against slavery and the slave trade in the District of Columbia, but others opposed the annexation of Texas, the interstate slave trade, the extension of slavery to the national Territories, the admission of Florida to statehood unless slavery were proscribed by her constitution—indeed, they were directed against any act or situation calculated to give comfort to the slaveholder.

Women played their part in the crusade. The work of obtaining signatures fell largely to them, and in 1837 they formed a national organization of their own. Carrying petitions from door to door, discussing slavery in their sewing circles and at their quilting bees, arguing with recalcitrant husbands and sons, the women brought a potent influence to bear.

Coöperating with Birney at the New York headquarters, Weld, Stanton, and Whittier stoked the forge. When financial stringency resulting from the panic of 1837 forced the dismissal of many agents, they filled the ranks with volunteers, and the petition flood showed no abatement. And by 1840, when every agent of the national society had either been dismissed or transferred to a state or local society, more petitions than ever were coming in. The abolition movement was no longer the cause of a few zealots and hired workers. The people were taking over.

Instead of stagnating in the New York office as he had expected to do, Weld wrote: "I have never done half so much for Abolition as since I have stopped speaking." Yet his was a lonely life. "I am a hermit here in the midst of throngs," he complained. He boarded with a colored man and woman, brother and sister, eating his meals with them in a little room with an uncarpeted floor and walls with newspapers pasted over the plaster cracks. He slept in a tiny attic room two miles uptown, with a colored man for his landlord. Every morning he was up at dawn or earlier, and after taking his customary bath he would go out and walk and run and hop for an hour or more, sometimes going four miles and never less than two before breakfast. In winter he split his own wood and carried it up the three flights of stairs to his room. He was always at the antislavery office by eight o'clock. Before and after office hours he visited sick and needy colored persons, so that he never returned to his lodgings before eleven o'clock at night.[23]

And besides the burden of his work, Weld was racked by mental turmoil. He had vowed never to marry till the slavery struggle was won; but an irresistible lady had entered his life.

10

TWO SISTERS

FROM SOUTH CAROLINA

Foremost *among King Cotton's loyal*
courtiers was the prosperous, pushing, perky little state of
South Carolina. Rich in her agricultural resources of cotton, rice,
and indigo, she was proud of her beautiful and prosperous city of
Charleston, teeming with commerce, graced by the mansions of
affluent planters clustered along the waterfront, its streets bor-
dered with tropical palms festooned with Spanish moss, and its
gardens bright with gorgeous oleanders. Boastful of her cultural
heritage and her brilliant statesmanship, typified in John C. Calhoun and Robert Barnwell Rhett, and not a little arrogant in assertion of her rights, South Carolina typified the slaveholding
South. Yet out of South Carolina were to come two of abolition's most effective champions, the sisters Sarah and Angelina
Grimké. And it was Angelina who had set Weld's heart aflutter.

Weld had first met the sisters in November, 1836, when they
attended his indoctrination lectures for the new agents, al-

though he knew them previously by reputation. Garrison introduced him to them after one of his meetings, and Angelina thrilled when Weld called her "my dear sister."

Sarah was forty-four years old, Weld's senior by eleven years, Angelina was approaching thirty-two. Both sisters were devoutly religious. Their friends remarked their beauty, and Angelina was described as tall and graceful, with a shapely head crowned with chestnut ringlets, a lovely complexion, and clear blue eyes that could either flash or dance. If the sisters were beautiful, however, their photographs are something less than flattering, for they represent both Sarah and Angelina as angular in body and of forbidding countenance.

Their father, John Faucheraud Grimké, was of Huguenot descent. Aristocratic and courtly, he was born in South Carolina and educated at Oxford. He began to practice law in London, but with the outbreak of the American Revolution he returned to South Carolina and served as a colonel in the Revolutionary army. With the winning of independence he opened a law office in Charleston and rose to be a justice of the Supreme Court of South Carolina.

Their mother, Mary Smith Grimké, sister of a North Carolina governor, was of Irish and English Puritan stock, so that they had a non-conformist heritage on both sides. High-strung and narrowly religious, Mrs. Grimké was as overbearing toward her children as she was toward the family slaves. Indeed, there seemed to be little affection between members of the family, save the mutual love of Sarah and Angelina and a reciprocal devotion between them and their brother Thomas.[1] A Yale graduate and brilliant orator, Thomas Smith Grimké was a unionist during the South Carolina nullification excitement. Enlisting in such causes as peace, temperance, education, and betterment of the condition of the Indians, his reform adjurations were stilled by his untimely death from cholera in 1834,[2] but not before he had exerted a lasting influence upon the sisters.

Both girls had known frustration. Sarah craved education, and, when admonished that learning was not for ladies, she had studied literature, languages, and even law in secret, until she was found out and rebuked. She rebelled at being a "doll, a coquette, a fashionable fool," and when her aspirations were denied she plunged into the Charleston social whirl of theater-going, balls, and parties in a sort of defiant abandon.[3] This merely induced a sense of guilt, especially when a Presbyterian minister tried to win her to that faith. She said later that she did not know to what this frivolous life might have brought her had she not been obliged to leave Charleston and accompany her father to Long Branch, New Jersey, where he went for the sake of his health. She nursed him there until he died; then she returned to Charleston, only to chafe anew at the social conventions that stifled her intellectual longings, and at the ritualistic formalism of the Episcopal worship in which she was brought up.[4]

Angelina, too, grew up in the social whirl. She fell in love. Her lover died; and she enshrined him in her memory with bittersweet nostalgia.[5] Now she too rebelled at luxury, and in a naïve effort at asceticism she would refuse rich cakes, wine, fruit, and nuts when invited out to tea. She could find no more comfort in the church than Sarah could, although her sense of religious mysticism was equally strong and deep.

From girlhood the sisters had pitied the slaves. They suffered agonies when slaves were punished, for Judge Grimké was a stern taskmaster. Yet they were reared on the Southern Bible argument, and did not think the institution sinful until they came under abolition influence. When Sarah was quite young her father assigned her a slave girl as a handmaid, and Sarah was anguished when the little creature died soon afterward. Sarah tried to educate some of the Grimkés' more intelligent Negroes, instructing them orally, and complaining about the South Carolina law that forbade her to teach them to read.[6]

Angelina was irritable and hot-tempered as a girl, and claimed she overcame these failings when a slave promised to make her a doll and dress it like a soldier, if she would learn to control herself.[7]

She would have nothing to do with slavery, even as a child, except in one case. Mrs. Grimké owned a slave she could not manage, and Angelina persuaded her mother to let her have the girl. She obtained a place for her in another family, but would not accept her wages. Finally she returned title to the girl to Mrs. Grimké on condition that the slave be allowed to remain where she was.[8]

In her late twenties, Sarah visited some Quaker friends in Philadelphia. Later she moved to that city and became a Quaker herself. She had already tried Presbyterianism and Methodism, but they furnished no more comfort than Episcopalianism, and she thought herself the vilest of sinners. Hers seemed to be a misdirected life; she yearned to be a useful member of society.

Under Sarah's influence, Angelina became a Quaker, too, and later joined Sarah in Philadelphia. Angelina might have been happy except for Sarah, who, with her passion for self-immolation, made Angelina doubt that true religion and happiness could be compatible. As it was, neither girl could feel contentment except in austerity and self-sacrifice. Both had the conviction that they were called to some great work.[9]

To come under Quaker teachings was to imbibe antislavery doctrine, for the Friends were pioneers in antislavery, and all of them opposed slavery in the abstract. Their hostility was of varying degrees, however, and the solutions they recommended ranged from colonization to immediatism. Indeed, the Quakers were so rent by antislavery argument that discussion of the subject was now discouraged. But in antislavery the thwarted Grimké sisters found release for their restless spirits. Determined to devote themselves to moral uplift, they became emphatic champions of abolition.

Some of their Quaker friends were quite provoked, not only because of their disputatious agitation of a controversial issue, but by other instances of non-conformity as well. The sisters did not use all the Quaker forms of speech, they wore bonnets better suited to protection from the cold than those prescribed by

Quaker style, and they resorted to vocal prayer in private devotions, a practice contrary to Quaker usage. To Angelina the efforts of certain Friends to still antislavery discussion were like the attempts of the Jews to close the lips of Jesus. She felt called of God to speak, and believed that one should not be swayed by others in matters of conscience.[10]

Factors in making Angelina an active abolitionist were the mobbing of Garrison in Boston and the assaults on George Thompson, the British antislavery agent. Angelina wrote Garrison a letter of encouragement, and Garrison printed her letter in the *Liberator*.[11] This was Weld's introduction to the Grimké sisters. The letter made an odd impression on him. He read it again and again. He seemed to hold communion with this unknown Quaker girl, he told her later.

The sisters were appalled to see Angelina's letter thrust before the public; but their sense of duty soon overcame their shyness. In 1835 Angelina published an *Appeal to the Christian Women of the South*, urging them to recognize their responsibility for slavery and use the power of moral suasion against it. Sarah wrote an *Epistle to the Clergy of the South* in which she voiced a similar appeal.[12] Recognizing the potency of arguments adduced by women of slaveholding antecedents, the abolitionists seized upon these pamphlets eagerly and spread them over the land. But the treason of the sisters outraged the South. Postmasters in South Carolina burned the pamphlets publicly, and the authors were threatened with imprisonment if they had the audacity to come home.

The Quakers were the only well-established sect that encouraged women to speak in meeting, and Sarah and Angelina availed themselves of that right. Persuaded that they had an aptitude for public speaking, they resolved to devote their talent to antislavery lectures. Of course they would confine themselves to women's meetings in conformity with the usage of the day.

Both sisters recognized the need for further training and indoctrination, and it was this that brought them to Weld's training course. Weld noted the two young ladies with their little Quaker bonnets in his audience, and upon acquaintance he found Angelina disturbing. He often encountered the sisters at the Tappans';[13] indeed, much as he tried, it was impossible to avoid them altogether. But Weld was not easily diverted from his life's purpose. He was wedded to a cause; and as the tantalizing fondness for Angelina grew with acquaintance, he strove with all the power of his grim will to suppress it. Moreover, this aristocratic girl was far above him. Like him, she had a mission to perform. And, being a Friend, she was forbidden to marry outside her faith in any event. Weld resolved to overcome his unseemly yearning by devoting his full powers to making the sisters potent anti-slavery instruments.

Under his tutelage Angelina became eloquent and quick in argument. Sarah was capable, too, although she lacked self-confidence, and often fumbled for words. Sometimes her speech was slow and hesitant; again she became excited and spoke too fast.

The sisters attended colored Sunday Schools and prayer-meetings in New York. They began to address small gatherings of women. Their meetings were better attended than they had hoped, but they found New York a difficult place in which to work. "Ten thousand cords of interest are linked with the southern slaveholder," they complained. They extended their area of service to smaller communities outside the city proper, laboring quietly to avoid publicity, devoting their spare time to study in order to be "fully harnessed" for their labors.[14]

Sometimes Weld and other young men at the headquarters office were obliged to act as their escorts. Angelina noticed how Weld's face, which was preternaturally stern in any event, became even more hard-set and impenetrable when she was with him. Yet, when he accompanied the sisters on visits to the colored poor, his perfect ease and lack of condescension impressed them with his innate goodness.[15] Angelina scarcely dared admit it to herself, but she believed she loved him. To be sure, it was an unrequited affection, for he would not even take her arm when they walked down the street, unless one of the other men reminded him to do it. When they went to church, he hung back until someone else had offered to take her home. And when he accompanied the sisters to the steamboat, as they left on a speaking tour of Massachusetts, his farewell was so impersonal that it seemed to stab her heart. She was glad she had not confided her feelings to Sarah. She would overcome this futile fancy with hard work.[16]

The sisters evoked a whirlwind in Massachusetts.[17] Women attended their lectures in such numbers that their courage almost failed before the crowds. Then men began coming too. At first they only gathered around the doors and listened at the open windows, with their heads above the lowered sash. Then some of the more courageous spirits began to venture in. Almost before they realized what was happening the sisters were speaking regularly before mixed audiences, a thing they had never planned to do.

At first they were a little shocked at their own boldness, for the ideals of that day held woman to be a pure and bashful creature whose charm derived from helplessness. Her place was in the home, her function that of mother and fond wife. She was supposed to shun the tumult of public controversy and hold her peace in mixed assemblages. Her influence must work in subtle ways.

American men were noted for their deference toward women, yet women won this deference by acquiescing in the notion of masculine superiority. Politics were exclusively men's affair; nowhere in America could women vote. Nor did married women enjoy the right of property, or even the right to their children, before the law. No institution of higher learning admitted women until Oberlin led the way, and except for teaching or domestic service, few jobs were open to them.[18] These usages enjoyed the sanction of the church, and ministers, whose influence was paramount with women, resisted any threat of innovation. Anything smacking of boldness or assertiveness in women was certain to evoke the clerical ire.

The sisters' lectures in Massachusetts were under Garrisonian auspices, and Garrison had already ruffled the clergy with his censures against clerical tenderness toward slavery. Indeed, the ecclesiastical authority had been flouted to a degree that these irreverent radicals must be rebuked. Even so good an abolitionist as the Reverend Amos A. Phelps was impelled to write a letter of remonstrance to the sisters, and the sensibilities of the gentle, kindly Samuel J. May were shocked by their boldness at first.[19] Delegated to express the views of his colleagues, the Reverend Nehemiah Adams, a preacher of the old school whose friendliness to Southern rights was to earn him the sobriquet of "Southside" Adams, prepared a "Pastoral Letter" which reprimanded both Garrison and the Grimkés. Garrison was chided for seeking to make the church a place of "doubtful disputation" by instigating abolition agents to make speeches in churches where abolition sentiments were unwelcome, and for undermining the deference due the pastoral office. The Grimké sisters were warned of the insidious effect of female lecturing on both the lecturers and their auditors. Woman's strength came of dependence, proclaimed Adams. God made her weak that she might command man's support; and by assuming the position of a public reformer she forfeited man's respect. For "if the vine, whose strength and beauty is to lean upon the trellis work, and half conceal its clusters, thinks to assume the independence and the everlasting nature of the elm, it will not only cease to bear fruit, but will fall in shame and dishonor into the dust." [20]

The "Pastoral Letter" centered a noisy contention upon the Grimkés. Conservatives regarded them as infamous; to Weld and his abolition brethren they were heroines. At the behest of his deacons, one clergyman invited them to speak from his pulpit; then, in defiance of his official men, he implored the congregation to stay away. Another pastor declared that if they spoke in his church, he would never cross its threshold again. At Groton, where they spoke in a barn because every church was closed to them, a clergyman consented to open the meeting with prayer, then took his leave, announcing as he strode to the door that he would as soon rob a hen-roost as stay and hear them speak.[21]

Traveling by boat from New York to New Haven, James G. Birney encountered the Reverend Leonard Bacon, pastor of the First Congregational Church of New Haven and later to be professor of theology at the Yale Divinity School. Bacon offered Birney his hand, but Birney drew back. "Mr. Bacon," he declared, "I cannot interchange civilities with you till I know the truth of what I have heard you said of Miss Grimké in your speech on Saturday."

"And what was that?" asked Bacon.

"I have been told," responded Birney, "that in speaking of fanaticism, at one time in New England, you said a Quaker woman had been known publicly to walk through the streets of Salem, *naked as she was born*—but that Miss Grimké had not been known to make such an exhibition of herself *yet*. Did you say this?"

"I did," replied Bacon. And after a pause: "And should I have said that she *did?*"[22]

Abashed at their unwanted notoriety, but resolute in faith, the sisters continued their campaign, speaking five and six times a week, traveling from one place to another in stages and wagons, sometimes in rain, sleet, or snow, putting up with poor and insufficient food and wretched lodgings, often ill with colds and sometimes so exhausted they would have to spell one another on the platform. On January 5, 1838, Sarah related their experiences at South Scituate to her friend Jane Smith. The notice of the meeting that had been arranged for them came late, and they missed both stage and steamboat. A friend volunteered to take them in a carryall, and they were thankful he had thought to cover them with a buffalo robe, for the wind came in bleak off the sea. It was an awful night, but the house was filled. "I spoke with great difficulty," Sarah wrote, "for the stove pipe was just above the pulpit & the doors and windows were all closed. My mouth became exceedingly parched & water would not relieve it. (Perhaps I was feverish too)." [23]

Sometimes the crowds were so large that Angelina spoke in one hall while Sarah held forth in another. At Woonsocket a joist gave way in a church, and when it was propped others began to creak, but still the people stayed.[24] At another town, where they spoke in a second-story hall, men who hesitated to come in crowded upon ladders at the windows and clung to their precarious perches throughout the meeting.

The longer they stayed in Massachusetts, the more they were subjected to Garrison's influence. Henry C. Wright, an agent of the American Antislavery Society but a man who was much closer to Garrison than to the New York headquarters group, made it his special duty to arrange their itinerary, to write reports of their activities for the *Liberator*, and to constitute himself their squire and counselor.[25] A tight-jawed man with short-cropped hair, lean cheeks creased with cross-hatching lines, and beetle brows overjutting his hard eyes, Wright had the austere visage of a Cromwellian Roundhead. Impetuous and headstrong, he was so fanatically zealous in reform that it was said of him that only after long wrestling with his soul could he bring himself to spend ten dollars on an ailing tooth, rather than give the money to some worthy cause.[26] He wrote prolifically for antislavery papers, taking care, Weld thought, to make his name conspicuous. Weld could not endure such vanity. And while he would have been horrified to be accused of jealousy, he resented Wright's intimacy with the sisters, and was instrumental in having the agency committee transfer Wright to Pennsylvania, an action which evoked the sisters' anger.[27]

Weld watched with apprehension as the sisters' minds inclined increasingly toward Garrison's views; for Garrison was becoming so incautiously intemperate that even fellow abolitionists were turning away from him. Assured of his omniscience, inflexible in his faith, Garrison seemed utterly unmindful of the consequences of his zeal. Tall and erect, prematurely bald, and so nearsighted that his children had discovered that when playing blind man's buff they needed only to remove his gold-rimmed spectacles instead of blindfolding him, he was punctilious in dress, manners, and personal deportment. He was so facile with words that his editorials were ready for the press when they left his pen. In his bitterest diatribes never so much as a comma or quotation mark was misplaced, and when pressed for time he could set his editorials in type without writing them out at all. The power of his speeches came as much from the utter self-forgetfulness with which he developed his theme as from their acrid bite; and the same voice that excelled in oratorical malediction, in private conversation breathed an almost feminine charm. He could argue without becoming excited or loud, and those who knew him only by reputation were agreeably surprised upon acquaintance to find him so bland and urbane.

Born and reared a Baptist, he based his reform philosophy on scriptural precepts. He hoped to find his staunchest allies in ministers and church members, and, when he was unable to shatter their indifference, he turned a critical eye on their theology. He stopped attending church, rejected Sabbath observance on the ground that true Christians should hold one day holy as another, and condemned the institution of a paid ministry with the argument that man needed no intercessor between himself and his Maker.[28]

The Grimké sisters came easily under his spell. Sarah felt a sort of elasticity in the Boston atmosphere. Accepting Garrison's opinion of the uselessness of ministers, which was akin to Quaker beliefs in any event, she rejoiced in the prospect of release from the obligation of attending public worship. She confessed that it had become a weariness to her soul, "and if that part of the machinery of piety is laid in the dust, then the necessity of a regular ministry . . . will cease, and that will be a wonderful relief to my spirit." Ministers had been anathema to her ever since she was reborn in abolitionism.[28] Sarah and Angelina became ecstatic in relating Garrison's virtues to Weld. What a pity, they wrote, that he suffered such torture from the scrofulous infection on his scalp. It was a complaint that continued to break out on various parts of his body for years afterward, and its cure was probably not promoted by his indulgence of the office cat, which he allowed to caress his bald forehead while he spun editorial yarn.

With a mind eager for new ideas, Garrison was surprisingly naïve, and fell an easy prey to fads and foibles. He had unbounded faith in patent medicines and nostrums. Phrenologists found tempting quarry in his smooth pate. Mediums could tune him to the spirit world. He tried dietary fads and water cures, and lost an infant son by the imperfect operation of a medicinal steam bath.[30]

A thoroughgoing pacifist, he had early acknowledged the virtues of nonresistance. "We justify no war," said he. "The victories of liberty should be bloodless, and effected solely by spiritual weapons. If we deemed it pleasing in the sight of God to kill tyrants, we would immediately put ourselves at the head of a black army at the South, and scatter devastation and death on every side." [31] In November, 1837, when Elijah P. Lovejoy was shot down by a proslavery mob at Alton, Illinois, while attempting to defend his abolition press, Garrison voiced regret that Lovejoy died with a weapon in his hand. In Garrison's sight, resort to force, even to defend oneself, was a rebuff to God. One must never doubt the power of His everlasting arms.[32]

Of all Garrison's idiosyncrasies, however, the one that was most generally alarming and most unpalatable to Weld and many others of his fellow abolitionists was his rejection of government—an end product of his vexation at those constitutional guarantees behind which slavery could take refuge when hard pressed, and a logical extension of his non-resistance beliefs. For if a man must not resist, he should not be coerced, he explained. Every human government was upheld by coercion or the threat of it. Governmental authority derived from the right to punish.

But Garrison denied this right to men or human agencies; vengeance and punishment belonged to God. Thus Garrison's righteous idealism brought him to a sort of philosophical anarchy.[33]

While Garrison's rejection of government was a logical consequence of his own ideas, his thinking in this direction was stimulated by young John Humphrey Noyes, an honors graduate of Dartmouth College who had begun to study law but gave it up to become a minister. Revolting at the Calvinistic belief in human depravity, Noyes became convinced that man could attain to perfect holiness and that he himself already enjoyed that estate. He also rejected the idea of monogamous marriage as being incompatible with human perfectionism, and was already developing a conception of "free love" which was to be put into practice later in his Oneida Community.

Noyes renounced allegiance to the Government of the United States and asserted "the title of Jesus Christ to the throne of the world." He wrote Garrison that when he thought of the United States Government he pictured "a bloated, swaggering libertine," trampling on the Bible and its own Constitution, "with one hand whipping a Negro tied to a liberty-pole, and with the other dashing an emaciated Indian to the ground." Every person who voted or held office acknowledged himself a subject of a slaveholding government, and Noyes could not but think that many abolitionists had heard "the same great voice out of heaven" that had waked him with the call, "Come out of her my people, that ye be not partakers of her sins and her plagues." Admonishing Garrison to assume leadership of a no-government movement, Noyes admitted that if Garrison did so, he would be deserted by many of his present friends, "but you will be deserted as Jonah was by the whale—the world, in vomiting you up, will heave you upon the dry land." [34]

Weld had no faith in Noyes' type of perfectionism. His brother Charles had seen the perfectionist put on a strange performance in New York. He was in a "highly spiritual" state, and to prove his insensitivity to perverse influences he had consumed large quantities of rum, raw whiskey, and cayenne pepper, topping off the whole by eating a handful of tobacco. Weld's brother was amazed that he survived, and Weld was convinced that Noyes was a charlatan.[35]

But Noyes' plea was not without effect on Garrison, for shortly thereafter Garrison became a leader in the formation of the New England Non-Resistance Society, which denied allegiance to any human government, refused to recognize national boundaries or distinctions of caste, race, or sex, renounced all war, forswore participation in celebrations of military victories, and pledged its members to hold no office under government, to use no governmental agencies for redress of grievances, and to abstain from voting.[36] Henry C. Wright was a leading organizer and first president of the society, and won the Grimké sisters to its tenets.

This topic was the subject of many argumentative letters between Weld and the sisters. Sarah was amazed that Weld could not perceive "the simplicity and beauty and consistency" of the doctrine that all government, whether civil or ecclesiastical, "conflicts with the govt. of Jehovah and that by the Christian, no other govt. can be acknowledged without leaning more or less on an arm of flesh." Angelina thought "No-government" was "a sublime doctrine" which would "bring us into that liberty wherewith Christ hath made us free."[37]

Weld retorted that it was a crazy phantasy. He was a peace man, he asserted, but not a no-government man. "The doctrine of personal *non-resistance*, of returning good for evil, of being smitten and turning the other cheek, I have not only advocated in private for years and in public debate at Oneida Institute and Lane Seminary, but for months when I first began lecturing in Ohio I was called to the *test* almost every day." But he shuddered at the idea of rejecting government, and prayed that the Lord would enlighten those "who are bewildered in its mazes and stumbling on its dark mountains." Weld feared that the sisters were succumbing to the blandishments of flatterers. They had not thought this thing through, he warned, or, if they had, then they were placing too much confidence in their own reasoning powers.[38]

As the sisters' right to speak was challenged, they were drawn into a defense of woman's rights. Sarah wrote a series of "Letters on the Equality of the Sexes and the Condition of Women," which were published in the *New England Spectator*. Both sisters asserted their rights as women from the platform and in the press, and Garrison, with his usual readiness to leap into the forefront of any new reform, not only urged them on, but himself became an aggressive leader of the woman movement.[39] Thus he exposed another angle to enemy fire. For, having antagonized the church and clergy, shocked the Sabbatarians, and horrified those who saw the American government as the perfect political organism, he now scandalized the guardians of the modesty and humility of womanhood. Accepting him as abolition's spokesman, people took his aberrations to be adjuncts of abolitionism. Supporters of the established order not only found reason to detest him, but were also confirmed in their horror of the movement he symbolized.

Watching Garrison's antics from the New York headquarters office, Elizur Wright feared that Garrison had forfeited his usefulness to the antislavery cause. It was downright nonsense to suppose that antislavery could be promoted "with forty incongruous things tacked on to it." "You can't drive a three tined fork through a hay mow," Wright explained to Phelps, "though turn it t'other end to, and you can drive in the handle. And I don't see why when Garrison knew his paper was regarded as the organ of the Mass. Society he did not have abolitionism and common sense enough to conduct it strictly as an abolition paper. . . . When I charge this mismanagement upon Garrison, I do not forget that he has done far more for the slave than I can expect ever to do. I love him too, like a brother. But I believe his noncombatism and his perfectionism are downright fanaticism, and I don't wonder that there should be a recoil among men who are not ready to concede so much to the Spirit of Liberty as you and I, but are pretty good abolitionists for all that."[40]

Weld, too, was aware of the dangers inherent in Garrison's scattershot zeal and in the Grimkés' agitation of the woman question. When the sisters wrote to Weld complaining of the way the clergymen were treating them, he accorded them scant sympathy. They must expect resistance if they tried to make an issue of women's rights, whereas, if they would simply "let the barkers bark their bark out," the opposition would soon cool down; for while there were many old-school ministers who would make violent opposition to any change in woman's status as being contrary to God's will, yet there were even more who would come over "if they first witness the successful *practice* of it rather than meet it in the shape of a doctrine to be swallowed." Abolition was the thing to talk about, Weld pleaded, and, being Southerners, the sisters would command attention and be believed. They could do ten times as much for antislavery as could women like Lydia Maria Child or Maria Weston Chapman, not because they were more competent than they or other Northern women were, but because the Grimkés were Southerners. But the moment they took up collateral reforms they sacrificed their advantage. Whittier also pleaded with the sisters to stick to abolition. In speaking for that cause, he pointed out, they were making the strongest possible assertion of women's rights.[41]

But the Grimkés were mortified and hurt by the clergy's censures and insisted they must be answered. The time to assert a right was when that right was denied, Angelina explained to Weld. "*We must establish this right,*" she wrote, "for if we do not, it will be impossible for *us* to go *on with the work of Emancipation.*"[42]

Weld was unconvinced, and proceeded to explain his reform philosophy. Garrison was ill-advised, he thought, to make himself a spokesman for every lofty cause that came along. "No moral enterprise when prosecuted with ability and any sort of energy

EVER failed under heaven," asserted Weld, "so long as its con-
ductors pushed the *main* principle and did not strike off until
they got to the summit level. On the other hand every reform
that ever foundered in mid sea was capsized by one of these gusty
side winds. . . . If you attempt to start off on a derivative
principle from any other point than the summit level of the
main principle you must beat up stream—yes up a *cataract*. It reverses the order of nature and the laws of mind.

"Now what is plainer than that the grand principle for which
we struggle is HUMAN RIGHTS," Weld asked, "and that the
rights of *woman* is a principle purely derivative from the other?
. . . You put the cart before the horse; you drag the tree by
the top in attempting to push your *woman's* rights until human rights have gone ahead and broken the *path*."[43]

Weld did not want the sisters to misunderstand him. He had
no prejudice against women. He was as staunch for equality of
the sexes as he was for abolition. Indeed, the rights and wrongs
of women were an old theme with him. Woman's rights was the
first subject he ever discussed in a little debating society to
which he belonged as a boy, and he had always taken the position
that woman might make laws, administer justice, sit in the
chair of state, plead at the bar or in the pulpit, or do anything
else for which she was mentally, morally, or spiritually qualified.
Why, he even conceded woman the right to initiate the marriage proposal! But in allowing themselves to be drawn off from
abolition to woman's rights, Sarah and Angelina were wasting
blows on the limbs of the tree and leaving the trunk to stand.
Blows dealt at the trunk would bring the whole tree down
eventually, whereas merely to lop off limbs would leave the
trunk to sprout anew. And if they went off on some of Garrison's tangential hobbies, they would be wasting strokes on
mere branches and leaves.

11

A REFORMER'S

COURTSHIP

H*ad Weld been less obtusely single-*minded, he might have noted the little affectionate touches that Angelina could not always keep out of her letters. She made such "wry faces and outcries" about his wretched handwriting that he bought himself a new pen. She responded to his arguments so saucily that it seemed to him that he got a stinging earboxing with every letter.[1] She was gravely concerned for his health, for he had lost ten pounds while working in the office and now weighed less than he did at the age of fifteen.[2] She recommended that he read Andrew Combe on "Health and Mental Education," especially the chapter dealing with "Excessive Exercise of the Brain."[3] Sarah's health was worrying Angelina, too, she confided to Weld. Sarah had suffered with a bad cough for several weeks, and Angelina was fearful that if she should be obliged to lay aside her work, their enemies would account it a judgment.[4]

Weld was touched by Angelina's concern for his health, and assured her he was sound. His only complaint was an occasional ache in his throat, but it came only when "I act like a fool and get discussing in my screech owl style." He was more worried about the sisters than about himself, for they were unaccustomed to the treacherous New England winter that was coming on apace. He had read Combe and trusted to have got some benefit. Along with his other eccentricities Weld had adopted the dietary regimen of Sylvester Graham and recommended Graham's health rules to the sisters. This health expert was coming to Boston to lecture, and Weld hoped Angelina and Sarah could hear him.[5]

Graham was a Yankee preacher and temperance lecturer who, from study of physiology and of the Bible, had evolved a formula for health and longevity. It might almost be said that he thought the way to salvation was through the stomach, or, as one of his disciples put it, that there was a physical as well as a moral "fall" in Eden for which only vegetarianism could atone. Many people of that day ate prodigiously of meat and starches, drank heavily, and rarely bathed. And from Weld's efforts in behalf of manual labor, we have seen that they took little exercise. Graham taught abstemiousness and cleanliness, and as a basis of diet prescribed bread made of the whole wheat kernel, unbolted and coarsely ground, instead of the baker's product. Meat, fish, butter, tea, coffee, pepper, indeed, all condiments and stimulants, came under his ban. Diet was only one of his concerns, for he wrote and lectured on what young men and women should know and sought to keep "American amativeness" within prudent and pious bounds. He advocated hard mattresses, open bedroom windows, cold baths, loose and lighter clothing, and daily exercise; and if his ideas drew jeers from the medical profession of his day, time would seem to have vindicated many of his pronouncements.[6]

One day when Graham had partaken heartily of cucumbers, green corn, and watermelon at the home of a friend, expounding his peculiar ideas with his accustomed fervor the while, he was seized with intense pains in his stomach and colon. So dreadful was his agony that he threw himself on the floor and writhed; yet his enthusiasm and confidence were so invincible that between his spasms he ejaculated: "Yes, gentlemen! Posterity will do me justice! (Oh, my bowels!) Yes, gentlemen! Posterity will build monuments to my memory! (Oh, these gripes!) Yes, gentlemen, my system will flourish and ultimately spread through the world!" [7]

Graham was once mobbed by the allied butchers and bakers of Boston, but the bakers were finally persuaded to manufacture Graham bread, and numerous Graham boardinghouses were established throughout the country.

Weld confessed to Sarah and Angelina that Graham's was not altogether a pleasant personality. He was egotistical and lacked "the unction of spirituality." But he was fearless and independent, and Weld credited Graham's instruction with improving his health. Sarah and Angelina should hear him, for he would give them "more knowledge of the laws of life in 12 lectures than you can get from books in *six months*."

Weld felt ashamed of wasting so many words about his own health. He was really quite all right, and wished to reassure the sisters on that score. Yet, he admitted, he was something of a faddist in this matter of careful living, and he had a long health lecture "in pickle" for them if they should ever meet again.[8]

The letters between Weld and the sisters were more frequent and voluminous than mere business required. Even though they were separated, they were coming to know each other intimately. Yet intermingled with Weld's pleasantries were candid criticisms. A woman's budding affection is often manifested in efforts to improve a man or make him over; but Weld usurped the prerogative with the Grimkés. He was sometimes almost brutally hypercritical, so much so that at last Angelina complained that she felt hurt.

With this Weld's resolution broke. He upbraided his own dim-witted earnestness, his merciless zeal. "Just enough pressure on the probe to reach the seat of the disease is *kindness*," he explained. "But to thrust through and through with a rude and lacerating violence— What shall I call it? Have I indeed done this to *you* Angelina?" he bemoaned.

And with that he confessed his love.

He had never intended to do it this side of heaven; and he foresaw that Angelina would be amazed. But from the time he read her letter in the *Liberator* he had felt her attraction, and with their acquaintance in New York he came to love her. Little could she know how he was tortured as he tried to still the yearnings of his heart. He had small hope that she could love him in return. Doubtless she esteemed him as a Christian brother, and respected his principles as a man. Perhaps she understood how he meant to help her when he pointed out her faults, even though he had been tactless and cruel. But he could hope for little more than her friendship and respect, and he was prepared to accept her answer, whatever it might be, as the will of God.[9]

Weld's confession came indeed as a surpries, Angelina replied. And yet, in another way, it was no surprise at all. She was amazed at his power to mask his emotions, but she could account for the feeling in her own heart only as an answer to something in his own. When she noted that his last letter was marked private, she had steeled herself against another chastening; but she was most delightfully deceived. During their days together in New York she was frightened at her own bliss. Since their separation she had tried to think of him impersonally. She succeeded for a time, but lately the old feeling had come back. She had often gone to her knees, sometimes praying to be delivered from it, again asking God if it was wrong to love. Oh, how she rejoiced that Theodore had spoken out at last! To think that he had purposed to conceal his feelings, save in another world! The customs of society gave him privileges denied to her; yet, except for her pride, she might have spoken out herself. Still it was not pride alone that held her back. She had such confidence in his judgment and emotional balance that she was sure he would announce his feelings at the proper time. "I *feel* my Theodore," said she, "that we are the two halves of one whole, a twain one, two bodies animated by one soul and that the Lord has given us to each other."

Angelina and Sarah lay awake all night upon the receipt of Weld's letter, exchanging sisterly confidences; for Sarah was as overjoyed as Angelina.

But when Angelina's answer came to Theodore, it was he who tossed all night in sleepless rapture. He held the letter in his hand for a long time, not daring to tear it open. When he did, he would have liked to cry for joy, but he had no tears. The news was too good to be true. Angelina did not really know him. For four days he could not bring himself to answer her. "My heart aches for *utterance*," he finally wrote, "but oh *not* the utterance of *words*! . . . I have so long wrestled with myself like a blind giant stifling by violence all the intensities of my nature that when at last they found *vent*, and your voice of love proclaimed a *deliverance* so unlooked for, so full, so free, revealing what I dared [not] *hope* for, and what I had never for a moment dreamed to be possible—that *your heart was* and *long had been mine*—it was as the life touch to one *dead*; all the pent up tides of my being so long shut out from light and air, broke forth at once and spurned control." His chief pride was in self-mastery; yet Angelina's letter had so unmanned him that he now held himself a novice in self-restraint. Instead of being master of himself, he was like an artless, simple child. He felt humble, unworthy, imperfect.

It was an odd betrothal. Weld's emotions almost overpowered him. "You know something of my structure of mind," he wrote to Angelina, "—that I am *constitutionally*, as far as emotions are concerned, a quivering mass of intensities kept in subjection only by the *rod of iron* in the strong hand of conscience and reason and never laid aside for a moment with safety." Yet not one of his colleagues at the antislavery office had the least suspicion of his new estate. He was not ready to impart the news as yet, although Angelina pleaded with him to accept some one of his friends as a confidant. Their feelings were so sacred that she understood his unwillingness to reveal them to the common eye. But why struggle against the very laws of his being? Surely, if he was not ready to announce their secret to the world, at least he could trust Henry Stanton, or someone else in the office, so that he might have an outlet for his bliss.

Both Angelina and Theodore had some misgivings that they might love each other more than they loved God. Yet their love must be of His making, they concluded. Weld wished to come to Boston to see her; but the sisters were scheduled to speak before a committee of the Massachusetts legislature which was considering petitions for the suppression of slavery in the District of Columbia; and Weld would not distract them from their duty.

Their first appearance was on February 21, 1838, about ten days after Angelina had received Weld's proposal of marriage. Sarah was scheduled to speak that day and Angelina the next, but Sarah fell ill and Angelina took her place. The novelty of the experience, the responsibility, and the emotional excitement of the past few days unnerved her, and her legs trembled when she rose to speak. But her old power returned, and she spoke for two hours. The abolitionists were delighted with her effort. She was thankful that Weld had not come, for his presence would have been too much for her, she wrote. She was so thrilled by Weld's letters that she did not know how she could stand it when he should put his arms around her. The pamphlets he had sent her were most helpful, she reported, and she was glad to learn that he was faithful in visiting his colored friends. When colored folk came forward after her speeches to press her hand in gratitude, she felt that she was overpaid for her work. Their thanks were more heartening than the praise of the rich and the great. She would speak to the legislative committee again on Friday afternoon, day after tomorrow. There would be a third hearing next week. Then she would be finished, and she hoped her Theodore would come to see her.

From the time of Angelina's first hearing before the legislative committee Weld had forborne to write, since he did not wish to add to her excitement. But the day before her third and last appearance he took pen in hand again, and poured forth his pent-up affection. Then he catalogued his faults, for he thought it unfair in any man to deceive his prospective bride. He could never marry with a curtain around his heart or a false gloss on his character. He was selfish, he declared, not in the money sense, but in wanting his own way. He was proud, impatient of contradiction, tempestuous in temper. His visage reflected a "deep wild gloom."

Weld claimed to be contemptuous toward opponents. He was self-indulgent, wilful, absent-minded. And in his craving for exciting forms of exercise he was as much of a "boy baby" as he was in the nursery.

Angelina had no idea of his deficiencies in education, he informed her. He had never learned arithmetic beyond the rule of three. Chemistry, geology, astronomy, botany, and all the other "ologies" and "ographies," even including geography, were beyond his ken, except for what information he had picked up. In Latin, Greek, and Hebrew he was somewhat better versed. Theology and sacred history were his strong points. He had also studied "Intellectual and Moral Philosophy," not under instruction, but by himself, with care, delight, and great profit.

Angelina was at something of a loss to match Weld's list of eccentricities and shortcomings. She confessed to selfishness, pride, impatience, and irritability. She was so impetuous that when she went walking she always outdistanced everyone, even the children. She loved to shout and hear the echo answer. She was not fond of children. She laughed when people called her learned. She often wounded Sarah; but after a spell of tearful remorse they soon made up again. Weld had already perceived a great many of her faults, she reminded him, and there was no need to enlarge on them. Indeed, in some of his chiding letters he seemed to peer into her soul. She agreed that those who would marry should know each other's failings. To perfect one another was an object of marriage. Blind love was transient and shallow. She intended to tidy Weld up when they were married, she warned him, but she did not really mind his dowdiness, as long as he was clean.

Angelina touched lightly on sex. "Why is it," she inquired, "that those of our own sex *cannot* fill up the void in human hearts?" Weld had never thought about the matter, he replied. He had never intended to marry and had purposely avoided the contemplation of "that relation of the sexes out of which the institution springs." Now he was giving it thought. "I feel like a simple child on the whole subject," he confessed, "and in all artlessness will sit down at any bodys feet and receive most gratefully the least crumb of *true* teaching on the subject." Weld was as much in the dark as was Angelina about the "philosophy" of sex. But he believed he could explain some of the facts. Sex must be an auxiliary to the higher affections, "bringing to their aid as allies the resources of the compound nature in its *every* department, pouring itself through channels of which the mind is not aware and producing effects, the *cause* of which the mind has not the least consciousness of. I suppose this to be a law and a necessity of our human nature, body and mind *in one*, our mingled nature with *mingled affinities* and tendencies mutually acting upon and moulding each other. I suppose that persons of the *same* sex cannot so intensely be drawn toward each other by a love that baffles all expression. . . . In a word my dearest," and here Weld put it neatly, "I suppose you and I feel for each other more absorbing affinities than tho' we were of the *same* sex . . . from that law of our nature sublimely assigned by God as the reason for creating a difference of sex."

With the conclusion of Angelina's labors before the Massachusetts legislature, Weld planned to visit her at Brighton, where she was staying at the home of friends. He hoped she would meet him alone, he wrote, and that they might be alone for a while.

He warned her that he might seem haggard and emaciated from loss of weight, but she must not worry because he really felt very well.

It was a joyful visit, filled with precious days. Weld admitted later that he had to keep "an extinguisher" on his spirit. Angelina confessed: "I never could get near enough to thee." They planned to be married about two months later at the home of Angelina's sister, Mrs. Anna R. Frost, "3 Belmont Row, Spruce Street," in Philadelphia. Theodore would try to find a house somewhere near New York, and Sarah would come and live with them. All too soon it was time for Weld to go. He had work to do in New York, and Sarah and Angelina must begin a new series of lectures, this time at the Odeon, in Boston.

There they were to draw their largest crowds. The main floor and the four galleries that rose tier on tier above it were filled. People sat in the aisles.[10] Angelina spoke with her usual effectiveness, but Sarah was having trouble with her throat. It was so serious, in fact, that her Odeon speech was her last public appearance.[11]

Back in New York again, Weld started house-hunting. There were plenty of large houses to be had, with high rent, and also plenty of cottages; but seven- or eight-room houses, such as they wanted, outside the city but within commuting range, were hard to find. The depression which had begun in 1837 still gripped the country, and many city workers with reduced incomes had located their families in the country, where living costs were lower. Weld must have a house with some ground, for he planned to raise enough vegetables to pay the rent. Angelina was marrying a farmer, he would have her know, and he recalled with pride how, when he was fourteen years old, he had had entire charge of a hundred-acre farm. He had found a house that they could share with another family, he wrote to Angelina; but he and Sarah and Angelina were "a strange trio, different from all the world I do believe." It would be venturesome to try to live with others.

Weld also looked at furniture, but decided not to buy until he obtained a house. The matter of furniture presented difficulties, too, inasmuch as everything was "so tricked out and covered with carved work or bedizoned and *gew gawed* and gilded and tipt off with variegated colors." They must have simple furniture; for Angelina was a Quaker and Weld hated ostentation. Simplicity in dress, equipage, manners, furniture, and style of living was with him "a very witchery of ravishment"; and by plain living they would bear testimony against the garish frippery of their day.

Their marriage, too, must be an example, Weld explained. Each of them was blessed with unusual powers, although it might seem immodest to admit it; and each of them was widely influential. They had uncommon notoriety, Angelina especially, for at the moment she was probably the best known female in the country. They were identified with powerful moral movements: abolition, temperance, woman's rights, the whole great battle with "factitious life." Theirs was a crisis age, and their marriage would be a crisis in itself. As a public lecturer to mixed assemblages, Angelina was a cynosure. Many men thought she was utterly spoiled for domestic life. A man had said to Weld not long ago that he supposed a woman like Angelina would never marry— at least he hoped she would not. Her forwardness unfitted her for home life. She would be "an obtrusive noisy clamorer." This person was destined for a surprise, asserted Weld, yet he suspected that even many abolition men harbored similar thoughts. Marriage would be a challenge to Angelina.

It would test Weld, too. He was known as a man of wilful obstinacy and his marriage would "be scrutinized with argus eyes," he said. He was totally unused to contradiction. He had always been deferred to as a leader—at school, at Oneida, at Lane, and in the antislavery office at the present time. "I always loathed and spurned it," he explained, "and from a child have always refused all office and worked in the ranks as a common soldier and yet in reality did actually control and give shape to a thousand things with which I *seemed* to have nothing to do. This has arisen from the fact that those around me and most intimate with me have always had unlimited confidence in me, have probably overestimated my talents, the correctness of my opinions, my wisdom, judgment, far sightedness, integrity, conscience, fearlessness, and freedom from unworthy motives." This must have affected his character and made him headstrong, he thought. He must learn to be compliant.

Angelina did not fear the test. She recognized her peculiar position. She knew what men thought of her. But they did not know what an ordeal it was for her to lecture. She yearned for privacy. She would joyfully renounce the platform for the kitchen. And in so doing she would show forth the versatility of woman. Their marriage would be proof that "well regulated minds can with *equal ease* occupy high and low stations and find *true happiness* in both."

Meanwhile, Weld had found a house. It was at Fort Lee, New Jersey, a little way up the Hudson River from New York City. It overlooked the river, and the grounds were in thick greensward. A little boat, the *Echo*, provided regular steamboat service to and from the city. Weld went up every afternoon to put in garden and supervise painting, plastering, and other repair work. Sometimes he stayed all night. As evening gathered, while he sat at the open window looking out over the Hudson, his thoughts turned wistfully to Angelina. The river stretched away below him in a broad and shimmering sheet. Light faded into shadow where the forest overhung the opposite shore a mile and a half away. As night fell, the silent, brooding river gleamed with moonbeams. Watch-fires glimmered from the bows of little fishing boats. Sloops and shallops dropped down with the tide.

Weld wrote with dithyrambic pen as he tried to bring the scene to Angelina. "The tall cliffs and thick woods that pallisade the shore, combine in a group that can be taken in at a glance, the lineaments of a night scene that could hardly be heightened in beauty by the pencil of fancy tho' dipped in her deepest hues.

Four steamers have just shot past, plunging like warhorses up the current and strewing their myriad fire-flakes upon the still air. Each seems like the Spirit of the mighty stream or like the Genius of the joyous spring, unloosing its evening tresses upon the bosom of the tide and flinging its starry robe all abroad upon the waters. I have just come in from an hours stroll along the beach. I had no eye for its beauties nor ear for the lulling music of the tide's soft pulsations upon the sand, nor the gentle plash of the oar, or the deep mellow song of the boatman. The moon was cloudless, and the kindled torches of the firmament flamed in glory above me, but still I paced wearily in sadness and tears, for YOU were not with me, and I wept with very longing for you My Love, *Life of my life*."

Their wedding day, May 14, approached. Their secret was out at last, and the abolition brotherhood was ecstatic. Delegates and visitors were pouring into New York to attend the annual convention of the American Antislavery Society, and it seemed that every one must see Weld to congratulate him. Angelina and Sarah had gone to their sister's home in Philadelphia, where the annual convention of Antislavery Women would assemble on the day set for the marriage. Weld's wedding suit was giving Angelina concern, and even he was showing unwonted interest in fine tailoring. Angelina recommended a brown coat to match her wedding dress—frock, if he wished to depart so far from his custom—a white cravat (her sister Anna would tie it for him), white waistcoat, white or light colored pantaloons, white stockings, and shoes lower in the instep than those he usually wore.

White vest and pantaloons impressed Weld as "a little *buckish* and dandyish," but he followed Angelina's instructions to the letter, availing himself of the choice she left him in the matter of pantaloons, however, by selecting light drab instead of white ones.

Angelina was delighted with Weld's description of their house. But he should not concern himself with furniture, she told him.

When they were all together at Fort Lee they would decide just what they wanted, and have it made by the cabinet-maker he had told her about, who lived two miles away. The only thing that troubled her was Sarah's room. Their large apartment seemed wonderful, but from the dimensions he had given her, Sarah's room appeared to be very small. However, she had a so-lution. It was for Theodore to take the little room and let the sisters have the large apartment. "Look in at the windows of my soul," she added coyly, "and see if I am in earnest."

Wedding preparations went forward. The invitations had been sent; but from time to time they remembered other friends who must be asked. Angelina had ordered the cake baked by a colored confectioner who used nothing but "free sugar" in his products. Weld must stay in New York until the antislavery convention was over—except for the agents' convention, it was the first one he ever attended—then he would come to Phila-delphia. Those who made a practice of attending conventions agreed that this was the best one ever held. Weld would not know, he said—at least the crowds were immense. But Weld was bored. He was present only about a third of the time. He tried to listen to the speeches and reports, but he kept looking at his watch, and, whenever a mail was due, he slipped out and ran to the postoffice to see if there was a letter from Philadelphia.

At last the great day came, and the guests assembled. Garrison was present, well-groomed as usual, beaming benignly through his spectacles and looking to Henry B. Stanton like the prophet Isaiah in a rapt mood.[12] The massive man with the mellow voice, large brilliant eyes, and soft brown hair, overhanging the By-ronic collar, was Gerrit Smith. He seemed to be in good health and spirits today—he was so often ill with colds and fevers, rheu-matism, headaches, giddiness, or hemorrhoids, that admirers of his oratory accounted it extraordinary that a harp which gave out such noble music could be so easily put out of tune.

The Birneys, the Lewis Tappans, the John E. Fullers were there. Stanton, Amos Dresser, Hiram Wilson, and George A.

Avery made up a Lane contingent. The tall, spare man in the mussy white suit was Charles Callistus Burleigh. His bushy black beard was somewhat better combed than usual, and his dark hair hung to his shoulders in womanish curls. He was the most bizarre of all the abolitionists in appearance, and also one of their best orators and logicians.[13]

The tall lady with the steel-blue eyes and well-balanced head crowned with light brown hair, which was twisted into dangling curls in front and twined into a projecting bun behind, was Maria Weston Chapman, who reminded the poet Whittier of Joan of Arc without her casque. The little Quaker lady with the well-shaped lips and somewhat stringy hair pulled back over her ears to the nape of her neck was Abby Kelley, whom we shall encounter later. Whittier was there. He would step outside when the ceremony began, for to remain would be a breach of Quaker discipline punishable by excommunication. Angelina and Sarah were certain to receive this punishment, Angelina for marrying a Presbyterian, and Sarah for attending the wedding; but both were reconciled to it.

Weld's brother Lewis came down from Hartford. And standing about somewhat self-consciously in spite of everybody's efforts to put them at ease, were several colored persons, two of them liberated slaves who had belonged to Judge Grimké. "They were our invited guests," Sarah explained, "and we thus had an opportunity to bear our testimony against the horrible prejudice which prevails against colored persons, and equally awful prejudice against the poor." There were some forty guests in all.

The ceremony was unorthodox. In keeping with Quaker custom, Angelina would not suffer a minister to perform the rites, and Weld deferred to her wishes. By the law of Pennsylvania, a marriage could be solemnized without benefit of clergy, or even a magistrate, if witnessed and attested by twelve persons. "Neither Angelina nor Theodore felt as if they could bind themselves to any preconceived form of words," wrote Sarah in describing the nuptials, "and accordingly uttered such as the Lord gave them at the moment." Weld renounced all those rights to Angelina's person and property with which the law endowed a husband, save such as the influence of love might give him. Angelina professed to love him "with a pure heart fervently." Then each offered a prayer for enlarged usefulness and continued faith in God. A colored Presbyterian minister also prayed, and then a white clergyman. Garrison read the marriage certificate, which all the witnesses signed. The simple ceremony was over. The twain were one.

12

''SLAVERY AS IT IS''

The wedding festivities ended, Theo-
dore and Angelina attended the sessions of the Women's Antislavery Society in Pennsylvania Hall. Built by the abolitionists
and their reformer friends, this edifice was dedicated to "free
discussion, virtue, Liberty and Independence" on the same day
that Theodore and Angelina were married. Weld had been invited to speak, but declined because of his voice. Explaining this
fact in a letter written for the dedication ceremonies, he exulted in the completion of this "temple of freedom," the only
building consecrated to free discussion and equal rights for all
"in a republic of fifteen millions." "God grant that Pennsylvania
Hall may be *free, indeed!*" he prayed.[1]

Fired by the murder of the abolitionist editor, Elijah Lovejoy,
in Alton, Illinois, six months before, and by other proslavery excesses, Weld wrote with impassioned grandiloquence on the
theme of mere lip-service to freedom. "The empty name is
everywhere," he scoffed, "—*free* government, *free* men, *free*

speech, *free* people, *free* schools, and *free* churches. Hollow counterfeits all! . . . *Free!* The word and sound are omnipresent masks and mockers, an impious lie, unless they stand for free *lynch law* and free *murder*, for they *are* free. . . ."

Two days after the dedication of the new building, Garrison, Maria Weston Chapman, and Angelina Weld were scheduled to speak before the Women's Convention; but no sooner had Garrison concluded his address than a mob broke in, "yelling and shouting as if the very fiends of the pit had suddenly broke loose," as Garrison described it. The intrepid antislavery women kept their seats, and the mob withdrew, only to surround the building, however, and bombard the windows with stones and brickbats. Mrs. Chapman spoke for ten minutes against the crash of shattering glass. Then Angelina, two days a bride, took over and continued for an hour. "As the tumult from without increased, and the brickbats fell thick and fast, . . ." recorded Garrison, "her eloquence kindled, her eye flashed, and her cheeks glowed, as she devoutly thanked the Lord that the stupid repose of the city had at length been disturbed by the force of truth."

The next day, when the convention reconvened, the streets around the hall were thronged, and rumors circulated that the mob designed to burn the building. Before the evening session the mayor demanded the keys, locked both delegates and rioters out, and requested the milling mobsters to disperse. After he had left, however, rioters burst open the doors with axes and applied the torch, then thwarted every effort of the Philadelphia firefighters to save the structure. Within two hours it was a gutted ruin.

With this outrage vivid in their minds, the Welds left Philadelphia for Manlius, New York, for a visit with Weld's parents. Their honeymoon was brief, and soon they were busy setting up housekeeping in their new home at Fort Lee. Sarah and Angelina were excommunicated by the Society of Friends, as they had foreseen, but they suffered no regrets.[2]

Angelina found cooking easier than she expected; Sarah commented that she boiled potatoes to perfection. Weld had won the sisters to Graham diet, and they extolled it as both health-giving and an emancipator of woman in that it lessened the time she must spend over the stove. Angelina's practice was to cook a week's supply of food in a day, inasmuch as they "took their food cool." Their orchard yielded an abundance of fruit, and their field beans flourished.[3] If "Theda" found any deficiencies in "Nina's" cooking, he was not a man to bicker about his victuals.

Weld made regular trips to antislavery headquarters in New York; and as evening came, Angelina would listen for the piston stroke of the *Echo*, breasting upstream from the city. As soon as the sound of its thumping came across the water she would run out and blow a whistle, and Theodore, also equipped with a whistle, tooted a reply from the deck to inform her that he was aboard. On moonlit evenings they walked along the water's edge together. On Sunday, if the day was warm, they climbed to the top of the palisades and sunned themselves on the rocks. In the evenings they revised Weld's *Bible Against Slavery*, preparing copy for the third edition.[4]

Weld was appointed to the executive committee of the American Antislavery Society, but declined to serve.[5] Oberlin was some thirty thousand dollars in debt, and the trustees asked him to go to England on a money-raising trip. This, too, he refused, but he wrote an "Appeal to the Philanthropists of Great Britain" in behalf of the institution that he rated as having done more for human liberty and truth than any other in the United States.[6] The American Antislavery Society wanted Weld to tour the country to enlist twenty agents, as he had done in 1836;[7] and speaking invitations streamed in from various quarters.[8] But Weld had resolved to give his throat a prolonged rest. "When I stopt speaking I found it required far more firmness to resist the importunity of friends," he commented, "than it ever did to face a mob." [9]

Notwithstanding the many tasks he declined, he was extremely busy. He not only edited the *Antislavery Almanacs* for

1839, 1840, and 1841, but also prepared a great deal of the reading matter that went into them.[10] The executive committee had resolved to publish a number of tracts refuting the objections to abolitionism, and the first, which Weld was commissioned to compile, was designed to represent slavery as it really was. It would be eyewitness testimony, and to collect his evidence Weld sent a lithographed letter to leading abolitionists throughout the country, asking them to furnish names and addresses of persons who had resided in the South and were willing to describe what they had seen. Especially to be desired was the testimony of such persons as ministers, editors, teachers, lawyers, and physicians, for Weld wanted only truthful witnesses.[11]

The response was less generous than Weld anticipated. Many abolitionists were willing to go as passengers on a pleasant sail, he complained to Gerrit Smith, but too few could endure the drudgery of coiling ropes. "They are willing to take the helm, or handle the speaking trumpet or *go up aloft* to see and be *seen*, but to bone down to *ship work* as a common sailor, especially in the *hold*," had small attraction. Weld asked Smith to bring his request for antislavery material before the meeting of the New York Antislavery Society, not just once, but at every opportunity; and he sent a similar plea to leaders of other abolitionist gatherings.[12]

Meanwhile, he had an idea. The New York Commercial Reading Room subscribed to scores of Southern papers, which, after being kept on file for a month, were sold for waste. Weld arranged to buy the discarded papers and bring them home. There he put Sarah and Angelina to work culling out news items, speeches in Congress and state legislatures, trials and court decisions, advertisements for runaway slaves, anything containing facts adverse to slavery. "Our present occupation," wrote Sarah to her friend Jane Smith on January 24, 1839, "looking over southern papers, is calculated to help us . . . see the inside of that horrible system of oppression which is enfibred with the heart strings of the South. In the advertisements for runaways we de-

tect the cruel whippings & shootings & brandings, practiced on
the helpless slaves. Heartsickening as the details are, I am thankful
that God in his providence has put into our hands these weapons
prepared by the South herself, to destroy the fell monster." [13]

"The fact is," recorded Weld when this, his most important
book, was finished, "those dear souls spent six months, averaging
more than six hours a day, in searching through thousands upon
thousands of Southern newspapers, marking and cutting out
facts of slave-holding disclosures. . . . Thus was gathered the
raw material for the manufacture of 'Slavery As It Is.' After the
work was finished we were curious to know how many newspapers had been examined. So we went up to our attic and
took an inventory of bundles, as they were packed heap upon
heap. When our count had reached *twenty thousand* newspapers,
we said: 'There, let that suffice.' Though the book had in it
many thousand facts thus authenticated by the slave-holders
themselves, yet it contained but a tiny fraction of the nameless
atrocities gathered from the papers examined." [14]

In his introduction, Weld impaneled the reader as a juror to
bring in a verdict on the question: "What is the actual condition of the slaves in the United States?" Then, from his eyewitness statements and newspaper clippings, he presented evidence that slaves were undernourished, overworked, poorly and
immodestly clad, inadequately sheltered, neglected in sickness
and old age, and inhumanly punished.

Weld denied the stock argument that it was to the interest of
the slaveholder to treat his slaves well. How about old slaves?
he asked. Or worn out slaves, diseased slaves, the blind, the
dumb, the deformed, the maimed? Was it not to the master's
interest to have them die as soon as possible? How about the
habitual runaways, slaves that were hired from other masters,
slaves who worked under an overseer whose wages were pro-
portioned to the crop raised? People were not always guided
by self-interest, anyway, Welt asserted. It was to the interest
"of the drunkard to quit his cups; for the glutton to curb his

appetite; for the debauchee to bridle his lust; for the sluggard to be up betimes; for the spendthrift to economize; and for all sinners to stop sinning. Even if it were for the interest of the masters to treat their servants well, he must be a novice who thinks *that* a proof that the slaves *are* well treated. The whole history of man is a record of real interests sacrificed to present gratification. If all men's actions were consistent with their best interests, folly and sin would be words without meaning." Self-interest was a strong impellent, Weld granted, but equally strong were lust, pride, anger, revenge, and love of power.

As a matter of fact, both slaves and masters were victims of a brutalizing system, Weld contended. From the files of Southern papers he adduced scores of instances of brutal shootings, duels, and fights, with a purpose to show that the masters were so accustomed to work their will upon the slaves that indulgence of passion had become second nature with them. Weld quoted hundreds of instances where slaves were maimed, beaten, and sometimes killed. From advertisements of runaways he adduced descriptions of slaves with lacerated backs, brands, cropped ears, knocked-out eyes and teeth. Anyone could kill an outlawed slave, he pointed out. Away from his own plantation, a slave might be "examined" by any white person, no matter how crazy or drunk the examiner might be, and if the black man dared to do so much as lift a hand against a white man, he could be killed with impunity. The laws which made the testimony of a colored person worthless against a white man meant in practice that a white man could work his will upon a Negro without risk of punishment so long as no white witnesses were present. Nor were the slaves protected by public opinion. It was public opinion that denied their manhood and made them chattels. How could they derive protection from public opinion such as that?

Weld's *Slavery As It Is: Testimony of a Thousand Witnesses*[15] was a devastating indictment. To be sure it was misnamed. A more descriptive title would have been "Slavery's Excesses."

For Weld portrayed the system at its worst. When Weld asked his Kentucky friend, James A. Thome, for instances of cruelty he had witnessed, Thome replied: "I have really witnessed so few cases of cruel treatment in Ky., that any account I could give from personal observation would, I fear, have the impression that *cruelties were rare*. I might have stated numerous facts which have occurred in *other places*, and of which I have *heard*; but this would not have been in pursuance of your request." [16] Weld was scrupulously careful to present trustworthy evidence; but his evidence was altogether on one side.

Although *Slavery As It Is* appeared without the author's name upon it, the abolition clan knew it as Weld's work and acclaimed it as a major accomplishment. It was a mass of solid facts, proclaimed *Zion's Herald*, amassed by a master-workman. It was an irresistible battering ram, constructed of materials the South itself had furnished, that would burst jagged breaches in the wall of slavery. No man could read it without hating slavery with undying hatred. No man who had not embraced antislavery principles should be without it, unless he was afraid of being convinced; and for an abolitionist to be without it, would be like a soldier refusing to use the ammunition provided for him.[17]

The *Christian Examiner* called the book "a very remarkable and terrible volume." [18] The *Emancipator* described it as "a terrible and faithful" picture of the South's "peculiar institution," but it was not shocked at what Weld had revealed. "That our brother was enslaved was enough for us to hear," declared the editor. ". . . Finding him a *brute*, we took for granted he had *brute* treatment." Weld had performed a mighty feat, to be sure. He spoke the strongest human language. But the delineator of slavery "must consult the lexicography of Hell." [19]

A correspondent of the *Emancipator* regarded Weld's book as the "greatest stumper of the slaveholders that was ever invented by man." When traveling in company with slaveholders this correspondent made it a practice to relate instances of cruelty that Weld had cited. Invariably his listeners called them lies;

whereupon he would pull Weld's volume from his pocket and give names, places, and dates from Southern papers. "This reply I have seen close up the mouth of a slaveholder as quick as though his jaws had been clamped with the lockjaw," he gloated, "—at the same time he would change color, like a man who has taken an emetic." [20]

The *New York American* wondered why so few political, literary, and even religious journals and periodicals had noticed the book. If it had described Russian serfdom or Turkish, African, or Chinese slavery, or if the same industry and talent "had been exercised in furnishing forth the adventures of some lewd minx," it would have received the widest notice. "But when the South struts menacingly before their vision, how many editors, even those of religious journals," the *American* derided, "have the courage of a kitten to cry *mew*?" [21]

Priced at 37½ cents a copy, or $25.00 a hundred, *Slavery As It Is* was spread over the North. Twenty-two thousand copies were sold within four months, and at the end of a year sales exceeded a hundred thousand copies.[22] It was as influential in England as in America, and when Joseph Sturge, the English abolitionist, read it he rated Weld the greatest of all American antislavery propagandists. Weld's arguments were irresistible, and his talent for succinct statement was unsurpassed. "He would be a bold antagonist who should enter the lists against him," Sturge declared; "he would be a yet bolder ally who should attempt to go over the same ground, or to do better what he has done so well." [23] When Charles Dickens published his *American Notes* in 1842, his chapter on slavery was taken almost entirely from Weld's book, although the celebrated Englishman made no acknowledgment of his source.[24] Until the appearance of *Uncle Tom's Cabin* in 1852, Weld's *Slavery As It Is* enjoyed preëminence in antislavery literature.

Indeed, Weld's book aroused such interest in England, where Weld's friend and former patron, Charles Stuart, was instrumental in publicizing it,[25] that the officers of the British and Foreign Antislavery Society requested information on the economic, social, and political effects of slavery upon the North. The executive committee of the American Antislavery Society, to whom these inquiries were addressed, commissioned Weld to reply, and authorized him to employ assistants for three months to collect materials in New York, Philadelphia, and Boston. Most of this research was done by James A. Thome, who, forced to flee from Oberlin when he was implicated in helping a fugitive slave escape to Canada, was glad to find employment until things cooled down to the point where he dared return to Ohio.[26]

"By the way," wrote Thome to Weld in the midst of his labors, "ever since the reception of your last letter, I have been admiring the perfect *nonchalance* with which you talk about cutting down the manuscript *one half*, 'as likely as not, and a little more;' and that too without having so much as seen a sheet of it! How perfectly characteristic! You have already begun to scent the slaughter at the distance of sixty miles, and doubtless you are licking your chops in anticipation of your gory feast." Would Weld make mincemeat of his brains? queried Thome in mock complaint. He knew what to expect from Weld in the way of compression from his experience with *Slavery in the West Indies*; but he chided that if he had Weld close at hand, he would twitch his whiskers.[27]

It was planned to send this new book to the World Antislavery Convention, which was scheduled to meet in London in June, 1840, but publication was delayed when Thome's materials were destroyed by fire. Furthermore, the national society was in desperate straits financially, for the aftermath of the panic of 1837 had left the Tappans, Gerrit Smith, and other large contributors in stringent circumstances. Weld's salary was reduced from a thousand to seven hundred dollars a year at his own request, and Thome worked for several weeks without pay. On May 15, the *Emancipator* announced that Weld's book would not be ready in season for the World Congress, but that an elaborate statistical work by Weld and Thome would be forwarded in its place. This was published in London in 1841 under the title *Slavery and the Internal Slave Trade in the United States.* Weld was the first choice of the executive committee to represent the American and Foreign Antislavery Society at the London convention, but he declined.[28]

Meanwhile, the executive committee of the American Antislavery Society had persuaded Beriah Green to do a companion book to Weld's *The Bible Against Slavery.* Elizur Wright explained to Green that Weld's book on the Old Testament had created a demand for "a finishing stroke"; people were asking if the abolitionists were afraid of the New Testament, inasmuch as Weld had expounded only upon the Old Testament. Green stipulated that Weld should edit his manuscript, and the executive committee authorized him to do so. But Weld refused at first. Who was he to criticize the work of a man like Green? he protested; but when Wright convinced him that Green had asked for his assistance, Weld gave it willingly.[29] Green's product was published in 1839 with the marathon title, *The Chattel Principle the Abhorrence of Jesus Christ and the Apostles: or No Refuge for American Slavery in the New Testament.*

Weld's books were all in great demand, and both *The Bible Against Slavery* and *Slavery As It Is* went through many printings. It was music to Lewis Tappan to hear the New York newsboys shouting, "Antislavery Almanac! Slavery Almanac!" as they sold ten thousand copies of the *Antislavery Almanac* for 1840 in two days. "We sell to poor men," one of them told Tappan. "Not a rich man has bought one." [30] Antislavery was the common people's cause.

Weld thought the national society should put a larger number of intelligent colored speakers into the field. "They would do more in three months to kill prejudice," he wrote to Gerrit Smith, "(and our cause moves only as fast as that dies) than all our operations up to now." And they would attract larger audiences than white men could command.[31] Weld continued to work for amelioration of the condition of free Negroes, helping to make it an objective of the New Jersey Antislavery Society of which he was now an active member. Nor were Angelina Weld and Sarah Grimké idle. They visited indigent colored people in their neighborhood and helped circulate antislavery petitions. "We have just finished our work of petitioning," wrote Sarah to Jane Smith on January 24, 1839. "It has done us good to go among our neighbors, altho' we had much to try us, the selfishness, unfeelingness & ignorance we met with almost every where were calculated to awaken the feeling of gratitude to God who had touched & softened our hearts & enlightened our minds. I never felt so much compassion for the ignorant before, altho' patience was sometimes sorely tried. One woman told me she had rather sign a petition to have them all hung than set free . . . she was a professing Methodist." [32]

Weld also brought another forceful worker into the antislavery cause about this time. At the Woman's Antislavery Convention in Philadelphia he had been forcibly impressed by the young Quakeress Abby Kelley, who made her first public address at that gathering. At the close of the meeting, Weld had urged Miss Kelley to give up schoolteaching and become an antislavery lecturer. Laying his hand on her shoulder, he declared· "Abby, if you don't, God will smite you!" But Abby had an aged mother to support. She needed time to decide. By January, 1839, however, she was writing to Weld to ask how best to prepare herself for antislavery work.[33] Soon she was enlisted in the cause. Coming under Garrison's influence, she would later marry the turbulent Garrisonian agent, Stephen S. Foster, who made it his special mission to heckle the clergy. Stomping into church in the midst of the service, Foster would demand the right to speak. Sometimes his wish was granted, but more often the outraged worshipers threw him out.

To Parker Pillsbury, who often accompanied him on his disputatious pilgrimages, Foster wrote in January, 1842, that he was laid up from a vigorous Baptist kick in the side, and doubted if he could continue his self-appointed mission much longer. In the past fifteen months he had been in four jails, and had been ejected from twenty-four churches, twice by way of a second-story window.[34] Under Garrison's and Foster's influence Abby Kelley became a fiery termagant. From her mild exterior Weld could never have guessed what a spitfire he was to loose upon the country.

On December 13, 1839, Angelina Weld gave birth to a son. They named the child Charles Stuart, after Weld's friend. Angelina was still a devotee of Andrew Combe, whose books on the rearing of children contended that most infants were overfed; so when young Charles was weaned, Angelina put him on a Spartan diet. He languished until, one time when Theodore and Angelina were away from home, Sarah began to feed him all he would eat. His health improved so rapidly that Weld insisted thereafter that the child must not be stinted in his fare.[35]

Weld had always hankered for a farm and thought farm labor might improve his voice. Moreover, he must find means to make a livelihood, for the American Antislavery Society lacked the money to employ him longer. Early in 1840 he learned of a farm for sale at Belleville, New Jersey. It comprised fifty acres with a seven-hundred-foot frontage on the Passaic River, and had once belonged to Nathanael Greene, the famous Revolutionary general.[36] The yard, elevated several feet above the highway which passed in front, was surrounded by a stone wall surmounted by palings. Flanking the gate were two gigantic weeping willows. Rosebushes climbed the pillars of the forty-eight-foot piazza, and the yard was filled with lilacs, pines, and hemlocks. South of the house was a garden, with grapes, raspberries, gooseberries, and fruit trees. On the west was a grass plot enclosed with lilac bushes. To the north was a woodlot. The house itself was originally a five-room two-story stone structure, but a wooden addition had been built on at the rear so that it now contained fifteen rooms. Fences, barn, and corncrib were in poor repair, but the dwelling itself was well preserved. In March, 1840, Weld and the sisters bought the property at sheriff's sale for $5,750. They grieved at giving up the majestic Hudson, Sarah told her friend Jane Smith, but here they were on "a sweet little river, gliding noiselessly by thro' rich meadow land." [37]

The purchase took all their ready cash, but Lewis Tappan agreed to loan Weld money for a cow and chickens, lime, horse feed, and fencing until Angelina and Sarah received their share of their mother's estate, and until the national society paid Weld what it still owed him. So Weld went to work with vigor, hoping not only to earn a living from the place but also to regain his voice by manual labor. Visiting Weld one day in July, 1841, the English abolitionist Joseph Sturge found him bringing in a load of rails on a wagon drawn by oxen. Disposing of his cargo, Weld took Sturge into the wagon and drove to the house. Two or three former Lane students arrived about the same time; indeed, the house was always filled with company. "In the household arrangements of this distinguished family," observed Sturge, "Dr. Graham's dietetic system is rigidly adopted, which excludes meat, butter, coffee, tea, and all intoxicating beverages. I can assure all who may be interested to know, that this Roman simplicity of living does not forbid enjoyment, when the guest can share with it the affluence of such minds as daily meet at their table." [38]

There is no evidence that the Fort Lee home, the Belleville residence, or any of the other places where the Welds were to reside, were stations on the Underground Railroad. Yet Weld helped, at least indirectly, in aiding slaves to escape. He was a member of the New York Committee of Vigilance, whose functions were to protect endangered free Negroes, obtain redress when they were wronged, and "to counsel and direct the stranger." [39] Four months before his marriage Weld wrote to Angelina under seal of secrecy that a half-dozen fugitive slaves were in New York City. They had arrived at Lewis Tappan's home on New Year's night, one man having swum every river between Tuscaloosa, Alabama, and the Pennsylvania line. They had been hidden and would be embarked for England, Weld confided, and once they were safely on their way he planned to write a pamphlet telling of their heart-rending experiences.[40] There were so many things like that to be done, if he could find the time.

13

POLITICS

OR MORAL SUASION

W*hile Weld strove to put his run*-down farm into production, momentous events were shaping up in abolitionism. The moral appeal had roused large segments of the Northern people; but many abolitionists insisted that moral precepts could only be made effective at the ballot box. An increasing number wished to implement their program by electing antislavery representatives to Congress and to the state legislatures. James G. Birney thought one good congressman was worth a hundred lecturers. "He has almost daily occasion for agitation," Birney argued, "and he speaks to the whole people. We can reach the South through no other means. The slaveholders gain their advantages in national politics and legislation, and should be met in every move they make."[1]   Adopting a strategy that had already proved effective in Ohio, Birney withdrew the national society's agents from organizational work and sent them forth to influence state and local elections, confident that the momentum already attained would bring spontaneous gains in membership of local societies without further direction from agents.[2]

Under this new policy, candidates were questioned regarding their views of Congress' power over slavery in the Territories and the District of Columbia, their attitude on the annexation of Texas, and, in the case of would-be state legislators, their opinions regarding the so-called "Black Laws" of the Northern states which discriminated against free Negroes. Abolitionists were urged in no circumstances to vote for anyone whose answers were unsatisfactory.[3]

This was well enough when antislavery and proslavery candidates opposed each other, but if two rival candidates both answered unfavorably, or if a candidate ignored the inquiries, as many of them did, the abolition voter was in a quandary. Still there was as yet no movement to put forward independent abolition candidates. "The cause of antislavery belongs to all parties and all sects," explained the *Philanthropist*, "and we should as much regret to see abolitionists drawing off from the parties to which they belong as we should to see them leaving the churches of which they are members to build up a separate antislavery church." [4]

As the antislavery voters gained strength they came to hold a balance of power in some electoral districts. Two often, however, candidates who owed their election to abolition votes forgot their benefactors once they were in office, while in other cases they found party discipline too potent to resist. Perplexed and disappointed, some abolitionists were ready to try independent nominations. Joshua Leavitt declared in the *Emancipator* that the antislavery movement was now like "the young of a noble bird, grown too large for the nest and feeling its strength and courage equal to . . . committing itself to the bosom of the air and training its powers in the region of thunders and lightnings and storms." Other leaders of the American Antislavery Society, notably Birney, Myron Holley, C. T. Torrey, Elizur Wright, and

Stanton, favored Leavitt's idea, convinced that questioning of candidates and the balance-of-power policy were too uncertain.[5]

The case of old John Quincy Adams gave point to their objections, for after enjoying the support of abolition voters he refused to vote for emancipation in the District of Columbia unless the people of the District were allowed to express their views, and even favored the admission of Florida to statehood with or without slavery. Then, to crown his recreancy, he attacked the abolitionists' tactics, charging that to urge immediate emancipation was like pouring oil in a volcano. The abolitionists recoiled in stunned amazement, all the more persuaded that they must cut loose from these old-line politicians.[6] But they encountered a stumbling block in Garrison, who, holding himself aloof from the contamination of government, would not besmirch himself with politics.

Still confident of the potency of moral suasion and distrustful of politicians, Weld watched from the sidelines as the matter came to an issue at the annual meeting of the Massachusetts Antislavery Society in 1839, when the political actionists, led by a group of anti-Garrison ministers, laid plans to seize control of the Massachusetts society. Political action was not the only issue; equally inciting factors were displeasure at Garrison's dictatorial methods and extra abolition hobbies. But Garrison was forewarned of the revolt, and rallied his cohorts to counteract this new emanation of "priestly bile."

Weld's friend, Henry B. Stanton, who attended the Massachusetts meeting as an informal representative of the American Antislavery Society, reported that it was "stormy enough," and brought out "the disease in the anti-slavery body, which has long been concealed under the surface." [7] The Reverend Amos A. Phelps led off with a blast at Garrison's dictatorial propensities, asserting his right to work for freedom "without doing it through your paper, and without coming and kneeling devoutly to ask your Holiness whether I may do so or not." He was as sin-

cere an abolitionist as Garrison was, he avowed, and he would
not be subservient to one "whose overgrown self-conceit had
wrought him into the belief that his mighty self was abolition
incarnate." Garrison's supporters were incensed, but they wrote
off the diatribe as simply another example of "the hautiness of
the cloth." [8]

The attendance was the largest of any meeting the Massachusetts society had ever held, for both sides were out in full force.
But the Garrisonians had the votes to control, and the dissidents
were forced to content themselves with what their rivals characterized as "boisterous and unmannerly demonstrations."

Stanton fought hard for a resolution making it the duty of
every abolitionist to exercise his right to vote; but his resolution
was defeated by "Garrison's train bands." Garrison, who claimed
he never tried to dictate in matters of conscience, then proposed a substitute resolution which declared it recreant in those
abolitionists whose consciences told them they should vote, not
to do so. Twice Stanton asked Garrison publicly whether he did
or did not hold it a sin to go to the polls, to which query Garrison smugly replied: "Sin for *me!*" When Stanton tried to prove
that Garrison had originally favored political action, he was answered by the Garrisonians with shouts of "It is false"; and when
he attempted to offer the files of the *Liberator* in support of his
assertion, he was "browbeaten down," indeed "well-nigh mobbed
down," as he described it.[9]

"But I cared nothing for this," wrote Stanton to the national
executive committee, "and only mention it as an illustration of
the unfairness with which the whole proceedings were conducted. But the point is,—the Society hauled down its flag and
run [*sic*] up the crazy banner of the non-government heresy, and
we had to rally round or be ostracized. The split is wide, and can
never be closed up. . . . Our cause in this State is ruined unless
we can separate the A.S. Society from everything that does not
belong to it. That is the issue now tendered to us, and meet it
we must, sooner or later. I am for meeting it here, now, on the

spot where the evil exists." Stanton informed Birney that he would come to New York to explain the situation more fully. But the national executive committee should distinctly understand "that Garrisonism and Abolition in this State are contending for the mastery." [10] Finding that Garrison held the Massachusetts Antislavery Society in an unshakable grip, the political actionists seceded, taking all those who had been antagonized by Garrison's foibles along with them. In May, 1839, they met in Boston and organized themselves as the Massachusetts Abolition Society, as distinguished from Garrison's Massachusetts Antislavery Society.[11] Returning to New York, Stanton wrote from headquarters to the secessionist leader Phelps that "all those with whom I have conversed fully approve of your doings in the organization of your new Society. Weld says you have taken the right ground, and he conjures you to maintain it and go ahead." [12]

Weld rejoiced to see the Massachusetts abolitionists renounce Garrison's irrelevancies, but he could not foresee the clamorous fight that was to follow. Transferring his allegiance to the "New Organization," Phelps declared that the "Old Organization" was no longer an antislavery society pure and simple, but "a woman's rights, non-government anti-slavery society." The Reverend Daniel Wise said that he would support the "New Organization" because he preferred to have the hairs served on one plate and the butter on another.[13] As a medium of expression the new society set up the *Massachusetts Abolitionist* and imported Elizur Wright from the headquarters office to edit it. With the establishment of this paper the rival factions mixed it lustily at close quarters, Garrison and the *Liberator* swinging heavily from one side and Wright and the *Abolitionist* pumping punches from the other.

Weld had scarcely bargained on such a mêlée as this. Hearkening to the din of battle coming out of Massachusetts, he despaired. "The spirit of the Massachusetts belligerents on both sides is absolutely ferocious," he lamented to Gerrit Smith. "Their calling each other *dishonest hypocritical* double tongued false witnesses, etc., is probably what each believes of the others, and *believing* it, let them say it; but the manifest *state of mind* toward each other in which it is all said, Oh how it crucifies the Saviour afresh. I instinctively recoil from its fiery contact and charge my soul 'come not thou into their secret.' . . . I have not *read* a single article in the whole controversy, but every week since it began I have turned to the Liberator as it came, with unspeakable yearnings and prayer that I might find in it the heart of Jesus, and as my eye ran hastily from column to column *almost* wherever it fell on anything touching the subject of controversy I saw the vibrations of serpents tongues and the darting of envenomed stings. The Mass. Abolitionist I rarely see, not being a subscriber to it. From my long acquaintance with Elizur Wright I can hardly conceive of his indignation against wrong . . . degenerating into that personal hostility which inflicts pain with a *relish*. If it has so degenerated in him, I know of no one in Mass. except dear Samuel May whose temper has not been poisoned by the fierce feud." [14]

Beriah Green took less of an alarmist view. "*Dead men* never quarrel," he wrote to Weld. "So many men of intelligence, independence, and decision of character—all and each alive to his responsibilities, which so heavily press upon them; sharp strife now and then must be expected and put up with. We must be willing to quarrel for the slave and endure the quarreling of others. God grant, we may be saved from contending for ourselves and against the slave!" [15]

As "No-government" became a vital issue, Weld tried to save his friends from this delusion. When Gerrit Smith came to New York for the annual meeting, Stanton reported that Weld had several conversations with him, and that "he is very much further from being a non-resistant than when he came to the anniversaries. W. is strong in the faith that Smith will come out right." [16] Thus Weld was influential in confining this Garrisonian heresy to New England; it never gained much favor among abolitionists elsewhere.

At the annual meeting of the American Antislavery Society in 1839—from which Weld stayed away as usual—the champions of political action and the Garrisonian non-voters came to grips again, with the outcome a virtual draw. At Garrison's insistence, and after a long, unpleasant controversy, the national society agreed by a close vote to interpret the word "person" in its constitution to mean women as well as men; and on the issue of political action it adopted—again by a close vote—a resolution to the effect that exercise of the electoral franchise was "a duty . . . we owe to our enslaved fellow-countrymen, groaning under legal oppression."

It was evident, however, that most members of the national executive committee, and especially the Tappans, were displeased with the action taken on the woman question, and that their sympathies were altogether with the "New Organization" in Massachusetts. Both Garrisonians and anti-Garrisonians flexed their muscles for a finish fight at the annual meeting of the national society in 1840.

In the interim each faction watched the other closely. The national executive committee was fearful of the outcome, and about three weeks before the 1840 convention it transferred ownership of the *Emancipator* to the New York City society, alleging lack of funds to finance it any longer. The Garrisonians were furious, charging the executive committee with bad faith in thus disposing of a paper that was the property of the society, and insisting with some reason that it could surely have survived its financial troubles for three weeks.[17]

Unmoved by Garrison's strictures, indeed, almost oblivious of them, abolitionists throughout the Northwest were almost unanimous for political action. The Illinois Antislavery Society declared the franchise to be a gift from the Author of all good and perfect things, while one local society after another passed resolutions declaring the exercise of the voting right to be a sacred duty.[18] Indeed, both East and West, except among the Garrisonians, the question was not whether an abolitionist should vote or not, but whether he might in conscience vote for anyone except a professed abolitionist. Most leaders of the movement thought he should not; but that inevitably raised the corollary question of what to do when no abolition candidate was in the field. Myron Holley again proposed to resolve the dilemma by the formation of an independent party, but other leaders, including the Tappans, thought such action ill-advised.[19] "Great efforts are making to form an abolition political party in this country," wrote Lewis Tappan to the Englishman, Joseph Sturge. ". . . The number of abolitionists is now so large here, and their views on so many points of policy so various, that it will be impossible, I think, to have them united long. In fact they are disunited already. There will probably be an abolition political party—a religious association—a Garrison party, etc. etc. We shall, I hope and pray, get along without quarrelling, for it will be a sad sight to witness the friends of human rights contending angrily among themselves." [20]

But Tappan's hopes were destined to be dashed. After much maneuvering and several false starts, a "National Third-Party Anti-Slavery Convention" was called to meet at Albany on April 1. Birney was selected as the presidential candidate, with Thomas Earle of Pennsylvania as his running mate.

Political action left Weld supine and indifferent. To Garrison, however, it was a challenge; and, with Birney, Stanton, Leavitt, and other leaders of the American Antislavery Society now committed to a political movement, he prepared all the harder for a finish fight at the 1840 convention of the national society. Both sides labored to get out the vote, but Garrison was more resourceful than his rivals. Two special trains conveyed the delegates of the Massachusetts society, together with others favorable to Garrison's views, from Boston to Providence, where a chartered steamer waited to take them to New York. More than four hundred persons crowded aboard, many of them women; for Garrison had taken full advantage of his victory on the woman question to bring out the ladies in force. Many of the delegates were colored, but both the railroad and the steamship company waived the color line. Whites and blacks mingled indiscriminately on both trains and boat, although this mixing of races occasioned excitement and some rioting when the delegates reached New York.

The staterooms of the steamer were insufficient, and many of the passengers spent the night on deck. It was a lively crowd, decorously jolly, happy in the thought of laudable purpose. Speeches and hymns enlivened the evening until it came time for the embattled Garrisonians to retire that they might husband their strength.[21]

The convention met in a Presbyterian church at the corner of Madison and Catherine streets. Again Weld stayed away. More than one thousand delegates attended, however, and all the remaining space was filled with spectators. The anniversary exercises in the morning passed off without incident, although the surcharged atmosphere betokened storms in the afternoon.

Arthur Tappan, president of the national society, did not attend, and when the business session opened Vice-President Francis Jackson was in the chair. The break came over the woman question, although this was only the immediate manifestation of many underlying differences, chief of which was the question of political action. Instructed to appoint a business committee, Jackson named several men and one woman, Weld's convert, the tempestuous Abby Kelley. Her nomination brought objections from the floor and then a lively debate. The delegates avoided indecencies, but the New York press, reporting the proceedings, indulged in innuendo as to what might happen in a committee room where Miss Kelley was the only woman with six or eight men.

The vote which settled the dispute not only upheld the chair, 560 to 450, but also showed that the Garrisonians had enough votes to control, whereupon the vanquished faction claimed that Garrison had packed the meeting. The Garrisonian contingent had "come on in a body," declared the *Emancipator*,[22] "not to meet their brethren from other sections, and take counsel and reason together, and act by the common voice, but by the force of numbers to *take possession* of the National Society to subject it to their own particular policy and particularly to displace the late Executive Committee."

The New York leaders could not abide defeat. At the invitation of Lewis Tappan they withdrew to a lecture room in the church basement to decide what they would do. Almost all the ministers and all but one member of the old executive committee joined the seceders. Out of their deliberations came the formation of a new organization, the American and Foreign Antislavery Society, with a constitution guarding against female intrusion.[23]

The Garrisonians, now in full control of the old national society, passed a resolution declaring that its constitution did not attempt to settle the question of whether an abolitionist must vote or not, and another resolution condemning the nomination of abolition candidates for political office. As a shot at the departed clergymen they declared the church to be "the foe of freedom, humanity, and pure religion."[24]

The American Antislavery Society that the Garrisonians took over was merely a shell. Its treasury was empty and it had lost its paper. But Garrison determined to revitalize it. The executive committee was reorganized in accordance with his wishes, an office was set up in Nassau Street, New York, and a new paper, the *National Antislavery Standard*, was established. Later the headquarters were moved to Boston.[25] Under Garrison's leadership the society continued to denounce political action and to rely exclusively on moral suasion, a strategy that reminded Birney of a Chinese army rattling tin pans to frighten the enemy.[26]

In the East Garrison had split the abolition ranks wide open, but the rift was far less serious in the West. The Ohio state society refused to take official action on the advisability of running abolition candidates, but Gamaliel Bailey, who had succeeded Birney as editor of the *Philanthropist*, put the influence of his paper back of Birney and Earle by calling a third-party state convention. The state societies of Illinois, Indiana, and Michigan also refused to endorse political action officially, but in each state individual leaders came forward to head the movement. Everywhere, however, organization was hasty and superficial, with few third-party candidates running for state and local offices.

As the excitement of the campaign mounted, with the Whig candidate, William Henry Harrison, "the Hero of Tippecanoe," running strongly against Martin Van Buren, the abolitionists were merely a faint whistle in the shrieking winds. Most abolitionists were Whigs, and, with such a good prospect of defeating the detested Democrats the great majority of them could not bring themselves to throw away their votes on Birney and Earle, who had no chance whatsoever. Others, prepared to vote for Birney, could find no third-party ballots or did not know the names of third-party electors. Birney mustered only 7,069 votes, running strongest in Massachusetts, Michigan, Vermont, and New York, although only in Massachusetts did he poll as much as one per cent of the vote. Harrison was borne into the White House by the popular tide, with both his nomination and election due in no small measure to the votes of antislavery men.

The rift among the abolitionists was lasting. Writing to John Scoble, an Englishman, on March 1, 1843, Lewis Tappan observed: "The warfare between the old organization—which is in possession of the *name* of the American Anti-Slavery Society—and the New Organization, including the Liberty Party—is unrelenting. They denounce us without reserve, and have no sympathy with us or English abolitionists who sympathize with us. All hope of reunion is out of the question." [27]

The family feuds of the abolitionists were a stench in the nostrils of the nation, declared Tappan to Weld;[28] and Weld agreed. Indeed, Weld was now almost a voluntary castaway so far as the abolition movement was concerned. He could not bring himself to join the Garrisonians with all their extraneous projects; he would not affiliate with the "New Organization" so long as it

denied the rights of women; and he had no stomach for politics—
too often politicians had used the slavery issue to promote selfish
or sectional aims.[29] He wrote to Gerrit Smith that he and Angelina and Sarah felt impelled to hold aloof from both national societies.[30] Nor would they take sides in the quarrels. When Joseph
Sturge discussed the antislavery situation with the Welds in July,
1841, he commented that "they may be justly accounted allies
by each party . . . and I could not but wish that those, of whatever party, who are accustomed to judge harshly . . . might be
instructed by the candid, charitable, and peace loving deportment of Theodore Weld." [31]

For the duration of the antislavery struggle the abolitionists
were destined to be divided into two major camps, almost as hostile to each other as they were to slavery. Garrison led the radical no-government men, whereas the political actionists, after
running independent candidates again in 1844 under the name of
the Liberty Party, were to join the Free Soil Party in 1848 and
then try to reinvigorate an independent party in 1852. Moreover, the political actionists themselves lacked unity, and often
split into factions.[32] Some men of abolition convictions remained
Whigs or Democrats until, in the end, all voting abolitionists
came together to form the radical wing of the new Republican
Party. As time went on, it would become increasingly difficult
to draw a sharp distinction between political abolitionists and
opponents of slavery extension, the so-called "free soil" men; but
the Garrisonians were readily recognizable for what they were.
Associated with none of these groups, but no less fervent for
emancipation, were a few strong-minded individualists like Theodore Weld.[33]

14

BACKSTAGE

IN WASHINGTON

When *Weld moved to the Belleville*
farm he planned to devote about three or four hours a day to
farm work. The remainder of the time he would write. But the
farm was in such pressing need of attention that before long he
was laboring eleven and twelve hours a day, ploughing, hoeing,
felling trees, splitting rails, boring post holes, digging and hauling
rocks.[1] He had little incentive to write, for with the débâcle in
the American Antislavery Society, who would publish his work?
Weld was soon a full-time farmer.

Then, almost as though it were a miracle, his voice returned.
On June 30, 1841, he wrote to Gerrit Smith that he had ventured to agree to speak at an antislavery rally at Newark on
July 4. It was a perilous experiment, but his throat was so much
better that he felt it a duty to try. He would talk only a few
minutes, perhaps not more than five, but, if he had no trouble, he
would speak, "God helping me, as often as I can treasure vocal

power enough to last me for a ten minute testimony against the climax of human villainy." Weld credited his recovery to hard muscular work to which the force of circumstance had put him. It was the will of Providence. For if he had followed his intended routine of a mere three hours of work a day, his voice would never have come back.[2]

It was five years to the day since Weld had talked in public when he stepped before the audience at Newark. Joseph Sturge, who came over from New York to hear him, reported that he spoke without serious difficulty for half an hour.[3] Lewis Tappan sent congratulations. "Thank you," replied Weld with heartfelt fervor. "I have 'got Well' again through the mercy of our Father." [4]

"And so your mouth is open again in the cause of Humanity," exulted Beriah Green. "Blessed be God! May he enable you to plead for the Dumb, long, earnestly and effectively!" Then, re-membering Weld's reckless disregard of self, he added: "Your past experience in this matter should teach you prudence. I hope that you will not pour yourself out at a single gush. That is a pro-tracted struggle to which you are Heaven-called. May God help you to spend your strength, economically!" [5] Rejoicing in his re-stored powers, Weld spoke again at Newark and in other nearby communities. He was active in the Essex County Antislavery So-ciety.

On January 3, 1841, the Welds had a second son. They named him Theodore Grimké Weld. They were overjoyed to have an-other baby to keep Charles Stuart company, but the child was destined to give them many hours of heartache.

Just as Weld was getting back into the swing of antislavery work, he received an important letter from Joshua Leavitt, who was in Washington covering the congressional session for the *Emancipator*. The abolitionists' third-party aspirations had been premature, but Birney's political spadework as secretary of the American Antislavery Society had yielded fruit. The strategy of questioning candidates and throwing abolition ballots to congressional aspirants of abolition sympathies had resulted in the election of a little group of Whig congressmen who were ready to do battle in the national legislature. Already they had proved their faith by staunch support of John Quincy Adams in the petition fight. But this was merely in the nature of a harassing operation, condoned if not approved by the Whig leaders as a means of embarrassing the Democrats.

In 1841, however, the House of Representatives passed the notorious "forty-second rule," which made the "gag" on anti-slavery petitions a standing rule, rather than a special rule applying only for the duration of a session as heretofore. With the adoption of this measure the little band of zealots resolved on a frontal attack. They would go beyond the right of petition and agitate the slavery question itself at every opportunity. They knew they must expect a galling counterfire and that they must fight alone, for to attack slavery itself was to defy party discipline by giving battle on what the Whig leaders had always avoided as untenable ground. But they were a stubborn band, even without the constant prodding they received from Leavitt.[6]

Leading them was Joshua Reed Giddings, representative from Ohio's Western Reserve, a reckless, truculent fighter who had been baptized in antislavery by Weld himself. Of stern and frugal Yankee antecedents, he was reared on a farm, and by hard study in the little time his father spared him from the chores he had equipped himself to teach school and then to practice law. Of a dogged rather than a brilliant intellect, and without the finesse of the successful party leader, he combined the farmer's hard-bitten independence with the didacticism of the schoolmaster and the lawyer's love of argument. He was six feet two, broad-shouldered and compact, with flowing white locks and features seamed with heavy lines. His excellent physique belied his uncertain health, however, for he was bothered with dyspepsia and an irregular heart. He was not a remarkable speaker and he sometimes groped for a word, at which time he would close his eyes as if to envision it, and wait until it came.[7]

He was serving his second congressional term, and was John Quincy Adams' closest friend in Congress. Like Adams, he dwelt chiefly on the moral wrong of slavery, but he went further than Adams in holding slavery to be illegal, inasmuch as no act of man's could make one human being the property of another. Even as a freshman legislator Giddings had noted how overbearing Southerners could sometimes be, and had resolved that he would brook no insolence. Already his aggressiveness had brought a warning from a Southern congressman that if he ever set foot in the South he would be hanged, and few of his Southern colleagues deigned to speak to him.[8]

Second of the group was Seth M. Gates of New York, whose antislavery ardor was born of evangelical piety. Although Gates had edited a paper and practiced law, he was so timid about speaking in public as to be almost inarticulate. But he labored in other ways, and so effectively that a Southern planter offered five hundred dollars for his delivery in Savannah "dead or alive."

William Slade of Vermont, who was serving his sixth congressional term, was the third member of the band. No orator, he could summon a prickly vituperation and a brackish wit that made even the most proficient speakers reluctant to tangle with him. Trained for the law, he had edited a vigorous political newspaper whose failure had bogged him in debt. He scorned bankruptcy and was still paying the debt off with what money he could spare from support of his wife and nine children. Since he was dependent upon political office for his livelihood, discretion must have warned him to play safe, but Giddings regarded him as the staunchest abolitionist in the House. And while his recreancy displeased the national Whig leaders, the faithful Vermonters later made him governor of the state.

Slade's colleague from Vermont was John Mattocks, a highly successful lawyer, a veteran state legislator and former Chief Justice of the state's Supreme Court, who had just been elected to Congress after having served previously fourteen years before. Robust and good-humored, he was a witty conversationalist, although he claimed never to have made a formal speech in his life. His antislavery convictions were as unwavering as his devout Congregationalism, and he assured his embattled colleagues that no abolition doctrine was too ultra for him. He too would later serve as governor of Vermont.

Sherlock J. Andrews of Ohio, a man of ability and some eloquence, whose latter talent was circumscribed by a throat ailment which the Washington climate aggravated until his voice was reduced to a whisper, Nathaniel Briggs Borden of Massachusetts, and Francis James of Pennsylvania were others who could generally be relied on for support. Giddings wrote to his wife that the group constituted a "select committee," not so much thought of at present, but destined to a larger place in history.

They became disheartened at times. Gates was so disgusted with the "hollow heartedness" of most of his Whig colleagues that he contemplated joining the Liberty Party. "I cannot, however, get along with all their views and positions," he explained to Birney, "and so I hold on where I am, receiving all the curses of the South for my ultra abolitionism, and the cuffs of the third party men of the North, for my Whigism."⁹ Everything they did drew criticism, too often from those who owed them gratitude. "Mr. Leavitt has once more done some of us a gross injustice in his remarks about the election of Speaker," Gates protested to Birney in another letter. He, Giddings, and Slade had labored manfully to obtain the nomination of a free-state man, and when the Whig caucus chose a slaveholder they had bolted and prevailed upon John Quincy Adams, as well as others of their group, to buck the party choice. Yet Leavitt was accusing them of apathy. "We get curses enough here for obstinacy, and bolting party," Gates complained, "without getting it from him."

But Leavitt did not mean to let them down, and he had hit upon a plan to make their opposition effectual. They were pressed with a multitude of minor congressional duties that left them little time to search out and assimilate the factual materials with which to implement their antislavery attack. Theodore

Weld, however, was skilled in antislavery research. Why not bring him to Washington and put him in charge of a sort of antislavery reference bureau? The Whig insurgents took to the plan at once. If Weld would come, they would pay his traveling expenses, see that he had access to the shelves of the Library of Congress, where investigators must be introduced by a congressman, and provide room, stationery, and all other facilities.[10]

Weld saw the possibilities as soon as Leavitt broached the proposition. "That those men are in a position to do for the A.S. cause by a single speech more than our best lecturers can do in a year, we all know," he wrote to Lewis Tappan. "The fact that these speeches, prepared for the press by the speakers themselves after delivery, will be . . . scattered all over the south as well as the north settles that point." And besides, Gates and Andrews, as well as Giddings, were Weld's own converts to abolitionism.

Yet the job presented problems. Three weeks of carpentry work were imperatively demanded at Weld's farm, besides the routine labor. He had planned to do all this himself; if he left, he must hire it done. To hire, he must borrow. Weld took his problem to Lewis Tappan, and as usual Tappan helped him with money. "Dear Theda . . . has concluded to go & see how far in earnest these men are," wrote Sarah to Jane Smith, "—if they are determined to do their duty he will most joyously devote himself to the service & labor behind the curtain—thou knowest this is just what he prefers, but if he finds no true hearted man among them he will return immediately." [11]

On December 30, 1841, Weld arrived in Washington, where he was ensconced in an alcove in the Library of Congress, his desk piled high with materials he had brought along and with books and newspapers selected from the Library's accumulation.

He lodged at Mrs. Spriggs' boarding house, where, a few years later, Abraham Lincoln of Illinois would be a boarder. Leavitt was with Weld, and Gates and Giddings also had lodgings there, along with a dozen or more other congressmen. "Mrs. Spriggs is directly in front of the Capitol," wrote Weld to his wife. " . . .

The iron railing around the Capitol Park comes within fifty feet of our door. Our dining room overlooks the whole Capitol Park which is one mile around and filled with shade trees and shrubbery." The park was adorned with summer houses, "jet d'eaus," basins filled with gold and silver fish, and was criss-crossed with gravel paths. A better place for exercise could not be had, and every morning before breakfast Weld went over to the park and ran and hopped and jumped for an hour or more. "I have a pleasant room on the second floor," he informed Angelina, "with a good bed, plenty of covering, a bureau, table, chairs, closets, and cloathes press, a good fire place, and plenty of dry wood to burn in it." 12

Indulging Weld's dietary peculiarities, Mrs. Spriggs set a deep bowl of milk before him at every meal, and into this he crumbled the Graham bread she always provided. Mush, apples, vegetables, almonds, figs, and raisins completed his fare, and if his messmates accounted him strange when he scorned the juicy roasts, the rich butter, and the aromatic tea and coffee that they relished, at least Weld noted no sneers.

Mrs. Spriggs was a Virginian. Five of her servants were free colored persons, the other three were hired slaves. Weld marveled at the uninhibited manner in which the boarders talked about slavery, abolition, and runaway slaves in the presence of these Negroes, and wondered that the slaves were not incited to run off.

On New Year's Day, Weld, Leavitt, and Giddings attended President Tyler's levée. None of them cared to touch the "presidential digits," so they avoided the reception line. Indeed, the "palace" was so thronged that they stayed only fifteen minutes, then went to pay their respects to the Adamses. Weld was pleased to note that the Adams house was modestly furnished and that Adams and his wife were plainly dressed, in contrast to the "pomp and tinsel" at the White House. Adams was glad to meet Weld. "I know you well, sir, by your writings," he remarked. On a later occasion Weld dined with the Adamses. "It was a genuine abolition gathering," he wrote to Angelina, "and the old patriarch talked with as much energy and zeal as a Methodist at a camp meeting." [13]

Weld loathed the very atmosphere of Washington. "The Worlds splendor which blazes around me," he lamented, "the pride and fashion, prodigality, ostentatious display and vanity, and desperate strugglings and vaultings of ambition, the envyings and fierce encounters of rivals for office and popular sway, are lessons to my soul that are to be learned here. May God help me to reap from them all those peaceable fruits of humility, faith, love, zeal, and patience of hope which those who are wise in the wisdom of the Lord may gather from them."

He was homesick from the first. "When the press of business pauses as it does at intervals (as at meals, and before breakfast, and after I retire at night, and at brief little snatches during the day) how my *heart beats* home," he wrote to Angelina. He assured her he had heeded her admonitions to keep spruced up. His socks were whole. His clothes were in good state. He shaved every morning, he reported.

Angelina feared he might be in peril of arrest or even assassination. His room was filled with abolition literature, and hadn't Amos Dresser been publicly whipped merely because abolition pamphlets were discovered in his luggage?

Weld reassured her. There was really no danger at all. And what if there were? "We are not the agents God has chosen for the deliverance of the slaves if fear of *anything* swerves us from duty." As an abolition lecturer he had often been in hourly danger of death, but he never let it cost him an hour's sleep. "Now I am free of all apprehension," he declared. "Not but that I think it not *utterly* improbable that I may be called before the legal authorities to account for the abolition books, etc., in my possession and if so shall certainly not be specially grieved at an opportunity to say something about inalienable rights. But of this, even, I think there is not any probability." [14]

According to his custom, Weld sought a colored church. He found two colored Methodist meetinghouses, and, while both pastors were "full of noise and shouting," still the congressional chaplains were scarcely better. Indeed, what passed for religion in Washington, Weld reckoned a pompous sham, "having the form of Godliness but denying the power thereof," and sustained merely for appearance and reputation. "Oh what mockery of God!" he groaned. And yet there were some sanguine signs. Gates came in one day to report that he had attended a meeting in a Capitol committee room to organize a congressional teetotal temperance society, and that Wise of Virginia—who, only a few days before, had been so enraged at Gates by reason of an abolition speech that he countered with a furious diatribe in the course of which he shook his fist under Gates' nose—this same Wise had been so drawn to Gates in common loathing of the Demon Rum that he had taken a seat beside him and talked quite civilly for some time.[15]

Weld himself attended a later meeting of the society, and shortly thereafter he visited a Methodist church where John Hawkins, the celebrated reformed drunkard, was lecturing. So plaintive was Hawkins' appeal that many eyes were wet with tears, including Weld's own. During his discourse Hawkins made an oral side-swipe at tobacco chewers, and at the close of his speech, while many of his auditors were signing the temperance pledge, a gentleman hastily wrote out a pledge against tobacco and handed it to Hawkins, who held it aloft while he voiced a lusty plea for addicts of the weed to renounce their vice and sign. Several came forward, and Weld noted that his neighbor squirmed uneasily. At length he turned to Weld, and with shame-faced look announced, "I can't go that." Whereupon Weld reasoned with him, and with such effect that he finally started from his seat, marched boldly up the aisle, and, emptying the tobacco from his pockets, turned it over to Hawkins, who held it up as a trophy before the audience. With that the aisle was crowded with repentant chewers, smokers, and snuffers, who, in a few minutes, had not only signed the pledge, but piled two quarts of burley on the altar.[16]

Weld worked in the Library of Congress as long as the doors were open—from nine until three—sometimes taking off an hour to visit the House or Senate for relaxation. After supper he worked in his room until bedtime, examining law books, treaties, judicial decisions, the *Journals* of Congress. He and Leavitt held frequent consultations. Much of Weld's time was devoted to the case of the *Creole*, a ship which sailed from Hampton Roads bound for New Orleans in October, 1841, with 130 slaves aboard.[17] In the course of the voyage the slaves revolted, took possession of the ship, and sailed her into the port of Nassau, where, according to British law, the bondsmen were entitled to freedom. A slaveowner on the vessel was killed in the mêlée, however, and the Bahaman authorities held the Negroes in custody pending instructions from London.

The owners of ship and cargo demanded the interposition of the American government and the State Department proceeded to urge their claims. The South regarded the case as a test—indeed, Southern firebrands wished to push the matter to the threat of war—inasmuch as the British had made it a practice to liberate Negroes whenever American coasting vessels that carried slaves had come within British jurisdiction because of weather or other unavoidable circumstance.

The case was expected to come before the House at any moment; Southern representatives had delayed this long only through fear of giving the abolitionists a chance to fulminate. It would come up in due time, Weld informed Angelina. "Meanwhile we are getting ready for them." The recommendations of the Secretaries of War and of the Navy for an increase in the military forces in the South were also destined for criticism. They would open up the question of taxation of the North to protect the South's "peculiar institution," and Weld was building up a mass of data to bolster the abolitionists' complaint. The antislavery phalanx was also preparing petitions to be signed by free colored seamen who had been imprisoned while their ships remained in certain Southern ports,[18] a precautionary measure designed to prevent their inciting slaves to run off.

Altogether, Weld was very busy, and before he had been many weeks in Washington the blustery sectional cross-winds reached crescendo in the House. On Friday, January 21, 1842, John Quincy Adams presented a petition from Habersham County, Georgia, praying his own removal from the chairmanship of the committee on foreign affairs because of his antislavery prejudice. He was "possessed with a species of monomania on all subjects connected with people as dark as a Mexican," the petitioners complained, and was therefore not to be trusted regarding our relations with Mexico.[19] This was just the sort of thing in which Adams delighted; it gave him a chance to evade the gag rule. Foreseeing this possibility, Southern members moved to lay the petition on the table, but Adams demanded the right to be heard in his own defense. Upheld by the Speaker of the House, he launched into a tirade until it seemed to Weld, who was watching from the gallery, that "slaveholding, slave trading, and slave breeding absolutely quailed and howled under his dissecting knife." Time and again Southern members tried to stop him by raising points of order or by screaming: "That is false," "I *demand* Mr. Speaker that you *put him down*," "What! are we to sit here and endure such insults?" "I demand that you shut the mouth of that old harlequin."

But Adams swung his cleaver without mercy as Weld rejoiced to hear it thud to the very bones. At least half the Southern members left their seats and gathered about Adams to threaten or glare, but the old man, his venerable dignity forgotten, drew himself up to his full five feet eight inches, and with bald head gleaming and eyes aflame beneath his lowering brows, he gave them glower for glower. Weld marveled at Adams' audacity as he replied to interruptions with "I see where the shoe pinches, Mr. Speaker, it will pinch more yet." "I'll deal out to the gentlemen a diet that they'll find it hard to digest." "If before I get through every slaveholder, slavetrader and slave breeder on this floor does not get materials for reflection it shall be no fault of mine," and so on until a vote for adjournment silenced him.[20]

The next day Adams continued, but at every opportunity some Southern member would interrupt, so that Adams was never able to speak more than five minutes at a time.

On Monday Adams was prepared to carry on, and, when the House refused to hear him, he resorted to his accustomed practice of presenting antislavery petitions, bringing them up one after another and proceeding as far as he could, until, in each case, as soon as the nature of the petition was made evident, the Speaker applied the gag. In due course, Adams drew from his file a petition from a group of citizens of Haverhill, Massachusetts, who asked Congress to take measures for the immediate dissolution of the Union, inasmuch as it no longer brought reciprocal benefits but drained off the resources of the North to support an institution detestable in the sight of that section, and because inevitable destruction was foreshadowed by the nation's proslavery course. During the ensuing uproar Adams moved the appointment of a select committee with instructions to answer the petitioners by showing the reasons why their plea could not be granted.[21]

An expert in parliamentary procedure, the crafty Adams had placed himself in an invulnerable position. Southerners had repeatedly threatened to dissolve the Union by force, and it ill befitted them to take offense at a proposal asking for a peaceable dissolution. As the observant New York merchant and diarist Philip Hone saw it, the Haverhill petition advanced the same disunion argument that the South Carolina nullifiers had put forward, but now that "the brat is born of Northern parents, these patriotic hotspurs are horrified beyond all example." [22]

Adams had acted solely as the agent of his constituents, being careful to make it evident that he did not favor their plea. But such was the rage of certain Southerners that they walked right into the trap. George W. Hopkins of Virginia asked the Speaker if it would be in order to burn the petition in the presence of the House. Henry A. Wise and Thomas W. Gilmer, a fellow Virginian, demanded that Adams be censured, and Gilmer introduced a resolution to that effect. Slaveholding members rejoiced that at last they had Adams in their grasp, and a Southern caucus was called to meet that evening to plan future strategy. Giddings tried to organize the Northern Whigs in Adams' behalf, but most of them refused to foment "a sectional quarrel." A few stalwarts did meet in Giddings' room, and Leavitt and Weld were asked to join them. Appointed a committee of two to give Adams what help they could, Leavitt and Weld called at his residence late that night. Adams was deeply moved, for he had expected to fight alone; and he asked them to check certain points and have the books and documents supporting their conclusions placed on his desk when the House convened the next day.[23]

Following a meeting of the committee on foreign affairs on Tuesday morning, Caleb Cushing, Adams' colleague from Massachusetts, warned the old gentleman that Southern members of the committee were plotting to displace Adams as chairman.

In order to avoid the appearance of partisanship, the Southern caucus had selected Thomas F. Marshall, a Kentucky Whig, to lead the attack in the House. A nephew of the late Chief Justice John Marshall, he was an ambitious, aggressive, and bibulous young man whose oratorical efforts had once been described by Adams as "alcohol evaporating in elegant language." After the transaction of some minor business on Tuesday morning, Marshall opened upon Adams by proposing substitute resolutions, more specific than Gilmer's in that they accused Adams of insulting the American people and disgracing his country in the eyes of the world by permitting himself to be made the instrumentality of a contemptuous and treasonable clique. Such conduct merited expulsion from the House, the resolutions declared, and Adams' colleagues would act with grace and mercy if they merely censured him and turned him over, for the rest, to the chidings of his own conscience and the contempt of all true Americans.

The galleries were filled with spectators and many senators had crowded into the lobbies when Adams rose to reply. Weld noted that he was unusually calm, and used none of the personal invective to which he so often resorted when dealing with the slave power. Instead he quoted the Declaration of Independence respecting the right of a people to change their government, and held forth on the question of personal liberty. "I said I thought it impossible the House should entertain the resolution," he recorded in his diary, "and after a few remarks postponing my address till it should be ascertained I stood accused, I finished." [24]

As Adams sat down, Wise rose to attack. Tall and lean, with a dangerous glitter in his eye, he was able, rash, and headstrong. Kind to his own slaves, he could tolerate no taunts at slavery. A Virginia aristocrat, he subscribed to the Southern code of honor, had wounded an opponent in a duel and served as second to W. J. Graves when he killed a fellow-congressman, Jonathan Cilley, in an affair of honor. He was excitable and high-strung, and later, when serving as governor of Virginia, would refuse to save John Brown from the gallows even when presented with evidence of his insanity. He chewed tobacco and swore lustily, and, if his oratory was in the current grandiloquent style, his invective could sear and scorch. The perspicacious Philip Hone thought he tried to ape John Randolph of Roanoke, and while he fell short of the eccentric Randolph in ability, he could "vomit fire" like a dragon. [25]

Almost quivering as he spoke, Wise denounced Adams as a "white-haired hypocrite" who had forsworn the teachings of his fathers and "preyed upon the dead." Adams' treason ranked with that of Benedict Arnold and Aaron Burr, and he should consider himself fortunate to be let off with a reprimand. Wise spoke for two hours, not only against Adams but also against abolitionists and abolitionism, and the next day he held forth for two hours and a half, speaking, so it seemed to Weld in the gallery, "with the ferocity of a fiend." Adams sneered that he would not interrupt until Wise "had disgorged his whole cargo of filthy invective"; and when he finished at last, Adams contended that if subornation of perjury and treason were to be the charges against him, only a regularly constituted court and jury could try him.

Marshall retorted that Adams was guilty of contempt, and the wrangle continued until it was shut off by a vote to adjourn.[26] It was not an edifying debate on either side, and it seemed to Philip Hone that the House had become a counterpart of the French National Assembly on the eve of the Reign of Terror. He thought Adams' deliberate provocation of the Southerners disgusting, and that Wise's language would bring blushes in a grogshop.[27]

Not all the Southern members agreed as to the wisdom of an aggressive course, and on Thursday Joseph R. Underwood of Kentucky, Thomas D. Arnold of Tennessee, and John Minor Botts of Virginia spoke against a vote of censure. Leverett Saltonstall of Massachusetts made such an able defense of Adams that Richard W. Thompson of Indiana moved to table the whole subject. Marshall and Gilmer begged Thompson to withdraw his motion. He refused. Whereupon the fire-eaters resorted to obstructive tactics to prevent a vote until it came time to adjourn.[28]

On Friday Weld was once more in the gallery as Adams and Marshall had at each other again, with Wise and Gilmer breaking in. Adams accused the slaveholders of attempting to destroy the right of habeas corpus, trial by jury, freedom of the mails, of the press, of petition, and free speech. Adverting to South Carolina's practice of incarcerating free Negro seamen while their ships were in her ports, he accused her of enslaving citizens of Northern states in violation of their constitutional rights. He contrasted the educational system, the internal improvements, the industry and thrift of New York State with the wretched highways, the tumble-down dwellings, the cultural stagnation, and the general poverty of Virginia, blaming the South's backwardness on slavery.

During this whole time Weld kept himself at Adams' service, searching out documents, marking passages in books, keeping the old warrior's ammunition coming up in bountiful supply each morning. Several times he called at Adams' residence in the evening to learn what Adams might need the next day.[29]

Having dealt with the outrages of the slave power, Adams passed to personalities. His reply to Hopkins' suggestion of burning the Haverhill petition was a mere reference to "the combustible gentleman from Virginia." In answer to Wise, he brought up the matter of his serving as second in the Graves-Cilley affray, pronouncing him as much a criminal as the man who pulled the fatal trigger, and denouncing one who, entering the halls of Congress smeared with human gore, would dare pass judgment on a fellow member. As for Marshall, Adams suggested that he return to Kentucky and *commence* the study of law, and also offered a few comments on his personal habits. Giddings overheard Isaac E. Holmes of South Carolina speak to Gilmer and Underwood in terms of grudging admiration of Adams, and Weld reported the slaveholders as utterly confounded. Threats, questions of order, motions to lay on the table, refusals to adjourn as a means of tiring Adams out, interruptions, accusations, explanations, all were ineffectual to silence the old man. "The Old Nestor has cast all their counsels headlong," gloated Weld, "turned all their guns against themselves, and smitten the whole host with dismay and discomfiture." [30]

The old man's stamina amazed him. "Last Friday," Weld wrote to Angelina, "after he had been sitting in the house from 12 o'clock till 6, and for nearly half that time engaged in speaking with great energy against his ferocious assailants, I called at his house in the evening, and he came to meet me as fresh and elastic as a boy. I told him I was afraid he had tired himself out. 'No, not at all,' said he, 'I am all ready for another heat.' He then began and went through with the *main points* which he designed to push in his speech the next day, and with as much rapidity and energy of utterance and gesture as though he had been addressing the house. I tried to stop him, telling him he would need all his strength for the next day, but it was all in vain. He went on for an hour, or very nearly that, in a voice loud enough to be heard by a large audience. Wonderful man!" [31]

Saturday brought further skirmishing. Then Sunday gave Adams a brief rest. "The pressure upon my mind in the preparation of my defence is so great that for several successive nights I have had little sleep," he recorded in his diary on Monday, January 31. "Last night brought me some respite and relief, and I slept this morning almost until sunrise." It was a late hour for him.

On Monday the House took up other business, and Adams had a further chance to rest, though he was active in several matters that came up. Adjournment came early due to the death of Senator Nathan Fellows Dixon of Rhode Island. On Tuesday the House transacted no business because of Dixon's funeral, but Adams' committee on foreign affairs held a meeting at 10 A.M. Here Gilmer sprang the scheme to depose Adams as chairman, but the net result was merely to provide Adams with a new weapon to use in the House. For the remainder of the week the old man sparred and slugged by turns, at one time producing an anonymous letter from Jackson, North Carolina, which threatened him with assassination, at another exhibiting a portrait of himself with the mark of a rifle bullet in the middle of his forehead and the legend, "to stop the music of John Quincy Adams, sixth President of the United States,

"Who in the space of one revolving moon,
Is statesman, poet, babbler and buffoon."

Adams contrasted his cordial relations with Washington, Jefferson, Madison, and Monroe with the "base conspiracy" of the three Virginians who now assailed him. He denounced the plot to remove him from his chairmanship. When Marshall launched another attack, Adams produced some published letters of Marshall's in which that gentleman himself had loosed "an exquisite blast" at slavery. "I saw my cause was gained," recorded Adams, "and Marshall was sprawling in his own compost. I came home scarcely able to crawl up to my chamber, but with the sound of 'Io Triumphe' ringing in my ear." [32]

On Monday, February 7, Weld called on Adams early to congratulate him on his defense of the past week. When the House met, Adams was prepared to carry on. But Botts moved to table the whole matter forever, and his motion carried, 106 to 93. The House then declined to receive the Haverhill petition, whereupon Adams proceeded to present a variety of others, bringing up nearly two hundred before the House adjourned.[33] The old man truly had "provoking pertinacity."

Weld saw Adams' triumph as the first victory over the organized slaveocracy since the foundation of the government, and predicted that slavery's downfall would date from that hour. Giddings, too, marked it as the beginning of a new political era. "Well we have triumphed," he wrote to his daughter, "the *north* has for once triumphed. . . . I entertain not the least doubt that a moral revolution in this nation will take its date from this session of Congress," he concluded. "I am confident that the charm of the slavepower *is now broken*. I may be too sanguine— quite likely I am,—but such are my candid sentiments." [35]

Weld was not so optimistic as Giddings. The tide was turning, to be sure, but he still foresaw an exhausting fight. "Every day reveals more new symptoms of alarm and shift of position among the slaveholders here," he informed Angelina, "but though they feel their foundation shaking they will strive to sustain it with perfect desperation. Satan never retreats without a death struggle, and even when cast out by power omnipotent, it is not without the prostration of his victims. Like those of Old they wallow foaming, and though cast into the fire and into the water he hardly departeth from them even then. That slavery has *begun* its fall is plain, but that its fall will be resisted by those who cling to it, with energy and desperation and fury such as only fiends can summon when they know their hour has come, the end will be slow. Woe to abolitionists, if they dream that their work is well nigh done." [36]

Weld reported that five slaveholders had resigned from Adams' committee to show their spite. The Speaker appointed five other Southerners to fill their places, and three of these also resigned. Congress had quieted down, but Weld expected a battle to flare up at any moment over the proposed annexation of Texas. The question of the rights of colored seamen also hung fire, with the abolition members waiting to make it the excuse for opening a discussion of the whole question of the constitutional rights of free Negroes.

With Adams vindicated, the antislavery congressmen continued their needling tactics, while the slaveocracy, smarting, waited for some victim of lesser ken to venture within their clutch. On February 27, Giddings challenged them by presenting another petition for the dissolution of the Union.[37] "It made some stir," Weld reported, "but the slaveholders had been so horribly burned by the fire before, they took special care not to move a vote of censure." [38] But a few days later Giddings dared them again, and now they believed they had caught him.

While diplomatic negotiations relative to the *Creole* case were in progress with Great Britain, Giddings presented a series of resolutions derogatory to the American position, and declaring that to reënslave the black men would be contrary to international as well as to American law, and incompatible with our national honor. Unquestionably he used materials prepared by Weld, and he probably had Weld's coaching before he spoke.

The starting-point of Giddings' argument was basically the same as that of John C. Calhoun—namely, that slavery was exclusively a state affair, and that the states had delegated no authority over slavery to the Federal Government. From this it followed that the Federal Government had no more right to support slavery than it had to abolish it. If the people of slaveholding states could claim exemption from federal interference with slavery, conversely the people of the free states should be spared the guilt and expense of sustaining slavery through federal agency.

Giddings' second proposition was that slavery, being an abridgment of the natural rights of man, could exist only by force of positive municipal legislation, "and is necessarily confined to the territorial jurisdiction of the power creating it." From this he reasoned that the laws of Virginia, where the *Creole* Negroes were owned, were inoperative on the high seas, and that the authority of the Federal Government was also inoperative inasmuch as the states had given it no power to deal with slavery. Therefore the Negroes on the *Creole* were not only outside the jurisdiction of both Virginia and the Federal Government, but also ceased to be slaves as soon as they were shipped on the high seas. Consequently they had violated no law of any kind in using force to make good their natural right to freedom.

It was a shrewd and cogent argument, and bears the mark of Weld's logic. It had broad implications, for, if the Federal Government had no power over slavery, how could it maintain slavery in the District of Columbia? And since the authority of Territorial governments was delegated by the Federal Government, from whence could come their power to pass regulations permitting the introduction of slavery? In the hands of an antislavery president, Congress, or Supreme Court, such reasoning could have far-reaching consequences.[39]

Perhaps the fire-eaters did not recognize these potentialities. It was enough for them that they had a chance to chastise Giddings, and they pounced immediately. "We are truly in the very pinch," wrote Gates to Birney. "The old hag has longed for a victim ever since Mr. Adams slipped out of her grasp, and she has at last got one."[40] A number of Northern Whigs wished to support Giddings, and for a time it appeared that the Whig party might divide along sectional lines. But Gates had witnessed similar situations before, and predicted correctly that most Northerners would yield to the pull of party ties. After long and bitter debate a vote of censure against Giddings carried, 125 to 69.

With the announcement of the result of the ballot, Giddings rose, took formal leave of the Speaker and the members of the House, shook hands with Adams, who had counseled him to take the course he did, bade farewell to a few personal friends, and walked out of the chamber. Soon afterward he sent in his resignation and returned to Ohio, where he presented himself for reëlection. The issue before the voters was party regularity—which meant silence on the slavery issue—*versus* the right to speak out on that question. Gates tried to rally support for Giddings in Washington, but was thwarted by the party whips. Anti-Giddings editorials appeared in the *Cleveland Whig*. Federal officeholders were warned not to support him. The heavy weight of party was used to crush him.[41] But the abolition seed that Weld and his coworkers had sown in the Western Reserve had made rank growth, and Giddings won a signal victory.

As Weld foresaw, the triumphs of Adams and Giddings were the beginning of slavery's end, for slavery could not stand against free speech. Heretofore both major parties had made silence on the slavery issue a test of party regularity. The Whigs could no longer do so. And as the Whig party lost cohesion it would grow increasingly weaker until it died. Eventually the Democratic party, also unable to muzzle its antislavery dissenters, would split. The second session of the Twenty-Seventh Congress marked a turning point in the battle for freedom. And insofar as Weld was instrumental in implementing the insurgent assault, he helped to bring slavery's demise.[42]

15

BELLEVILLE
AND WASHINGTON
AGAIN

By *April, 1842, Weld was back in* Belleville, busy planting his crops. He had been asked to speak in Philadelphia en route to his home, but as usual he preferred to expend his efforts in smaller places and came "through the interior." "My poor throat still gives me trouble," he wrote to Gerrit Smith, "but I manage to talk about twice a week, which is too much for it; but by talking short and taking care not [to] get into a tempest I slowly move up stream." He was speaking at Paterson every Sabbath evening on the moral bearings of the slave question, and planned to continue to do so for several weeks. "The leaven of abolition is working even in New Jersey," he rejoiced.[1]

In August Weld went to Manlius, New York, to help his parents sell their house. While there he gave a temperance lecture and planned to speak on abolition. But he had been afflicted all summer with fever and ague,[2] and he was seized so frequently with shaking fits that he had to desist. Lewis Tappan again brought up the matter of his taking a church in New York, and Angelina hoped her husband would consider it. The farm was a fit place to regain his health, but it was not where he belonged.[3]

The pulpit, however, no longer attracted Weld. The generality of preachers were too insincere. There were outstanding exceptions, he conceded, but "there is among the professed ministers of Christ such connivance at cherished sins, such truckling subserviency to power, such clinging with mendicant sycophancy to the skirts of wealth and influence, such humoring of pampered lusts, such cowering before bold transgression when it stalks among the high places of power with fashion in its train, or to sum up all, such floating in the wake of an unholy public sentiment, instead of beating back its waves with a 'thus saith the Lord' and a 'thou art the man'—that even men of the world who are shrewd discerners, regard them rather as the obsequious cooks and confectioners who cater for a capricious palate, than as the faithful physician who administers the medicine demanded by the disease, however much the patient may loath[e] it, and steadily pushes the probe to the core, whatever his struggles or upbraidings." [4] Weld wanted iron in his religion. The perfection of religion was to be like Christ—humble, charitable, forgiving, but ruthless with sin.

On December 27 Weld was back in Washington for the short session. Mrs. Spriggs had reserved him a warm, light room on the second floor, where board, lodging, lights, and shoe-brushing cost him eight dollars a week. The antislavery activities of Mrs. Spriggs' roomers during the last session had caused her place to be called the "Abolition House," and her friends had thought this might ruin her. But instead her house was filled, and she was one of the few landladies who had not been obliged to cut rates. The slaves she had employed before had all run away, as Weld had foreseen that they might, and now she made it her practice to hire only free colored help. "Stick a pin there!" exulted Weld when he wrote to tell Angelina.[5]

Abolition was the talk of the town, and Weld thought there might be "warm work." It would be nothing like last winter, however, for the Southern members were more tractable. They made a half-hearted effort to remove Giddings from the chairmanship of the committee on claims, and also showed displeasure over Northern manifestations of sympathy for the fugitive slave George Latimer who had been captured and subsequently ransomed in Boston. Weld thought the slaveholders had been so smitten with Adams' bolts at the last session that they were unable to rally, but actually the Whig leaders had decided not to harass the Whig insurgents needlessly, inasmuch as their votes would be needed for the passage of party measures.

Weld found plenty to do. A number of disputed claims for reimbursement to masters whose slaves had been killed in government service were scheduled to come up, and the abolitionists were girding to combat them. A petition from certain citizens of Boston in behalf of free Negro sailors was referred to the committee on commerce, of which Andrews was a member. He, Gates, Giddings, Slade, and others were planning to give battle when it came before the House, and Weld had fortified them with a long memorandum expounding the constitutional aspects of the subject. Also coming up from the committee on Territories was a resolution to inquire into the expediency of repealing those laws of Florida Territory which forbade the immigration of free blacks into that region and imposed a capitation tax on free colored persons already residing there. When these matters came before the House the Boston petition was tabled, eighty-five to fifty-nine, and the Florida resolution suffered the same fate by a vote of 113 to 80; but eighty votes mustered for a resolution of this sort was, in Weld's opinion, "the best vote for liberty that has ever been taken in Congress since the anti-slavery question came up." [6]

Weld left for home about two weeks before the session ended

on March 3, and with his departure the antislavery offensive lost
something of its verve. Giddings wrote that things were not the
same without him.[7] Leavitt told Angelina that his research and
counsel had been of basic importance. "He has been doing foundation work," he wrote, "and we all feel that our future labors
will be the more available for the services of a wise master-
builder." [8]

Weld's work so clearly demonstrated the utility of an antislavery agency at the national capital that the American and
Foreign Antislavery Society established a new paper, the *National Era*, there in 1847, with the capable and affable Gamaliel
Bailey to perform the functions of editor, lobbyist, adviser to
antislavery congressmen, and factotum of the antislavery enterprise. With the passing years the composition of Congress also
testified to Weld's work, as districts where he or his disciples
had proselytized rolled up a rising total of antislavery votes. Into the House to aid Giddings and his colleagues came bellicose
Ben Wade of Ohio, one of Weld's own converts. Caustic, vengeful Thaddeus Stevens, won to abolition by an agent whom Weld
had trained,[9] was elected to the House from Pennsylvania, and
brought to bear a derisive eloquence and a proficiency in parliamentary tactics that Giddings lacked. Owen Lovejoy, himself one of Weld's former workers, who had vowed eternal enmity
to slavery at his martyred brother's grave, would win election
from Illinois in 1857. State legislatures were similarly infil-
trated.

Shortly before leaving Washington, Weld wrote to Lewis
Tappan that he would be very busy at home for about six weeks,
for he planned to set out a hundred peach trees and a similar
number of apples, pears, plums, and cherries, besides grafting and
trimming some fifty others. The farm kept him busy all through
the summer and autumn, but with the harvest finished he took
up the antislavery cudgels again, speaking all too frequently for
his ailing throat. One of his addresses was to be before the Newark Lyceum, and he had chosen as his subject "Truth's Hin-

drances"—a philosophical query into those prejudices that closed men's minds, a plea for the right of free discussion, and a challenge to follow conscience and reason even in the face of hatred, contempt and ridicule. "I reckon it will be the last time they will be guilty of the indiscretion of asking me to talk to them," Weld predicted.[10] Tappan reminded Weld that New Jersey would soon elect representatives to a state constitutional convention. Were the antislavery men "up and doing"? he inquired. How about Weld's writing a pamphlet analyzing and criticizing the present state constitution? Tappan seemed to think Weld was not as active as he should be, and hoped he would soon burst forth again "like the sun after a partial eclipse." [11]

In fact, Weld had worries at home. He was concerned about his two boys. Neither of them seemed to have "a benevolent disposition," and they would not share their toys. Angelina was in "high tension" over William Miller's prediction that the second coming of Christ would occur sometime between March, 1843, and March, 1844. She was expecting a child about the latter date, and it may be she suspected that she had been chosen as the instrumentality of a world-shaking event.

In addition to Weld's domestic worries, other matters gave him poignant concern. A series of unsavory disclosures had put reform in bad odor. A leading reformer of Brooklyn, pastor of one of the "free churches," was discovered to have been molesting young girls of his Sunday School. It came out that the late editor of the *New York Evangelist* had been drinking intoxicating liquor, attending the theater, and consorting with loose women for several years. The editor of the *Oberlin Evangelist*, an outstanding moral leader and spokesman of the Liberty Party, was found to be an adulterer and a thief. Weld and Lewis Tappan agreed that the nauseous facts must be proclaimed to the world, for reform must never seek to cover up its dirt.[12]

Other reform leaders were in trouble through no fault of their own. Elizur Wright was obliged to earn a precarious living by peddling copies of his translation of La Fontaine's *Fables* from door to door. Marius Robinson was in poor health and had retired to a farm near Putnam, Ohio, where he contemplated raising silkworms for a livelihood. Edward Weed, another Lane rebel, who lived near Weld as pastor of a free church at Paterson, was inconsolable by reason of the death of his wife, the former Phoebe Mathews, one of the girls whom Tappan had sent to work with the Cincinnati Negroes. James A. Thome and George Whipple were hanging on desperately at Oberlin, where faculty salaries were crushingly in arrears, and both would soon be obliged to find other employment to sustain their families.

In January, 1844, Leavitt, Tappan, and Giddings all urged Weld to return to Washington. Giddings believed the antislavery forces could abolish slavery in the District of Columbia during the present session of Congress if they could command the services of a dozen men like Weld. Someone was needed to go among the people of the District to speak and circulate petitions and to visit wavering congressmen at their lodgings. Weld could do incalculable good, if he would return.

But this time Weld said no. Others could do the work as well as he could, he told Tappan, and he would not leave home until Angelina was delivered of her child.[13] Besides, he was surfeited with Washington and the politicians who infested it. Except for the little band of Whig insurgents, politicians were a noisome lot, he wrote to Giddings, afraid to vote their convictions, crouching on their marrow bones before public opinion, fawning at their masters' feet and "wriggling for the privilege of licking their spittle as it falls." "Just such creatures are nearly the whole democratic delegation in Congress and a majority of the Whigs," he complained, "if I see with true eyes."[14] This detestation of politicians and political methods still kept Weld aloof from the Liberty Party, and he declined numerous invitations to speak at Liberty rallies.

The Welds' third child, a girl, was born on March 22, 1844. They named her Sarah Grimké. Angelina had an easy delivery, "Not half as bad as the extraction of a tooth," but at first she could not nurse the baby. She was almost ready to give up when a poultice of cabbage leaves applied to the breast brought the milk abundantly.[15] When William Miller's millennial date came and passed with nothing noteworthy occurring, Angelina concluded that Christ's coming would be in the hearts of the people.

With Angelina and the baby safe, Weld accepted Lewis Tappan's reiterated invitation to speak in Brooklyn. There would be no riot, Tappan assured him, for the Hutchinson Family Singers, giving a concert at the Brooklyn Lyceum a few nights previously before an audience of eight hundred, had let go in full chorus with

"We are for Emancipation—
The Friends of Human Rights"

and not an egg had been loosed.[16] Tappan engaged the Lyceum for April 11, but when Weld announced that he would repeat his speech on "Truth's Hindrances," Tappan wondered whether such a subject would draw a crowd. "If you will only (!) take a little brandy & water . . . swear a little—get on a spree, etc. or stand up very straight with a white neckcloth, and turn up your nose at a 'nigger,' I could have the Lyceum filled," Tappan declared, "provided you would lecture upon 'The Glory of America'—'The Vast Fertility & Resources of the Western Continent'—'Sketch of American Statesman' . . . etc—But TRUTH'S HINDRANCES!! or Hindrances to Truth—it smells of radicalism—mad dog." [17]

The lecture was delivered as planned,[18] but it was Weld's last speechmaking effort for a long time. Six months later Tappan was asking him, "Why stand ye here all the day idle?" But Weld was destined not to speak again for eighteen years. Again he had overtaxed his throat, and while he tried exercise, water cures, and remedies of every sort, he concluded at last that he was finished as a speechmaker.

He settled down to farm work, but expenses kept piling up. He was obliged to provide a home for his parents until his father died and his brother Charles rented a nearby house and took their mother in. A ninety-six-year-old uncle and his eighty-year-old wife also lived with the Welds for a while, as well as Mrs. Anna Frost and her daughter. At one time or another they cared for an invalid nephew, for Theodore's sister Cornelia, also an invalid who later became insane, and for an impoverished friend of the Grimké sisters' Charleston days and her daughter. Samuel Dorrance, a young man from Paterson, also lived with the Welds to undergo instruction in temperance and antislavery lecturing. Charles Stuart Renshaw, a former Lane student and missionary now become an antislavery lecturer, made their home his headquarters and probably paid no board. "We know not whom else the Lord may send among us," Sarah wrote, "and only pray Him to help us fulfill his will towards all whose lot may be cast among us."

Sarah and Angelina had asked their mother to will them all the family slaves. She did so, but had disposed of all except four of them before her death.[19] These wished to remain in South Carolina, but since the law of that state forbade manumission, the sisters conveyed them to one of their brothers, who lived in South Carolina, with the understanding that the Negroes should be allowed to keep their earnings. Betsy Dawson, another former Grimké slave, became the Welds' servant, but they treated her as an equal, insisting that she eat at the family table and sit with them in the parlor. Later they employed another former Grimké slave, a worthless lout named Stephen, whom no one else could tolerate.[20] The sisters dispensed much quiet charity, giving freely of their small means to aid the sick and poor, especially the needy colored folk. Angelina wrote a petition against the sale of intoxicating liquors in Belleville Township and both sisters canvassed the neighborhood to find signers.[21]

Then Sarah Grimké had a sick spell. Little Theodore was never healthy. And Angelina was obliged to go to a sanitarium for several months. Knowing that Weld was hard pressed to make ends meet, the ever-helpful Lewis Tappan asked if he could put him in the way of earning something by writing. But Weld was bogged in frustration. He had many mouths to feed and must work desperately to make the farm produce. He could not speak; and neither writing nor speaking paid more than a pittance in any event.

About this time the passage of a new and more stringent Fugitive Slave Law as a component of the Compromise of 1850 sent a blast of hot hysteria across the North. Free Negroes in the Northern states began an exodus to Canada or to places affording quick access to it, for to prove one's right to freedom was not easy under the new law. Moreover, every man was under potential obligation to be a slave catcher. The judicial scales were weighted to favor the slaveowner.

Garrison trumpeted louder than ever for separation from the South. Giddings swore that the freemen of Ohio would flout the law, and advised fugitives to arm themselves and shoot down their pursuers. Theodore Parker said the new enactment was "framed in iniquity," and declared he would shelter and defend the fugitive with every means he could command, and every decent man should do the same. Henry Ward Beecher avowed from his pulpit that he would fulfil his constitutional duty of running after slaves, but confessed a liability to be taken suddenly lame on such occasions, illustrating his debility by limping across the pulpit.[22] The *Lowell American* asked if men would tolerate the "monstrous" law; surely no man with a heart in his bosom or a Bible in his home would do so.[23] Vigilance societies were organized in Northern cities to aid and defend the Negro. The Massachusetts Antislavery Society called the law "a piece of diabolical ingenuity"; the abolitionists would defy it and rest their case on the judgment of God and future ages.[24] Several sensational rescues of apprehended Negroes took place in Northern cities, and some attempts at rescue were frustrated.

It was a time for antislavery men to be up and doing, and Weld moped in fretful impotence. Angelina, under treatment in a sanitarium, wrote that she was distressed to see him working as he was in such a state of mind, "because you feel constantly that you are *not* in your right place, you are not *now* doing the Lord's will, but your own—& it seems to me this is the thing that is eating at the root of your peace—it grieves me sorely dearest to see you thus & I entreat you no longer to kick against the pricks of conviction & condemnation that are tearing & wearing your spirit all the while." [25]

Perhaps Weld would have felt better had he known what was taking place at Brunswick, Maine. For there a little plain-faced woman, "thin and dry as a pinch of snuff," was writing a book. Often suffering with headaches, worn with household cares, constantly interrupted by servants, tradesmen, and the demands of her numerous children, worried about bills because her husband's salary, meager as it was, often went unpaid, she was pouring out her heartache in *Uncle Tom's Cabin*.[26] And much of Theodore Weld's own antislavery passion was going into her book.

Harriet Beecher Stowe had not previously been identified with the abolitionists, though she always abhorred slavery. At Lane Seminary she came under the influence of the debates, and she visited a slave plantation across the river. This and another trip into the South were her only close views of slavery. The Stowe home had been a haven for fugitive slaves, however, and she had also tried to educate free Negroes. It was the Fugitive Slave Law that awakened her. Her husband had recently accepted a new post at Bowdoin College, and she left Cincinnati to join him in the midst of the excitement evoked by the new law. Stopping in Boston to visit her brother Edward Beecher en route to Bowdoin, she learned of the many Negro families that were breaking up and fleeing toward Canada. Arriving in Brunswick, she received a letter from Edward's wife beseeching her: "Hattie, if I could use a pen as you can, I would write something to make this whole nation feel what an accursed thing slavery is."

Now she was writing out of a bursting heart, the narrative rushing upon her, so she said, scenes and incidents flashing and fading in her brain by day and by night so that she must write fast to capture them while they were vivid. Sometimes the tears stole down her cheeks and wet the paper as she drove her pen. She was tired, overwrought, baffled by her own restraints, eager for escape herself, a condition likely to quicken her imagination. One writer thinks her own self-pity found expression in the character of Uncle Tom, a man sustained by gentle faith.[27]

The story was planned only as a sketch at first, to be run in installments in Gamaliel Bailey's *National Era* for perhaps three months. It ran for ten. As encouraging comments induced the editor to prolong it, Mrs. Stowe visited the rooms of the American Antislavery Society, now located in Boston. Here she obtained Weld's *Slavery As It Is* and other abolition tracts. Weld's source materials for his book were also on deposit there, and Mrs. Stowe pored through them.[28]

When proslavery persons sneered at *Uncle Tom's Cabin* as a grotesque distortion of slavery and the true character of the Negro, Mrs. Stowe prepared a 262-page defense. Its long but descriptive title was *A Key to Uncle Tom's Cabin: presenting the original Facts and Documents Upon Which the Story is Founded together with corroborative statements verifying the Truths of the Work.* This book contains twenty-one citations to Weld's *Slavery As It Is* and two references to Weld and Thome's *Slavery and the Slave Trade in the United States.* It also has a chapter comparing American slavery with Hebrew servitude in the manner of Weld's "Bible Argument," and another chapter, patterned after a chapter in *Slavery As It Is,* to show the impotence of Southern public opinion to protect the slave. Following Weld's method, Mrs. Stowe printed hundreds of advertisements culled from recent issues of Southern newspapers to prove her points, so that in effect this portion of her *Key to Uncle Tom's Cabin* was a continuation of Weld's researches.[29]

Only a small part of the material in her *Key* influenced her in writing *Uncle Tom's Cabin.* Most of what went into the later book was in the nature of corroborative afterthought. But this was not true of Weld's work. She drew upon it as she wrote. George Harris's account to Eliza of his violent beating at the hands of his master's son was suggested by a letter from John M. Nelson to Weld on page fifty-one of *Slavery As It Is*. The character of Simon Legree, and slave life on a plantation managed by the sort of man he was, were suggested in large part by facts that Weld had gleaned. Later Mrs. Stowe told Angelina Weld that while writing *Uncle Tom's Cabin* she slept with *Slavery As It Is* under her pillow, and it is said that when she wrote *Dred, A Tale of the Great Dismal Swamp*, another but less influential antislavery novel, in 1856, she came to Weld for advice.[30] Perhaps she did; perhaps these statements are apocryphal. The important point is that she made extensive use of Weld's work, and that through her and her novel his influence touched millions of people.

For *Uncle Tom's Cabin* enjoyed phenomenal success. Presses could not keep pace with the demand for it. All over the North, people devoured it. In England it sold over a million copies. Young men who would later make up the hard core of the Union Army during the Civil War felt its impact in the impressionable years of boyhood and youth.

The politicians who had hoped to make the Compromise of 1850 a final settlement of the troublesome slavery issue were thwarted at the very moment of success. For as moderates of both sections rallied behind the Compromise measures, the tumult engendered by the Fugitive Slave Law had begun to calm down; but now thousands in the North who had been hostile or apathetic to antislavery were aroused,[31] not to vindictive clamor but rather to a quiet hardening of purpose to put slavery down. At a pen stroke Mrs. Stowe reaped the fruits of twenty years of abolition labor. No longer could antislavery discussion be stilled. A novel had reached an audience that would have scorned a tract.

Influence is often an unmeasurable, intangible quality, but in whatever degree Weld influenced Mrs. Stowe, through her he helped move the world. And this was the way he would have wanted it. He had no wish for popular acclaim for himself.

Insofar as the Weld-Grimké correspondence shows, neither Weld nor Angelina nor Sarah so much as suspected until years afterward that Mrs. Stowe had even seen Weld's book. They were tussling with problems of their own. Along with their other individualistic idiosyncrasies, the Welds wished to educate their children after their own fashion and spent several hours each day instructing them. In their pinch for money they concluded that it would require only a little more labor to teach other children as well. Pupils were easily obtained, and soon Theodore, Angelina, and Sarah were conducting a school.[32] Still none of them was altogether happy. Angelina thought their talents were too circumscribed. "Altho' home education has some advantages," she wrote, "yet I am satisfied that it never can expand the hearts of our children as we want to see them expand, & as they must be expanded in order that they may be useful in developing the great principles of Love practically in their generation." [33]

They were living too selfish a life to know true happiness. She would gladly endure any sacrifice, if only Theodore could find his proper niche.

16

EAGLESWOOD

In the latter months of 1852 it seemed
that the broader field for which Angelina was yearning had
opened at last before the Welds. Marcus Spring, a philanthropic
New York businessman, enticed by the current fad for communal living, planned to establish a "Union" for the promotion of
industry, education, and social life in Middlesex County, New
Jersey.[1] Two hundred and seventy acres of land had been acquired on the shores of Raritan Bay, and here it was proposed to
erect a wharf, workshops equipped with modern labor-saving
machinery, studios for artists, a large dwelling unit, a laundry, a
bakery, and a refectory.

The idea was to form a joint-stock company and open subscriptions at twenty-five dollars per share. The promoters hoped
to raise a capital of five hundred thousand dollars but the project would be started when fifty thousand dollars had been subscribed and fifteen thousand paid in. The several units of the
enterprise—farms, workshops, laundry, and so forth—would be

rented out to individuals or groups. An office for the sale of products would be set up in New York City.

The society would have a religious base, non-sectarian, but of a nature to foster "that loving communion, which is the only true law of life in God's kingdom."

Education was a primary objective. "The intention," the prospectus stated, "is to organize such a thorough system of training—gymnastic, industrial, scientific, literary, artistic, social and spiritual—as shall promote vigorous development, and a practical preparation for whatever sphere the tastes and abilities of the young, of either sex, seem best to qualify them." The school would be open to children of members, and to as many others as could be accommodated.

It was hoped that the community would commend itself to capitalists as a safe and profitable investment medium, to farmers, mechanics, and artists aspiring to "a freer, larger, more harmonious form of human existence," and also to New York and Philadelphia businessmen who wished to rear their families in quiet, healthful surroundings.

An abolitionist himself, Marcus Spring was married to a daughter of Arnold Buffum, first president of the New England Anti-slavery Society. Well acquainted in abolition circles, he knew about the Welds' educational endeavors and now offered Weld the chance to take over the school, which, like the other departments of the project, would be rented out. Weld's few years of teaching had awakened a desire to bring better educational advantages to children of the middle class, an aim which accorded with Spring's ideals. And the opportunity was all the more appealing to Weld by reason of its similarity to the Oberlin idea— a Christian community supporting a liberal school.

Spring promised to put twenty thousand dollars into the school if Weld would take charge,[2] and by December, 1852, Theodore, Angelina, and Sarah were committed to the venture. Sarah subscribed a thousand dollars. Theodore and Angelina put in two thousand, although they were obliged to borrow part of their subscription from Sarah.

Weld and the sisters found the site of the new community delightful. Located at the confluence of Raritan River and Raritan Bay, it was twenty-five miles from New York by water and sixty miles from Philadelphia by rail. The woods and shore were beautiful, with a view of the Navasink Highlands rising in foliated grandeur south of Sandy Hook across the bay. The ever-varying surface of the bay was a constant enjoyment, now sparkling in bright sunlight, sliding soft swells along the sand, now dancing sprightly with little waves flipping dainty white petticoats, again overcast with sullen clouds and lashed by heavy winds that rolled up booming surf along the shoreline.[3]

The Raritan Bay Union was housed in a large stone building, 250 feet in length, with a turret and porticos. One wing contained apartments for families and rooms for single occupants. The other wing housed the school. In the center were parlors and a dining room.

Weld opened his school—they called it Eagleswood—in the fall of 1854. It accommodated fifty-six boarders. Since his manual labor days Weld had never lost his faith in exercise; and gymnastics, calisthenics, rowing, and swimming were important features of his curriculum. The institution was coeducational, for to separate the sexes was "to ignore a law of reciprocal action vital to the highest weal of both." [4] Weld taught English grammar, composition, and literature, placing special emphasis on Shakespeare in which he had three different classes each day.[5] Angelina's subjects were writing and arithmetic while Sarah instructed in French and kept the books. Two or three younger teachers completed the staff. Nathaniel Peabody, father of the celebrated Peabody sisters of Massachusetts, was a member of the Union, and his daughter Elizabeth taught at Weld's school for a time.

The non-sectarian religious ideals of the community comported with the Welds' philosophy; for they, and Sarah too, were becoming ever more unorthodox. Weld scorned religious creeds and forms. Like Garrison, he had come to reject Sabbath observance and refused to take the Bible literally in its entirety. More and more his religion was coming to be the simple precept: "Thou shalt love the Lord thy God with all thy heart, and with all thy mind, and with all thy soul, and thy neighbor as thyself." Sarah found herself adopting his views, although he never tried to influence her in matters of faith. "When I began to understand what the gift of the Holy Spirit really *was*," she wrote, "then all outwardism fell off. . . . I could not help it; it was unexpected in me, and I wondered to find even the Sabbath gone." [6] The sum of Sarah's religion was "God is love."

The Raritan Bay experiment did not turn out as Weld had hoped it would. Not only did he and the sisters derive no dividends from their investment, but his rent was fixed at such a figure that he was obliged to put his tuition rates beyond the means of the middle class whom he had hoped to benefit. The managers whom Marcus Spring employed were inefficient. All winter the place had insufficient heat. Gas lights were not installed as promised. And the water supply was so precarious that every drop must be conserved.

Weld was severely overworked. He not only carried a full teaching schedule, but all problems of discipline also fell to him. Administrative work absorbed his evenings. He was half sick all winter, suffering recurrent attacks of fever. At one period he was too weak to shave, and grew a beard; and Sarah and Angelina persuaded him "to wear his snowy honors." [7]

The inmates of the Union were uncongenial. Several had moved in from the unsuccessful North American Phalanx at nearby Red Bank, and they were a troublesome lot.[8] Jealousy and selfishness were rampant. Sarah reported that the place was filled with "innumerable sponges who suck up every spare moment." Weld complained that Sarah was always cross. Weld himself worked at such a pace that he had no time for his family. By the end of the first school year they were ready to give up.[9]

Marcus Spring persuaded them to stay for one more year, but by the summer of 1856 the Union itself had gone under. The more famous Hopedale Colony of Adin Ballou, in Massachusetts, was also in precarious circumstances at this time, and Weld and Ballou exchanged letters in an effort to discover the fallacy in the communal idea. "I was under a mistake about the evils of competition and love of money being the chief ones," confessed Ballou. "Love of command, love of ease, and the inclination to throw off care and responsibility upon others are equally potent and mischievous. . . . Few people are near enough right in heart, head and habits to live in close social intimacy. So far as household and industrial organization on the basis of united pecuniary interests is concerned, Association is impossible and undesirable at present. It costs more than it comes to. I give it up. The integrity and due privacy of the family ought to be sacredly preserved. Likewise the proper individuality of human nature in its sphere. I concur with you in the opinion that we shall ere long find a way to carry our divine principles into social arrangements so as to secure all the good without the evils of Association as attempted in these unsuccessful experiments. At this let us aim, and for this labor. We will unshackle and elevate the slave. We will raise woman to her destined sphere. We will educate the young. We will regenerate the public conscience, heart and opinion. We will do all in our power to make individuals and families what they ought to be,—and thus elevate society itself to the glorious state hoped for. . . ."[10]

The demise of the Raritan Bay Union was really a blessing to Weld. For with this he began his real career as a schoolmaster. In default of other possibilities of income, the proprietors rented him the school on a sliding scale commensurate with the number of his students. A lady rented the remainder of the building as a boarding house, and the Welds also took boarders during the summer months. The gas lights were installed at last, the water system was improved, and a new gymnasium was completed with apparatus for both sexes. Weld planned to build "upon the basis of God's model school—the family."

It was still hard going, however. At the end of 1858 the Welds' books showed a thousand dollars uncollected. A few of the Associationists still stayed around, but as they were sloughed off people of more congenial temperament moved in, until at last Sarah was able to report that "now we have a charming circle of friends." [11] Several of their neighbors were artists or poets.[12] In 1853 Weld's old friend James G. Birney and his wife moved to Eagleswood from Michigan, where they had lived since Birney left the antislavery headquarters in New York. Birney had twice been the Liberty Party's candidate for president, but in 1845 he had suffered a bad fall from a horse. His injuries caused intermittent paralysis, and he finally lost the power of speech. He died at Eagleswood in 1857.[13] Arnold Buffum, Spring's father-in-law, brought his family to Eagleswood in 1854, and when Buffum died in 1859 he was buried beside Birney.[14]

A son of Birney's was enrolled in Eagleswood School, and other friends of Weld entrusted their children to him for instruction. Gerrit Smith and Henry B. Stanton each sent a son, and Augustus Wattles sent a daughter. Rosanna Gould, another pupil, was the daughter of a Lane rebel.[15]

Weld was a superlative teacher. He was now in his middle fifties and his character had mellowed. His once impetuous zeal had given way to quiet patience. His detestation of wrongdoing was tempered with pity, so that his discipline was firm but also kindly. His own stern self-control induced self-restraint in his students. He inculcated high principles and noble purposes. His thoroughness gave him an easy familiarity with whatever subjects he taught. His perseverance kept him working with laggard pupils when others would have despaired. All his better qualities blossomed now that he had again found a way to serve mankind.

His pupils loved him. In the Weld-Grimké collection are scores of letters from former pupils expressing gratitude and affection, some of them confessing they never realized how much Weld's teaching meant to them until years afterward. A grateful parent, a New York editor of whom Weld asked permission to use his name as a reference, replied: "Just give me a chance to recommend you and your school—and see how high I will set you up—Not only by word of mouth, but by editorial word will I help you, thou good man and perfect teacher." [16] Eagleswood lacked Brookfield's rich traditions, but the abolitionist firebrand Theodore Weld had become a sort of real-life counterpart of Mr. Chips.

Weld gave up his Graham diet to the extent of eating meat once a day. But Angelina and Sarah had a new fad. It was the costume sponsored by Amelia Bloomer, which they first took up in Belleville as a symbol of female equality and a utilitarian housedress. Angelina called the costume an experiment. When woman was no longer merely "man's pretty idol," "coaxed and gulled with sugar-plum privileges" while denied her intrinsic rights, and when at last she took her place as man's equal, then she would also assert her right to practical dress, elegant, if she wished it so, but in any event not of an "absurd circumference and length." The sisters wore their "Bloomers" for several years, but eventually renounced them for conventional dress.[17]

Every Sunday Weld conducted religious services in the school, even though he himself held the Sabbath to be no holier than any other day. Sunday afternoon was open house, when visitors and neighbors gathered in the spacious parlor and everyone was free to speak his mind. Weld also organized a lyceum, a feature of which was a course of agricultural lectures on drainage, subsoiling, care of trees, and kindred topics instructive to the neighboring farmers.[18]

The Sunday gatherings and lyceum courses attracted famous guests. William Cullen Bryant, editor of the *New York Post*, came down from New York. Horace Greeley, editor of the rival *New York Tribune* and oracle of the backcountry, was another visitor. Greeley had lost money in the North American

Phalanx, close by at Red Bank, and deplored the failure of the associationist experiment on Raritan Bay.

Many of Weld's guests were Unitarian clergymen, whose diverse reform hobbies and pet "causes" of one sort or another made Eagleswood a potpourri of liberal thought. Among them were Edwin Hubbell Chapin, Robert Collyer,[19] Henry W. Bellows, James Freeman Clarke, William Henry Channing, and Octavius B. Frothingham. Their interests ranged through temperance and prohibition, eradication of social diseases, woman suffrage, education, abolition, improvement of the condition of the workingman, freedom for the oppressed minorities of Europe —every worthy movement of that day. They were intellectually restless—some of them, like Chapin and Bellows, brilliant and original thinkers; others, like Clarke and Frothingham, prolific writers. Bellows was a champion of self-help education, as Weld had been, and was one of the founders of Antioch College at Yellow Springs, Ohio. With the coming of the Civil War he would found and head the United States Sanitary Commission, forerunner of the Red Cross, with Collyer as one of his lieutenants. With varying intensity these men believed in man's perfectibility—Clarke, especially, sought truth and goodness in all persons, sects, and creeds; while Channing, nephew of the celebrated William Ellery Channing, made a fetish of the equality of men and the ultimate harmony and happiness of the human race through faith and love. Channing had tried communal life at Brook Farm, then set up a "Religious Union of Associationists" of his own that failed.

Bellows, Clarke, Channing, and Frothingham were Harvard graduates, and Harvard influence was paramount at Eagleswood. Weld's old friend Beriah Green was horrified to learn that Weld, Mrs. Birney, and Gerrit Smith were all planning to send their sons to Harvard. "To Harvard University!" Green gasped. "Was not Charles Follen there spurned? Were not Horace Mann and R. W. Emerson there hissed? Thence, did not Webster derive encouragement in supporting the Fu[gitive] Sl[ave] Bill? And

then said young Weld & Birney & Smith just entering! . . .
When the Son of Man cometh, shall he find fidelity upon the
earth! How could you throw such a stumbling block before your
weaker brethren?" asked Green reproachfully.[20]

Henry David Thoreau spent several weeks at Eagleswood.[21] In
October, 1856, Marcus Spring, who had taken up his residence
near the school, invited the eccentric Yankee sage to give a
course of lectures and do some surveying for him. Thoreau's
Walden, or Life in the Woods had been published two years before in protest against the industrialization and commercializa-
tion which he saw engulfing the country. Widely traveled in
New England and Canada, a frequent lyceum lecturer, Thoreau
was now living with his parents in their yellow house in Concord, where the family earned a precarious living by making pen-
cils, an occupation in which Henry David took little part, for he
had much thinking to do and often sat bemused at the back door
under a poplar tree.

Simple to the point of naïveté, a rustic dreamer who loved sol-
itude, Thoreau distrusted group action and demurred at all communal schemes. Eagleswood was still tinctured with "associa-
tionism," with some associationists still hanging on, and Thoreau thought it "a queer place." Everything revolved around
Weld's school, he wrote to his sister, with the Quaker spirit much
in evidence. When he lectured, his audience was mostly children,
"not so bright as New England children," he opined. "Imagine
them," he wrote, "sitting close to the wall, all around a hall,
with old Quaker-looking men and women here and there. There
sat Mrs. Weld and her sister, two elderly gray-headed ladies, the
former in extreme Bloomer costume, which was what you might
call remarkable; Mr. Arnold Buffum, with broad face and a
great white beard, looking like a pier-head made of the corktree
with the bark on, as if he could buffet a considerable wave;
James G. Birney . . . with another particularly white head and
beard; Edward Palmer, the anti-money man[22] . . . with his ample beard somewhat grayish."

On Saturday night Thoreau went to the schoolroom for the weekly dance, for it was thought strange, he said, if one did not attend. Children, teachers, and patrons were all on the floor, Weld, with his long white beard, romping and tripping as gaily as any of them.[23]

On three successive Sundays while Thoreau was at Eagleswood, his neighbor, Amos Bronson Alcott, came down from Concord.[24] A seer, a mystic, so unconcerned with worldly things that his wife and daughters were obliged to support themselves by sewing, teaching, and domestic service until Louisa wrote *Little Women*, Alcott liked to visit Eagleswood, not so much to lecture as to observe Weld's school. For Weld's methods, aiming at a symmetrical development of moral, esthetic and intellectual qualities, mixing gymnastics and organized play with classroom work, enforcing discipline with kindness, posing questions designed to make a pupil think, seeking to bring pleasure and beauty into the educational process, were much the same as those that Alcott had tried at his Boston Temple School some years before.[25]

It must have been a rich, full fare at Eagleswood, if one could assimilate it, full-flavored and well spiced as it was. Of course there were not always famous visitors; they came at relatively rare intervals. Usually it was only the local people who gathered in the parlor of a Sunday, and at such times things might be a trifle boring. At least Sarah found them so when she noted that "in all free meetings there will be those who love to hear themselves talk, and who are not specially improving or attractive." Still she thought it better than being obliged to listen to the same preacher every Sunday, and it was vastly stimulating when Theodore dipped back into literature or philosophy to "give us some of the great thoughts that have been conceived and buried alive."[26]

17

ONCE MORE

IN ANTISLAVERY

HARNESS

The cloistered life at Eagleswood was
not altogether unruffled by the turbulence that rocked the
country in the fifties. All of Weld's distinguished visitors at
Eagleswood were aggressively antislavery, and some of them,
like Greeley and Bryant, occupied strategic posts of leadership in
Republican inner circles. Gerrit Smith came up to visit Weld
while serving a term in Congress, and could enlighten him on
events and tendencies in Washington. Garrison, withdrawn from
politics but apperceptive as a weathervane, sometimes came to
Eagleswood from Boston. Augustus Wattles, Weld's friend of the
crusading days, was now an editor of the *Herald of Freedom* at
Lawrence, Kansas, and his wife Susan was in constant correspondence with Sarah Grimké.

With the repeal of the Missouri Compromise in 1854 and the
subsequent outbreak of bushwhacking in Kansas, the disorders

and afflictions of that far-off territory were a source of conversation and concern at Eagleswood. Sarah was now convinced that "the lurid torch of slavery" could only be quenched in blood, and she hoped the end would come quickly before too many lives were lost. She still believed the slave would have his freedom in her lifetime, but the festerings of racial hate would take generations to heal.[1]

As more blood was spilled in Kansas, the Eagleswood household worried for fear Wattles might meet foul play. They rejoiced when he assured them he was safe, had never thought it needful to carry arms, and was doing all in his power to compose the vengeful spirit on both sides.[2] Perth Amboy organized to collect a Kansas fund, but the chairman was so dilatory that Weld lost patience and proposed at one of the Sunday meetings that the children be sent out to solicit. Little twelve-year-old Sarah Weld and her friends not only canvassed the community but also knitted, sewed, and pasted to make knickknacks to be sold for the benefit of free-soil emigrants to Kansas.[3]

With the Dred Scott Decision in 1857 it seemed that the battle was lost; slavery was now entitled to protection in the Territories like any other form of property. Sarah Grimké concluded that nothing less than a slave market in the city of Boston would rouse the Northern populace to a realization of its cowardice. She rejoiced in the Supreme Court's decision, she wrote to Susan Wattles, and she would rejoice to see Kansas come into the Union as a slave state. "Rejoice," she affirmed in bitter submission, "because I believe the more heavily the North is ironed with the chains of slavery, the sooner she will shake off the bonds & rise up in the majesty of Freedom. The question is now assuming the dread importance that belongs to it. It has brought a sword into our country & it cannot be sheathed until Liberty waves her banner over the Free States. It seems to me that it must end in disunion." [4]

Weld was engrossed with the problems of his school all through these years and apparently wrote few letters, so we have no record of his opinions; but Sarah's views were not dissimilar to Garrison's. To be sure, she did not preach disunion as he did, but she saw no hope for peace except in separation. The North had no right to coerce the slave states. They, in their turn, could not "compel us to sustain an institution so abhorrent to the genius of the age." The South had sealed itself in medieval obscurantism and refused to face the realities of modern thought.[5]

In March, 1860, Eagleswood was jolted out of its routine when two corpses in pine boxes were brought up from Virginia to be interred. They were the bodies of two of John Brown's men, executed at Charlestown for complicity in Brown's attempt to seize the federal arsenal at Harpers Ferry and instigate a slave revolt. Weld had never met John Brown, though he saw him once in Boston; but Weld's friend Gerrit Smith was so intimately involved with the venerable zealot that fear of being implicated in his harebrained escapade drove Smith transiently insane. And Mrs. Marcus Spring, who had frequently corresponded with John Brown from Eagleswood, had such compassion for the old man and his courageous if foolhardy band that she went to Charlestown to minister to the wounded men in their prison; and on the eve of their execution she offered Aaron D. Stevens, who took six bullet wounds at Harpers Ferry, and Albert Hazlett a place of honorable burial at Eagleswood.[6]

It was an anxious time at Eagleswood as Brown awaited his fate. Angelina took to her bed. Sarah called the misguided patriarch the John Huss of the United States. Here was a man prepared to write his antislavery testament in his life's blood, and she could not put him from her, even in her dreams. "Last night," she wrote to Sarah Douglass, her Philadelphia Negro friend, "I went in spirit to the martyr. It was a privilege to enter into sympathy with him; to go down, according to my measure into the depths where he has travailed, and feel his past exercises, his present sublime position."[7]

When proslavery sympathizers in Perth Amboy made loud threats to throw the bodies of Stevens and Hazlett overboard when they were unloaded at the wharf, the Eagleswood community girded for a fight.[8] Peace was restored at Eagleswood; but over the country the war drums resounded ever louder as both North and South prepared for a showdown at arms.

Perhaps it was avoidable, as some historians insist—who can be sure? In any event, there is one lesson to be learned: namely, that when a controversy becomes a moral issue wherein opponents each see right and justice as altogether on their side, then there is no further hope of compromise. As long as slavery could be dealt with as a constitutional, an economic, or a political issue, there was always room for give and take. But as the North was won to the abolition view of slavery as a sin, its resolve became more stubborn and more grim; for with sin one must not compromise. On the other hand, as more and more persons in the South were willing to believe that slavery and the Southern way of life were a positive good for all concerned, and that those who would disturb these things were evil bigots, then the South likewise became inflexible. With no further possibility of compromise, war came.

Weld must have exulted that Oberlin, still fecund with the antislavery seed that he had planted, was in it early with a company—the Monroe Rifles, assigned to the 7th Regiment, Ohio Volunteer Infantry. Other Oberlin recruits would join other companies and regiments later, and Oberlin blood would wet the battlefields of Chancellorsville and Gettysburg and Lookout Mountain. Out of 151 enrolled at Oberlin, thirty-three would die, sixty-eight would suffer wounds, and forty would be taken prisoner. The Monroe Rifles were the only company in their regiment to report not a single deserter. Oberlin College and community also furnished twenty-one men for the first Northern colored regiment, the 54th Massachusetts.[9]

We should like to know the full war record of the abolitionists, but such a study is beyond our scope. Among the old-line abolitionists whose names have appeared in these pages, however, the following had sons, grandsons, or sons-in-law in Union service: Arthur and Lewis Tappan, Gerrit Smith, Joshua Leavitt, John Rankin, Samuel J. May, Simeon S. Jocelyn, Charles Follen, Joshua R. Giddings, and William Slade.[10] Two of James G. Birney's sons rose to the rank of major general, two others, a captain and a colonel respectively, died of wounds and disease, and a grandson was a captain of cavalry. Harriet Beecher Stowe's son Fred left Harvard to enlist and suffered a head wound at Gettysburg that impaired his reason. When Henry Ward Beecher's son asked his father if he could join the army, the bellicose preacher said he would disown him if he did not.[11] A number of abolitionists became officers of colored regiments, positions of uncommon danger inasmuch as the Confederate government decreed that white officers of colored regiments who were captured should suffer death.

With the relatives and offspring of his former fellow workers flocking to the colors, Weld was pained that his own son, Charles Stuart, now a student at Harvard, was a conscientious objector, resolved not to enlist himself nor to hire a substitute if drafted. The father could do no more than reason with him, and Charles rode out the war in safety.[12] But Weld, now in his fifty-eighth year, resolved to do something if he could. Levi Coffin, "president" of the Underground Railroad, and James M. McKim, corresponding secretary of the Pennsylvania Antislavery Society, found places in the Freedmen's Bureau,[13] and this would seem to have been a situation well suited to Weld by reason of his former work and intimacy with Negroes. More appealing to him, however, was hospital or health work, and in the summer of 1861 he wrote to his friend Henry W. Bellows, who was working to organize the United States Sanitary Commission, in the hope of obtaining a place as an inspector. Soon after the receipt of Weld's letter, Mrs. Bellows explained that her husband "did go to Washington & felt round for a handle for you; but it turns out that in the Inspection of Camps with reference to matters of Health, that the officers are very jealous of any but strictly Medical advice & in this way some of the most useful & energetic men have found they could not work to any advantage." [14]

Several of Weld's friends urged him again to take up public speaking; a man of his oratorical ability could help inspirit the Northern people to a greater effort and turn the people's minds to the necessity of making the war a crusade against slavery. Sarah Grimké prayed "that some good spirit may send Theodore again into the field to plead for the poor & the dumb." [15] She and Angelina were busy circulating antislavery petitions, and Angelina wrote "A Declaration of War on Slavery." [16] Like many other abolitionists, even while they deplored the horrible bloodletting, they did not want the war to end too soon. The Lincoln administration seemed reluctant to touch slavery except as a last recourse, and a quick end might leave it intact. Like the sisters, Weld found the war reverses hard to bear, "but without them slavery will never fall," he wrote. "So every reverse is a victory." [17]

Much as he would like to help, Weld hesitated to return to public speaking. He was all too mindful of his former trouble with his throat, and he feared that the accumulated rust of seventeen years might have deadened the old fire. As for his school, he was quite ready to give it up, for the war had posed burdensome financial problems and he had scant resources to tide him over. But a complicating problem was his younger son, almost an invalid from birth, who needed constant care.

It was Garrison who finally brought Weld to the firing line again, shortly after Lincoln issued his preliminary edict of emancipation in September, 1862—Garrison the former pacifist, disunionist, non-voter, and "no-government" man, now a staunch if critical supporter of Lincoln's administration. For the war brought new alignments in the abolition ranks. Most voting abolitionists had been in the Republican Party almost since its inception; they now made up its radical wing, seeking to control it and to make the issue of the war the extirpation of slavery as opposed to Lincoln's design to save the Union with or without slavery.

Contending with Garrison for leadership of the abolition extremists was Wendell Phillips, who denounced the Lincoln administration unsparingly and saw no good in anything it did. Garrison, however, gave the President the benefit of the doubt, and sought to persuade his followers to coöperate with him. Postponing the annual meeting of the American Antislavery Society in May, 1861, Garrison called for patience, pleading that "nothing be done, at this solemn crisis, needlessly to check or divert the mighty current of popular feeling which is now sweeping southward with the strength and impetuosity of a thousand Niagaras." And to his coworker Oliver Johnson he wrote that what was needed now was Northern unity. "We need great circumspection and consummate wisdom in regard to what we say and do, under these unparalleled circumstances. We are rather, for the time being, to note the events transpiring, than seek to control them. There must be no needless turning of popular violence upon ourselves, by any false step of our own." [18]

Garrison was still a man of peace, but with war upon the nation he was for seeing it through, even though his toleration of arms-bearing required some rationalization. Yet, as the months passed and Lincoln made no move for freedom, he could not be altogether mute. When, in September, 1861, Lincoln rescinded General Frémont's proclamation of emancipation within his military district, Garrison printed Lincoln's order between heavy black lines and declared the President guilty of "a serious dereliction of duty." When, in December, 1861, Lincoln's annual message to Congress proposed as a palliative to border-state Unionists that Congress consider colonization as a means of disposing of the Negroes who were flocking to Northern camps, Garrison wrote to Johnson: "He has evidently not a drop of anti-slavery blood in his veins; and he seems incapable of uttering a human or generous sentiment respecting the enslaved millions in our land." [19] Still Garrison's strictures were no harsher than those of Gerrit Smith, who, while adhering to the Republican Party, lost no opportunity to call attention to the administration's shortcomings, describing parts of Lincoln's annual message as "twaddle and trash," denouncing Lincoln's "worship" of the Constitution and his efforts to act within its bounds, and declaring the Constitution to be no more a proper guide for the conduct of a war than some old almanac.[20]

With the assembling of Congress in December, 1861, Garrison drew up a memorial that was extensively circulated and signed by the abolition brotherhood, appealing for use of the war power for the immediate and unconditional emancipation of the slaves of secessionist masters, and, "while not recognizing the right of property in man," allowing compensation to loyal masters.[21] It was a long stride for Garrison to favor compensation, and to seek to restrain men like Phillips and Stephen Foster when they tried to commit the abolitionists to a resolution to refuse the government all support and to "heap upon it that obloquy which naturally attaches to all who are guilty of the crime of enslaving their fellow men." [22] And since Garrison was anxious to have Weld lift his voice again, we may judge that the two men's thinking was along closely parallel lines.

Even while he fulminated, Garrison conceded that Lincoln could not act decisively until unity of sentiment was achieved. "I am willing to believe," he said, "that something of this feeling weighs in the mind of the President and the Cabinet, and that there is some ground for hesitancy, as a mere matter of political expediency." But he thought Lincoln should do his duty, come what might, and if others betrayed him, let the blame be theirs.[23]

By a happy coincidence—for Garrison had no foreknowledge of Lincoln's purpose—the same day that Lincoln proclaimed preliminary emancipation, on September 22, 1862, the *Liberator* declared that every obstacle to constitutional emancipation had been removed and the government, to be true to itself, must be for liberty; and that such a government was worthy of the support of every abolitionist, whether in a moral or military point of view. Not long afterward Garrison's eldest son accepted a second lieutenancy in the 55th Massachusetts Infantry, the second colored regiment to be organized, and his formerly pacifist father did not try to hold him back.[24]

It was ten days after Lincoln warned the South of his intention to free their slaves that Garrison wrote to Weld, inviting him to speak in Music Hall in Boston, the former rostrum of Theodore Parker, and to be his guest during his visit. Weld took four days to decide: he feared his voice might fail in such a large hall; and he was so out of practice that he dared not speak extemporaneously. If he accepted, he must read his speech, and *"keep my finger on the line!"* It would be like doing something entirely new and not a little distasteful. But at last he decided to accept. "The responsibility of saying something about these teeming times presses me," he wrote, "and I shall not be indolent." If the Music Hall experiment was successful, Weld would accept other speaking appointments throughout the state of Massachusetts.[25] The Welds planned to close their school on November 6. The ailing younger son was sent to a sanitarium in upper New York State. "If Theodore finds that he can use his voice as a lecturer," Sarah informed a friend, "& any field of usefulness opens for him Nina & myself will joyfully & gratefully resign him. The slave! The slave! is holding out his wounds & his chains & pleading in dumb eloquence that he may be rescued. . . . Who then that has an offering to lay upon the altar of liberty will not rejoice to place it there? We surely will. The people need Truth more than armies. We are dying by inches a coward's death, because we will obstinately & impiously reject the means of our redemption. But it is well. I see in disaster and defeat, in Lincoln & McClennan [*sic*], the ministers of Jehovah to afflict & to humble. Had we by our own right arm conquered the South & marched with rapid strides to victory & flaunted our stars & stripes over the revolted states, we should if possible have been more inflated with pride than we were before the rebellion. But our faltering government, our traitor generals, are leading us by slow steps along the painful path of repentance. . . . I am frequently asked Are you not weary of this war? Weary, no! I trust weariness & discontent will not come until I see some signs of repentance in the nation. . . . People think the elections are going wrong, I am sure they are going right, going so as to answer the purposes of God. This contest is world wide in its bearings. Humanity is its watchword. . . . The duty of every government is to combat false ideas & to direct the public mind to the contemplation of Truth by placing itself boldly in the van in the great conflict with error. Ours has failed to do so." [26]

Weld's speech was set for Sunday morning, November 9, 1862, and it so happened that a raging storm kept many persons from attending. Still Music Hall was fairly well filled, and Weld spoke for an hour and twenty minutes without discomfort. He had chosen a fighting theme—"The Conspirators—their False Issues and Lying Pretences"—and the *National Antislavery Standard* reported that he was heard without difficulty in all parts of the hall as he gave "a masterly refutation of the Calhoun doctrine of State rights, and an eloquent vindication of the supremacy and sovereignty of the Federal government; closing with a scathing satire of the secession appeal to the Declaration of Independence for justification and defence." [27]

Emboldened and encouraged by his success, Weld planned an extensive speaking tour. On the way home to prepare for it, he spoke at Lynn, Massachusetts, and Orange, New Jersey.[28] On November 22 he was back at the Music Hall for another Sunday service, and from there his route led west to Feltonville, Fitchburg, Leominster, and Worcester, then to the Cape Cod region, where he spoke at Manchester.[29]

At Essex, where he spoke before the Essex County Antislavery Society, he fell in with Parker Pillsbury, a bearded, brown, broadshouldered veteran of the early days, and the two men worked together through Danvers, Abington, Plymouth, Milford, and South Reading.[30] For the most part they spoke in churches, and to sympathetic audiences. It was not like the old days that they both so well remembered when an antislavery lecturer risked his life. There were no stones or brickbats, no spitballs or tobacco quids, and nothing at all similar to an experience that Pillsbury had once had with Stephen Foster when the two men came out of a meetinghouse to discover that the upholstery of their buggy, the whip, the reins, and even their valises had been daubed with a pungent unguent furnished by a gluttonous grass-fed cow.[31]

Weld alternated between his speech on "The Conspirators— their False Issues and Lying Pretenses" and his old discourse on "Truth's Hindrances," which he had refurbished to fit the issues of the times. Both speeches were read, and the antislavery press noted that his appeal was more to the intellect than to the emotions. Still the old magnetism was not lacking, and his years in educational work had increased rather than diminished his persuasive powers. "Mr. Weld's speech and manner are in the highest degree impressive," the *Liberator* observed.[32] "Both his thought and style evince high culture, yet refinement has not taught him to discard energy of expression, nor the most thorough plainness of speech. He is able to interest and instruct any audience, whether in city or country, and though his discourse is read, it receives such aid from voice, countenance and gesture as to produce the effect of an animated extemporaneous speech.

Angelina was overjoyed at Weld's success. "He is doing the very thing my heart wants him to do," she wrote to Gerrit Smith. "Now is the accepted time and the day of Salvation from Slavery." What a day of Jubilee there would be on January 1, 1863, if Lincoln did not lose heart and fail to issue the definitive edict of emancipation as he had promised! She waited in fear and trembling lest the President falter and prayed for him to stand firm and for the nation and the army to sustain him. "You see how warlike I have become," she said. "O, yes—war is better than Slavery." [33]

As Weld worked his way through eastern Massachusetts, then turned south to give two speeches at Providence, Rhode Island, things did not go well with the Union cause. The Army of the Potomac failed to follow up its victory at Antietam, and early in December suffered a staggering defeat at Fredericksburg. The Republicans received a serious setback in the fall congressional elections. New York, Pennsylvania, Ohio, Indiana, and even the President's home state of Illinois, all of which had gone for Lincoln in 1860, now returned Democratic majorities to Congress. Weld's own state of New Jersey went Democratic, and Wisconsin's delegation was evenly divided. The Democrats made impressive gains in several Northern state legislatures. Not a little of the blame for these reverses was heaped upon the abolitionists because of the antislavery pressure they exerted upon Lincoln. But other factors were the military deadlock, new calls for troops, the threat of a wholesale draft, and arbitrary arrests of some of the more noisy and dangerous dissentients.[34] It was a crucial period, and the Union party could not endure many more severe reverses.

The election in New Hampshire, scheduled for March 10, 1863, promised to be close. The Democrats had nominated Ira Eastman for governor, together with a strong slate of congressional candidates. The Republicans had nominated Joseph H. Gilmore, superintendent of the Concord Railroad, an able businessman with political ambitions but few personal attractions. Quite a number of persons left the nominating convention with the idea of supporting some other candidate, and since the War Democrats were also displeased with Eastman because he opposed the Emancipation Proclamation, a third candidate was put forward in the person of Walter Harriman.[35]

In this contingency Weld wrote to James M. McKim that "the friends of the slave & the govt." were urgent that he should visit New Hampshire to do what he could to promote the Republican cause.[36] When Weld was seeking antislavery agents in New England in 1836 he had found no more friendly spirit than Dr. Nathan Lord, president of Dartmouth College at Hanover, New Hampshire. Since then, however, Lord had become convinced that slavery was sanctioned by the Bible, and he was now among the bitterest critics of the abolitionists. Lately he had written "A True Picture of Abolition," which appeared first in the *Boston Courier* and was then circulated widely in New Hampshire to aid the Democrats. "No marvel," observed the *Liberator* of Lord's proslavery activities, "that New Hampshire was so long the pliant tool and active accomplice of the Southern band of men-stealers and cradle-plunderers; nor is it surprising that she is with difficulty kept from virtual rebellion at this awful crisis in the life of the nation, through the prevalence of a most venomous 'copperhead' spirit in all her towns and villages." [37]

The crisis in New Hampshire was the sort of challenge Weld would have welcomed in his younger days, and he did not shrink from it now. Mid-January found him in the thick of the political campaign, traveling in the dead of winter, speaking once and sometimes twice a day, visiting Concord, Manchester, Nashua, Portsmouth, and many smaller places.[38] For three weeks he stumped the state, adding to his previous repertoire a lecture on "The Issues of the Times," and pressing his campaign on Dr. Lord's home grounds with a speech in the Dartmouth College chapel on February 14. "President Lord will, I learn, fight shy of my meeting," he wrote to James M. McKim.[39]

How much he influenced the outcome of the election it is impossible to say. Eastman, the Democrat, polled 32,833 votes; Gilmore, the Republican, 29,035; and Harriman, the candidate of the War Democrats and the disgruntled Republicans, received 4,372, enough to prevent Eastman's having a majority and to throw the election into the legislature. Here the Republicans had a clear majority, and they elected Gilmore with 192 votes to Eastman's 133 and Harriman's one.[40] The congressional races were extremely close, but the Republicans captured two of the three seats.[41]

Weld's last New Hampshire speech was scheduled for February 28, and he informed Angelina that he would be home four days later. She was relieved to learn that he was well and that he had been speaking to crowded meetings. "Really I think it must be delightful for you to experience this kind of resurrection," she wrote, "and to feel that you are beginning once again to feel among the heart strings of the people as you did twenty years ago." Weld had told her he would be home only two days, and would then start for the West. Two days seemed very short, she said, but she would be thankful for the least favor now that he was in the field again. She hoped he could keep on till peace was won. She trusted some day to hear him speak in Charleston, "for after the war is over, I believe many true souls will hunger & thirst after the truth which has been so long withheld from them, & I pray God that *you* dearest, may one day have a mission in my native state & my birth city." [42]

After two days' rest at home Weld was on his way again, speaking at Newtown, Bucks County, Pennsylvania, on March 7, and then in Spring Garden Hall in Philadelphia on the eighth and ninth.[43] The antislavery Unitarian clergyman William Furness wrote to Garrison that he sat entranced while Weld talked for two hours, marveling the while at "his intimate knowledge of the whole letter and spirit of the Pro Slavery iniquity." The man's words were like music. They must contrive to make him better known. For if they could bring him to the fore, "our Union Leagues, even with Edward Everetts at the head of them, will listen with delight to such men as Theodore D. Weld." [44]

Weld made a one-day stop at Cleveland, then spoke five times in four days at Oberlin, where the *News*, announcing his arrival, declared that such an announcement, made twenty years ago, would have brought out every man, woman, and child in the town. The editor missed the extempore bursts of eloquence that so thrilled Weld's audiences in the old days, but there was "the same profound perception of his subject, the close thought, the masterly marshallings of argument, and the marvellous sweep of language." To the older people Weld's visit was a sort of "Auld Lang Syne." Their cause had now become the nation's; "their harvest, God be praised, is ripening." [45]

But eighteen weeks of steady speaking were beginning to take their toll from Weld. He wrote to his son that the incessant talking and the excitement of renewing acquaintance with old friends had quite used up his throat, and he was obliged to cancel a lecture engagement in Cleveland. After four days' rest, however, he spoke in Cleveland's First Congregational Church, where his friend and Lane classmate, James A. Thome, was pastor. Then he was off on a swing through upstate New York, with lectures at Rochester, Syracuse, and Cazenovia, and finally a visit at Peterboro with the Gerrit Smiths.[46] Then came a sojourn with his invalid son at Pompey Hills, New York, and at last, in early April, he was home again. "You will be glad to know," he wrote to Garrison, "that my throat did me good service during my Western tour tho constantly hoarse as it probably always will be. Yet it failed me entirely but once, when I was forced to recall some appointments. A week of silence came to the rescue and brought my voice back again." [47]

On May 12, Weld yielded to Garrison's entreaties to attend the annual meeting of the American Antislavery Society in New York City, much as he still loathed the trappings and vacuity of conventions. At the first session at the Church of the Puritans he sat on the platform with Garrison, Wendell Phillips, the Negro orator Frederick Douglass, Samuel May, and other veterans of the antislavery movement, and even consented to speak, holding forth for three-quarters of an hour on the political life of John C. Calhoun, whom he compared to Robespierre as a man whose high ideals and noble principles were rotted and subverted when he allowed himself to become the oracle of a system having its philosophical base in arbitrary power.[48]

As the elections of 1863 approached, Weld received a letter from his former mentor, Professor John Morgan, telling how much he had enjoyed Weld's Oberlin visit and entreating him to come once more to Ohio, where the arrest and banishment to the Confederacy of the incendiary Clement L. Vallandigham had put the Democrats in such high fever that in a spontaneous outburst of resentment they had nominated the disloyal Vallandigham for

governor. Another stunning Northern defeat at Chancellorsville brought encouragement to Peace Democrats and Southern
sympathizers; and all over Ohio, but especially in the southern
counties, the Copperheads were rampant, with violence breaking out in several places.

It was a time of dangerous tension, and Morgan pleaded with
Weld to lend a hand. Was his voice all right? he asked. And if so,
would he not renew his old battle on the old battleground by
stumping the state in the ensuing campaign? "Perhaps among
our copperheads there might be danger enough to renew the old
sensations," he challenged. "I am sure it would be most interesting to blow the anti-slavery trumpet where you first waked the
echoes with it near thirty years ago. It is apparent you left
something to be done in southern Ohio. Is the trumpet cracked
or ready for new blasts?" [49]

But Weld was pretty well used up. He made a few more
speeches near Philadelphia and in New York City, but they were
before small audiences where his voice was not unduly taxed.[50]

The Welds and Sarah Grimké moved to West Newton, Massachusetts, in the autumn of 1863; and in March, 1864, they moved
again, to Fairmount. From Charleston, South Carolina, they
had been receiving arrogant letters from Angelina and Sarah's
sisters, Mary and Eliza, who, rebels to the core, boasted that
they were safe and happy. But their tone changed as the block-
ade tightened, and they did not refuse the articles their Northern sisters managed to forward to them through the strangling
ring of Northern ships. Their slaves deserted them, their money
declined in value, and with the coming of Sherman's army they
lived on little more than hominy and water for several weeks.
Still they professed their willingness to die for slavery and the
Southern cause, and Sarah mourned that thousands like them
were worshiping a false god of their own creation. As soon as
hostilities were over, Angelina and Sarah sent money to their sisters and invited them to come North and share their home.[51]

Weld seems to have taken no part in the presidential election

of 1864; he was apparently played out. But he and the sisters rejoiced at Lincoln's reëlection, not so much, it seems, from admiration of the man as at the triumph of the forces of freedom.
Sarah wrote: "That she [the country] has had the courage & the
strength to place Lincoln at the head of her government augurs
well for the future. True he has not come to the rescue of the
negro with a heart full of sympathy for him, with that deep
sense of justice, which would enable him to see that Human
Rights belong equally to the black & the white. . . . This divine
unction of love Lincoln lacks toward the negro, but when we
compare him with his corrupt, traitorous & hypocritical prede-
cessor we may well thank God & take courage, hoping that four
more years of agony may give birth to a Ruler, as much above Lincoln as he transcends Buchanan." [52]

At long last came victory, and on April 14, 1865, a joyful ceremony was enacted in Charleston, South Carolina, as the Stars and
Stripes were raised again at Fort Sumter. Garrison was an invited
guest of the government and a lion of the occasion.[53] But Weld
was not among the speakers in Angelina's native city, as she had
hoped he would one day be. As might have been expected, he
preferred to celebrate under less spectacular auspices, and in
August he set out for the commencement exercises at Oberlin.
The old antislavery stronghold was in high fettle as tidal currents
of alumni surged up and down the college walks, eddied into the
bookstores and around the corners, stopping to shake hands with
old acquaintances and recall the combats and contentions of the
crusading days. "Even the least discerning could see that 1865 put
a period to an epoch in the history of the nation and of Oberlin,"
reported the Lorain County News. "The aging Theodore Weld
returned to join in the reunion of the Lane Rebels and, under the
auspices of the men's literary societies to deliver a 'Grand Ora-
tion' . . . to thousands of delighted hearers . . . which, though
nearly two hours long, held the audience spell-bound." [54]

Weld would have been something less than human not to have
enjoyed the adulation he received. Yet more pleasing to him was

a letter from his daughter Sarah, now twenty-one years old, that stirred the depths of memory. "How nice it must be for you to go through the old places and see the people that used to hear your lectures," she wrote. "Have you seen any of the men that mobbed you? I am especially interested in the one that blew the horn in your ear whenever you were approaching a rhetorical climax. I think that proceeding evinced real genius. I haven't the same respect for those who used rotten eggs as the most telling arguments. Have you been anywhere near Alum Creek? I think you said that the people who saved you were either dead or had moved farther out West. I wish I could be with you to see the ford you tried to cross and the bank you lodged upon. Do you suppose that the alder bushes are still there that you climbed up into?" [55]

James A. Thome's daughter wrote to Sarah Weld that she was sorry Sarah and her mother could not be present to hear her father speak. He would have stirred their souls and won their pride. "I can assure you that the Lane Seminary Boys who were present were proud of their Chief. . . . And our people were much pleased with his discourse delivered here on the Higher Law." [56]

18

THE SUPREME TEST

Informing a friend of the Welds' intention to move to Massachusetts, Sarah Grimké wrote that Theodore had purchased a "lovely little house" in Fairmount, seven miles south of Boston on the Neponset River.[1] (The town was later consolidated with Hyde Park which is now a part of Greater Boston.) The move was occasioned by Weld's decision to return to teaching, and it came about by reason of an offer from Dr. Dioclesian Lewis, well known in that day as a homeopathic and hydropathic practitioner and champion of physical culture and temperance.

Born in Auburn, New York, in 1823, Dio Lewis studied medicine with a local doctor, attended the Harvard Medical School for a single term, and then, without further warrant until he received an honorary M.D. from the Homoeopathic Hospital of Cleveland in 1851, practiced medicine at Port Byron and Buffalo, New York, at the latter place also editing a monthly magazine, *The Homoeopathist*. At intervals he traveled through the

South, the Midwest, and Canada, lecturing on temperance and physical education, invariably closing his discourse on the latter subject by inviting the audience to join him in calisthenics.

In 1861 he incorporated the Boston Normal Institute for Physical Education with the backing or approval of such men as Bronson Alcott, President Cornelius Felton of Harvard, Walter Channing, a former dean of the Harvard Medical College, Edward Everett, Dr. Oliver Wendell Holmes, and the publisher James T. Fields. This school was destined to graduate 420 persons in its seven-year existence.

A conspicuous figure, tall and sturdy, with an inordinately large head, Lewis was dramatic, quick-witted, and persuasive as a lecturer. He was also a prolific writer and had recently published a book on *The New Gymnastics* that was winning wide acclaim.[2]

With the success of his Boston school assured, Lewis projected a young ladies' boarding school at Lexington. He had known Weld for several years, for in the early fifties the Welds, experimenting with every mode of treatment for their invalid son Theodore, had sent the boy to a hydropathic institute that Dr. Lewis operated for a time in New York City. Familiar with Weld's success at Eagleswood, Lewis now persuaded him to teach English at his female seminary, which the prospectus described as "a noble structure, with every advantage of grounds, sunshine and ventilation, . . . ten miles from Boston, at Lexington, the site of the first Revolutionary battlefield. It is a quiet farm village, famous for its healthfulness, in a picturesque region, threaded by delightful rides and walks."

Doctor and Mrs. Lewis taught anatomy, physiology, and physical training; Mr. Carlton, the assistant principal, and his wife instructed in languages, mathematics, and science; while Weld was advertised to "give familiar lectures on Mental and Moral training, and take charge of Composition and Recitation, with the Critical reading and Analysis of Shakespeare and other masters of thought and speech." With physical culture a feature of the curriculum, Lewis' prospectus promised that girls with

drooping shoulders and weak spines and chests would be brought
into "a vigorous and symmetrical development" under the advantages of "the Movement Cure, the New Gymnastics and the
popular games of the English and German peoples." [3] Lewis had
been a fervent abolitionist, and, while the majority of his students came from aristocratic families, the color line was never
drawn at the school and a few colored girls were accepted as students, a policy which must have gratified Weld.[4]

Thus, with the conclusion of the war and the passage of the
Thirteenth Amendment to the Constitution, which abolished
slavery, Weld, along with almost all the other abolitionists, returned to normal pursuits. Unlike Wendell Phillips, who was ex-
ceptional in regarding emancipation as merely preliminary to the
larger struggle for full social and political rights for Negroes and
continued to agitate for Negro betterment, Weld, like Garrison, seemed content with a formal victory. True, he was active
in the local Freedman's Association, which gave relief and legal
aid to needy black men,[5] but his zeal for Negro advancement was
manifested only in individual cases which came within his notice
and did not operate on any general scale. Again in contrast with
Phillips, whose reformist urge now found expression in an attack
upon "wage slavery," Weld had no complaint against the capitalistic system and showed no interest in the labor movement. Perhaps he thought that the white laborer, once he had awakened
to his full potentialities, was quite capable of fighting his own battles at the ballot box. But in extenuation of Weld's almost aban-
doning a cause which he had done so much to initiate and whose
consequences were still problematical, we can plead only his
advancing years.

For a time the whole Weld family had employment at the
Lexington seminary: Angelina as teacher of history, and Sarah
Grimké as housekeeper and general manager. They were away
from their Hyde Park home from Monday to Friday, returning
only for the weekends, while the affairs of their own household
were managed by Eliza Grimké, who had come from Charleston

to make her home with the sisters.[6] For three years Weld aided Dio Lewis at Lexington, and then, in September, 1867, the seminary burned.[7] The school term was completed in temporary quarters, and then the Welds lost their employment when the seminary was disbanded.

This was a fateful year for Theodore, Angelina, and Sarah—a time when they were put to the acid test of their convictions. The most significant endeavor of their lives had been for the elevation of the Negro, the winning of his freedom, and the recognition of his right to a place in human society equal to that of the white man. Now, one winter evening as Angelina was browsing through the columns of a Boston newspaper, she came by chance upon the name of Archibald Grimké. It was in a syndicated article telling of the unusual record of a colored boy of that name at Lincoln University, a school for Negroes at Oxford, Pennsylvania.

At first Angelina thought the student might be one of the Grimkés' freed slaves who had taken the family name. Then she began to speculate. Could it be that this colored student really was a Grimké? Things like that had happened under the slave system in the South. Henry Grimké, brother of Angelina and Sarah, had remained in South Carolina until his death in 1850, and they knew but little of the sort of man he had turned out to be. Could it be, Angelina wondered in anguish, that this colored youth was her own brother's son? Aghast and panic-stricken at the possibility, she confided her suspicions to Weld and to her sister.

There were some anxious councils at the Weld fireside. It would have been easy to throw the paper aside and forget the matter or keep it secret. No one would ever be the wiser. But that was not the Welds' way. Weld and the sisters agreed that Angelina should write a letter to this colored youth.

His answer came quickly, confirming her fears. Yes, he and his brother Francis, also a student at Lincoln University, were sons of Henry Grimké by Nancy Weston, a beautiful family slave, and they had another full brother, John, who was still in South Carolina with their mother. On their father's death he had bequeathed his three slave offspring to his son Montague, their own half-brother, and the war and Lincoln's edict of emancipation had brought them freedom.

Angelina and Sarah were horrified at the disclosure: more to think that their brother Henry could be guilty of such a sin than because these colored boys were their nephews. Nevertheless, to acknowledge the kinship put their equalitarian idealism to the strongest test; but not even momentarily did they or Theodore flinch. All three agreed that these youths were rightfully their relatives and must be recognized as such. Angelina wrote a letter that Theodore and Sarah endorsed. She would not dwell on the past, she said; what was done could not be undone. She was glad the boys had taken their rightful name, and she hoped they would never dishonor it. In June, accompanied by her elder son Charles Stuart, Angelina attended the commencement exercises at Lincoln University in order to become acquainted with the boys. Archibald Henry, the elder, was nineteen, Francis James was his junior by one year; and Angelina reported that both of them were good-looking, intelligent, and gentlemanly.[8]

Angelina remained at the university a week, learning how, with the coming of freedom, the Negro mother had reared her children in a dilapidated little house in Charleston; how Gilbert Pillsbury, brother of Weld's acquaintance Parker Pillsbury, came to Charleston to be mayor during reconstruction, and his wife Frances, opening a school for colored children, had given the Grimké boys their first opportunity for education. Through her efforts Archibald and Francis were sent North into white families who agreed to see to their education in return for the work they did, but who ignored this obligation once the boys were under their control. Discovering the unfaithfulness of these supposed white friends, Mrs. Pillsbury had eventually got the boys admitted to Lincoln University, despite the inadequacy of their preparation. Here they made outstanding records, earning part of their way by waiting on table and teaching small Negro schools in the South in summer.

Both boys became student-teachers at Lincoln, and Archibald served as librarian. The professors at Lincoln were all white men, and one of them was so impressed by the older boy's remarkable aptitude that he wrote about him to Congressman Samuel Shellabarger of Ohio; and the congressman, in admiration of the manner in which the colored boy had improved his meager opportunities, prepared the syndicated article that Angelina had read in the Boston newspaper.[9]

Angelina showed her true nobility of character throughout the visit, but it was a harrowing experience none the less, and she was ill all the following summer.[10]

Before she left the colored school she invited her Negro nephews to visit the Welds in Hyde Park, and the boys accepted eagerly. This was a great occasion in their lives, and, anxious to make a favorable impression on their white relatives, they pooled their small savings to buy high silk hats, canes, and custom-made boots. Thus accoutred they journeyed to Hyde Park, and, however they may have astonished the Welds and Sarah Grimké, who represented the epitome of quiet taste, the white folk welcomed them heartily. The boys were not slow to learn, and their visit was a lesson in the virtues of simple living.[11]

But the Welds and Sarah Grimké did more than merely acknowledge their relationship to these aspiring colored youths. They helped their nephews complete their education. Both boys graduated from Lincoln University in 1870, and then Francis James, assisted by the Welds' and Sarah's benevolence, went on to graduate from Princeton Theological Seminary in 1878. He was pastor of the Fifteenth Street Presbyterian Church in Washington, D. C., for almost fifty years; served as a trustee of Howard University, a Negro college in Washington; was a member of the American Negro Academy; and wrote numerous articles treating diverse phases of the problem of Negro betterment.[12]

Archibald Henry Grimké, aided like his brother by his white

relatives, obtained an M.A. degree from Lincoln University in 1872, then entered the Harvard Law School, where he received his LL.B. in 1874. By this time Sarah was dead, Angelina was sixty-nine years old, and Theodore Weld was seventy-one. Their labors in behalf of the colored race were at an end. But through these nephews, whom they helped to educate, and especially through the elder one, the cause of Negro improvement was carried forward. For Archibald Henry Grimké won renown.

A practicing lawyer in Boston, he resided for a time in Hyde Park; and when he was away from home on business trips, the Welds took care of his infant daughter, whom he named Angelina Weld Grimké. When Weld drew up his will on December 6, 1889, he made a bequest of about $850 to Archibald Grimké for the education of this daughter, going to special pains, it would seem, to designate the father as "my nephew, Archibald Grimké." [13]

Angelina and Sarah did not live to see this nephew realize their high hopes for him, but Weld, assisting and encouraging him in inconspicuous ways, was gratified at his election to the presidency of the local branch of the National Association for the Advancement of Colored People and later to a vice-presidency of the national society and to membership on its board of trustees. From 1883 to 1885 Grimké was editor of the *Hub*, a paper devoted to the advancement of the Negro race. He was a crusader against racial discrimination, race prejudice, and the double standard of sex morality of which he was a victim. He became a student of the antislavery movement in which his benefactors had been so prominent, contributing articles to the *Boston Herald*, the *Boston Traveler*, and the *Atlantic Monthly*, and writing biographies of Garrison and Charles Sumner. Under the auspices of the American Negro Academy he lectured and wrote numerous pamphlets in support of full voting rights for Negroes.

In 1884 Archibald Grimké was alternate delegate to Henry Cabot Lodge at the Republican national convention, and in 1894 he was appointed consul to the Negro republic of Santo Domingo by President Cleveland, serving in that capacity for four years. Returning to Boston and moving later to Washington, D. C., he took up again his labors in behalf of his race, serving as president of the American Negro Academy from 1903 to 1916 and winning the respect of whites and blacks alike.[14]

Many honors came to him for his work: membership in the Authors' League of America and the Authors' Club of London, the presidency of the Frederick Douglass Memorial and Historical Association, trusteeship of the Estate of Emmeline Cushing for Negro Education. In 1919 he was awarded the Spingarn medal of the National Association for the Advancement of Colored People for the highest achievement of an American citizen of African descent.[15]

Recognition of these colored nephews and the advancement of their education was a fitting climax to the lives of Theodore and Angelina Weld and Sarah Grimké. It was as though fate had decreed for them a supreme trial of their sincerity, an ordeal by fire, where constancy assured the carrying forward of their ideals.

The remainder of their story is soon told. For several years Weld conducted a small school in a rented room. He delivered frequent lectures to small audiences in and around Boston.[16] He was a leader of the movement to organize the Hyde Park Free Public Library, and served as chairman of its board for nine years.[17] He was a member of the school board and an officer of the town.

Sarah Grimké was a contributor to the *New York Tribune*, the *Independent*, and the *Woman's Journal*. She made an abridged translation of Lamartine's biography of Joan of Arc.[18] "My mind has recently dwelt much on the so called 'Social Evil,' " she wrote in 1872, "too mild a term for a crime which degrades man to an animal, & woman even below him, altho' by nature his superior, which only renders her the more guilty. I have after much reflection come to the conclusion that woman in the matter of licentiousness is the greater sinner—1st because the sexual passion in man is ten times stronger than in woman 2d. Because he only accepts what she prepares for the gratification of his lust." [19] Sarah's opinions were quite positive for an old maid of eighty-one.

The woman's movement had always held a strong attraction for Weld and the two sisters, and their interest was reinvigorated in February, 1870, when Lucy Stone, the silver voice of woman suffrage, gave a lecture in Hyde Park.

Beginning with a protest against woman's enforced silence in public meeting, in which Weld and the Grimké sisters had played a part, the woman's movement had developed into a demand for the vote, and as a result of Mrs. Stone's lecture a number of Hyde Park women determined to make a demonstration at the next election. A few days beforehand a large caucus of both men and women was called, a slate of candidates was drawn up, and Weld made a ringing speech.

On election day, March 7, a terrific snowstorm blanketed the town, but the protestants assembled at a hotel near the polling place. Each woman had a masculine escort who presented his lady with a bouquet. Thus adorned they formed a procession, and with Weld and Angelina in the lead and Sarah and her escort in the second rank, they marched to the polls through swirling snow. As they reached the polling place, each man dropped back, while his lady, proceeding on, dropped her ballot in a special receptacle provided through the influence of the wife of one of the selectmen. From the crowd that had assembled for the spectacle came mingled jeers and cheers as the procession, re-forming, returned to the hotel.[20]

In Hyde Park, as in Fort Lee, Belleville, and Perth Amboy, the sisters were constantly occupied with visiting the sick and dispensing quiet charity. They liked to remember old friends with simple gifts. But Sarah's hearing and eyesight began to fail, and Angelina was often sick.

Sarah was the first of them to pass to her reward when death came to her on December 23, 1873. The funeral services were in the home, and she was buried in Mount Hope Cemetery in a plain coffin and with simple ceremony. Garrison and Lucy Stone paid tributes, and Weld sobbed like a child as he declared: "Her heart embraced all good. She knew no creed, but loved all and identified herself with all." Her colored nephew, Archibald Henry Grimké, came from Cambridge to pay his last respects.

Not long after Sarah's funeral Angelina came home one day, weary and overwrought from several hours of ministering to a neighbor who was a hopeless consumptive. Next morning when Theodore awoke she said very quietly: "I've something to tell you." Her tone frightened him, and she said quickly: "Don't be alarmed. I'm not. It's all for the best. Something ails my right side. I can't move hand or foot. I must be paralyzed." She had suffered a stroke in the night.[21]

She lived six years in helplessness, finally losing the power of speech, and died on October 26, 1879. Again there was a simple service in Weld's home, around a plain coffin draped with smilax, with wreaths of English ivy and tuberoses and a sheaf of ripened wheat at the foot. Angelina left a paper stating: "I have purposely selected my oldest clothes to be buried in, that my good ones may be given to the poor, that they may do good after I am gone." [22]

His life's companions gone now, Weld, still hale and active at the age of seventy-six, lived with his son Charles and his daughter-in-law.[23] Elizur Wright, who had brought him into the anti-slavery battle, had built an imposing home at nearby Medford, and here Weld, John Greenleaf Whittier, and Henry Wadsworth Longfellow were frequent visitors and liked to swap their old men's tales as they drank lemonade and ate cookies.[24]

Near Medford was Bear Hill, an eminence surrounded by many acres of beautiful, rugged, heavily wooded land which Wright envisioned as an everlasting asset to the people as a public park. Interesting Weld, Whittier, Samuel E. Sewall, Thomas Wentworth Higginson, and Edward Everett Hale in his project, Wright got some four hundred people collected on the spot and organized the Middlesex Fells Association. This inspired a series of forest festivals, the third one being held on June 17, 1882, in honor of the passing of a Massachusetts forestry law the month before. Unable to attend the festival, Weld wrote:

"Dear Elizur,

"Would that I could be with you next Saturday. . . . Your Middlesex people are the first in the field, pioneers, scouts, advance guard, marshalled and already dealing blows that tell. That's right. Muster all you can to the rescue of the forests. . . . The death of our forests is a great national calamity . . . and it rushes on apace. If this universal vandalism that sweeps down the forests, millions of acres every year, can't be stopped, and that speedily, the life of the whole nation is sapped. . . . Blessings on your Middlesex Fells Association—the first to cry aloud in preaching the gospel of *national salvation*. Ring the alarm bells loud and long. . . ." [25]

Thus, in his old age, Weld added conservation to his list of reform causes.

Tributes came to Weld with his old age—letters from old friends and invitations to attend ceremonials of one sort or another. He was an honored speaker and a pallbearer at Garrison's funeral; and Wendell Phillips asked him to write a life of Garrison, venturing, he wrote, "to advise an older & better soldier than myself." Phillips himself died in 1884, and the following year, at memorial services on Phillips' birthday, Weld was the speaker of the evening. Introducing him, the chairman said: "I have the great pleasure of presenting to you Mr. Theodore D. Weld. At the age of eighty-two he comes to speak to us as no living man can of Wendell Phillips. Mr. Phillips always spoke of him as the most eloquent and impressive of the early antislavery orators and cherished for him the most reverential regard. Let us not forget how much we owe to him and his noble wife, Angelina Grimké." [26]

Weld's birthday became a day of reunion for the abolition brotherhood as the years ticked off, and friends and neighbors delighted to do him honor. But the ranks were thinning fast, and by 1889 Weld and Whittier were about the only ones left. And outside the restricted circle in which he moved, Weld's name was almost unknown.

Weld lectured occasionally up to his ninetieth birthday, mostly on Shakespeare or education, subjects upon which he was accounted an authority. Then advancing feebleness confined him to the house. On the night of February 3, 1895, the silent stranger came, and he passed away in his sleep, aged ninety-one years and two months.[27] His life had almost spanned the nineteenth century, and he had participated in almost all the major reform movements of that ebullient age.

In the autograph album of Weld's grandson, Whittier had written in April, 1884;

> "*What shall I wish him? Strength and health*
> *May be abused and so may wealth.*
> *Even fame itself can come to be*
> *But wearying notoriety.*
> *What better can I ask than this?—*
> *A life of brave unselfishness,*
> *Wisdom for council, eloquence*
> *For Freedom's need, for Truth's defence,*
> *The championship of all that's good,*
> *The manliest faith in womanhood,*
> *The steadfast friendship changing not*
> *With change of time or place or lot,*
> *Hatred of sin, but not the less*
> *A heart of pitying tenderness*
> *And charity, that, suffering long,*
> *Shames the wrong-doer from his wrongs:*
> *One wish expresses all—that he*
> *May even as his grandsire be!*"[28]

4

Notes

chapter 1

[1] The description of this incident is based upon Weld's own account in a letter to Henry B. Stanton printed in Gilbert H. Barnes and Dwight L. Dumond, eds., *Letters of Theodore Dwight Weld, Angelina Grimké Weld and Sarah Grimké, 1822–1844*, I, 60–65. This two-volume collection of letters is cited hereafter as *Weld-Grimké Letters*.

[2] Genealogical table in the Weld Manuscripts, William L. Clements Library, University of Michigan. Unless otherwise indicated, the citation "Weld MSS" will refer to this major collection of Weld correspondence at the Clements Library.

[3] Lewis (1796–1853) and Charles (1799–1871) were graduates of Yale. The former became prominent by reason of his work among the deaf, serving as principal of the Pennsylvania School for the Deaf and Dumb at Philadelphia from 1822 to 1830, and then as president of the American Asylum for the Deaf and Dumb at Hartford, Connecticut. Charles taught school for several years, but both he and Cornelia (1807–1863) were periodically incapacitated by ill health. Ezra (1801–1874) was a merchant, first at Utica, then in Cazenovia, New York.

[4] *Weld-Grimké Letters*, II, 594–95.

[5] *Ibid.*, II, 596.

[6] *Ibid.*, II, 593–94, 597.

[7] *Ibid.*, II, 577–78.

[8] Henry B. Carrington, *Theodore D. Weld and a Famous Quartet*, 6.

[9] *Biographical Catalogue of Phillips*

Andover Academy, 1778-1839;
Claude M. Fuess, Men of Andover,
135-46.
¹⁰ "Mr. Theodore Dwight Weld,"
Boston Herald, Sept. 15, 1889.
¹¹ Weld-Grimké Letters, I, 3.
¹² Boston Herald, Sept. 15, 1889.
¹³ Weld-Grimké Letters, I, 273.
¹⁴ Unidentified newspaper clipping
in Weld MSS.
¹⁵ Henry B. Stanton, Random Recollections, 41-42.
¹⁶ Charles E. Beecher, Autobiography, Correspondence, etc., of Lyman Beecher, II, 96.
¹⁷ W. G. Ballantine, ed., The
Oberlin Jubilee, 306-07.
¹⁸ Beecher, II, 94-95.
¹⁹ Elizur Wright to Beriah Green,
March 7, 1835, Elizur Wright MSS,
Library of Congress.
²⁰ Finney's great revival is described in G. F. Wright, Charles
Grandison Finney, 31-61.
²¹ Weld's own account of his conversion, upon which my narrative is
based, is in Beecher, II, 310-12.
²² Weld to Zephaniah Platt, Nov.
16, 1829, Finney MSS, Oberlin College Library.
²³ Weld to Finney, Feb. 28, 1832,
Finney MSS.
²⁴ Beecher, II, 311.
²⁵ Article by Prof. Fred Landon of
the University of Ontario in the
Collingwood Enterprise-Bulletin,
May 13, 1843; copy in Weld MSS.
²⁶ Weld-Grimké Letters, I, 43, 48-
49.
²⁷ William G. Stone, "Historical
Reminiscences of the Village of
Whitesboro N.Y." (unpublished
MS); First Report of the Trustees
of Oneida Institute of Science and
Industry, March, 1928.
²⁸ C. A. Bennett, History of Manual

and Industrial Education up to 1860.
²⁹ Lewis Tappan to Benjamin Tappan, Sept. 7, 1831, Benjamin Tappan
MSS, Library of Congress.
³⁰ Robert S. Fletcher, A History of
Oberlin College, I, 37-38.
³¹ Beecher, II, 312.
³² George W. Gale to Finney, Jan.
21, 1830, Finney MSS.
³³ Gale to Finney, Jan. 29, 1830,
Finney MSS. The Third Annual Report of the Baptist Board of Foreign
Missions, 1831, reported that two
thousand dollars in labor and materials and one thousand in money
were collected by the school's agents
during the previous year. Weld had
so much to do with this that the
students resented President Gale's
omitting to mention him specifically
in his annual report. Weld to Finney, March 2, 1831, Finney MSS.
³⁴ Weld-Grimké Letters, I, 20, 22,
32.
³⁵ The Elucidator (Utica, N.Y.),
March 30, 1830. Clipped from the
Oneida Observer.
³⁶ Weld was a voracious tea
drinker, but at one of his temperance meetings he renounced both
tea and coffee when a tippler agreed
to sign a temperance pledge on condition that Weld would add tea and
coffee to it and sign the pledge himself. Weld never touched either
beverage again. His daughter told
how, in his old age, she implored
him to take a cup of tea for his
health's sake, inasmuch as the other
man must be long since dead. But
Weld refused. The other man's
death did not absolve him from his
oath, he said, and he would die an
honest man. Weld was often af-
fronted by tobacco fumes in the
stagecoaches in which he was

obliged to travel, and took up smoking in self-defence. But one day he resolved he would not become a slave to the weed, and gave it up. Memorandum in Weld MSS, probably written by Weld's daughter.

[37] "A Scrapbook of Weld Lectures," Rev. Henry Cowles MSS, Oberlin College Library.

[38] Sylvester Eaton to Finney, Jan. 21, 1831, Finney MSS; *Weld-Grimké Letters*, I, 49–50.

[39] *Western Recorder*, April 5, 1831.

[40] *Weld-Grimké Letters*, I, 33–35, 41–42, 46–47.

[41] Finney to Weld, July 21, 1831, Weld MSS.

[42] *Weld-Grimké Letters*, II, 596.

[43] Finney to Weld, March 17, 1831, Weld MSS.

[44] *Weld-Grimké Letters*, I, 50–52, 54–56.

[45] Among those present at this meeting were George Bourne, a Presbyterian minister who had been known as an antislavery agitator for fifteen years; Joshua Leavitt, editor of the *Sailor's Magazine* and secretary of the Seaman's Friend Society, who had come out for emancipation six years before; Simeon Jocelyn, another clergyman, whose ambition was to provide educational facilities for free Negroes; and William Goodell, well known to Weld as editor of the *Genius of Temperance*.

[46] Gilbert H. Barnes, *The Antislavery Impulse*, 33–36.

chapter 2

[1] Alice Felt Tyler, *Freedom's Ferment*, 76.

[2] Wendell P. Garrison and Francis J. Garrison, *William Lloyd Garrison, 1805–1879*, III, 25, Referred to hereafter as *Garrison*.

[3] Bertha-Monica Stearns, "Reform Periodicals and Female Reformers, 1830–1860," *American Historical Review*, XXXVII, 678–99.

[4] Barnes, *The Antislavery Impulse*, 17–19.

[5] Lewis Tappan, *The Life of Arthur Tappan*, 33–43, 103–09.

[6] Lewis vaunted himself upon his boldness and freedom. "I fear no man—court no man," he boasted to his brother, Benjamin Tappan. ". . . I would not flatter 'Neptune for his trident nor Jove for his power to thunder.' In joining a church or society or association I do not surrender any right or privilege but maintain entire freedom of opinion and action. Is it so with you?" he challenged Ben, who was a politician. Lewis Tappan to Benjamin Tappan, Nov. 13, 1835, Benj. Tappan MSS.

[7] Eugene Portlette Southall, "Arthur Tappan and the Antislavery Movement," *Journal of Negro History*, XV, 162–97.

[8] Lewis Tappan to Benjamin Tappan, Jan. 8, 1833, Benj. Tappan MSS.

[9] Merle Curti, *The Growth of American Thought*, 381.

[10] Lewis Tappan to Benjamin Tappan, Dec. 28, 1838, Benj. Tappan MSS.

[11] Tappan, 73–90.

[12] Barnes, 22–23.

[13] L. F. Anderson, "The Manual Labor School Movement," *Educational Review*, XLVI, 369–86.

[14] *Weld-Grimké Letters*, I, 56–59.

[15] *Ibid.*, I, 59–60.

[16] Angelina Weld to her mother, July 15, 1839, Weld MSS.

[17] On May 26, 1832, George W. Gale wrote to Finney: "I had a letter the other day from Brother Weld post marked Danville Kentucky May 4th. It had no date. He is not recovered from his disaster, thinks it doubtful whether he ever does—Writes with great difficulty—speaks also with less strenth [sic], altho from what he says I judge that he speaks often and with great effect both on temperance and manual labor causes. . . . He is a marvellous man in many respects! He will do his work I think fast." Finney MSS.

[18] William Birney, *James G. Birney and His Times*, 105–08.

[19] Lewis Tappan to Finney, March 16, 1832, Lewis Tappan MSS, Library of Congress; *Weld-Grimké Letters*, I, 66–68.

[20] Lewis Tappan to Finney, Aug. 17, 1832, Finney MSS.

[21] Lewis Tappan to Finney, March 22, 1832, Lewis Tappan MSS.

[22] *Weld-Grimké Letters*, I, 66–68.

[23] A résumé of Weld's manual labor lectures was printed in the *Hudson Observer and Telegraph* of Oct. 18 and 25 and Nov. 1. His temperance lectures were reported in the same paper for Nov. 15, 22, 29, Dec. 6, 20, 27, 1832, and Jan. 3, 1833, and reprinted widely in other newspapers.

[24] Barnes, 39–40.

[25] Beriah Green told of his conversion to immediatism, together with that of Wright and Storrs, in a letter to the Reverend S. S. Jocelyn of New Haven, Conn., dated Nov. 5, 1832, giving credit to the influence of the *Liberator*, Garrison's *Thoughts on African Colonization*, and a pamphlet by Charles Stuart. The letter is printed in the *Liberator*, Jan. 5, 1833.

[26] *Hudson Observer and Telegraph*, Oct. 4, 11, Nov. 8, 15, 1832, and Feb. 7, 1833; P. G. Wright and E. Q. Wright, *Elizur Wright*, 59–62; Fletcher, I, 144–45. See also Arthur C. Cole's review of F. P. Weisenberger, *The Passing of the Frontier, 1820–1850* (*The History of the State of Ohio*, vol. III) in *Ohio State Archeological and Historical Quarterly*, LII, 380.

[27] Beriah Green, *Four Sermons preached in the chapel of the Western Reserve College* (Cleveland, 1833).

[28] *Weld-Grimké Letters*, I, 94–97. Another factor making for Weld's conversion was Charles Stuart's argument for immediatism, *The West Indian Question*, published in England in the winter of 1831. Stuart sent Weld a copy which was used as a text for an American edition. *Ibid.*, I, 74n.

[29] *Ibid.*, I, 99–101.

[30] Theodore Dwight Weld, *First Annual Report of the Society for Promoting Manual Labor in Literary Institutions* (New York, 1833).

[31] Anderson, 369–86.

[32] Earle D. Ross, "The Manual Labor Experiment in the Land Grant College," *Mississippi Valley Historical Review*, XXI, 513–28.

[33] *Emancipator*, Nov. 17, 1832.

[34] *Weld-Grimké Letters*, I, 87–89.

[35] Dwight L. Dumond, ed., *Letters of James Gillespie Birney*, I, 27.

[36] *Weld-Grimké Letters*, I, 58–59.

[37] Beecher, II, 321.

[38] *Ibid.*, II, 315.

chapter 3

[1] John Vant Stephens, *The Story of the Founding of Lane*, 1–24.

[2] A. Tappan to the Reverend O. Eastman, July 14, 1832, Lane Seminary MSS, Virginia Library, Mc-Cormick Theological Seminary; Lyman Beecher, *Plea for the West*, 33.

[3] "Journal of Cyrus P. Bradley," *Ohio State Archaeological and Historical Quarterly*, XV, 218–22.

[4] Thomas J. Biggs to F. Y. Vail, July 23, 1834, Lane Seminary MSS; Beecher, II, 304–09; "Journal of Cyrus P. Bradley," 222–23.

[5] Carlos Martyn, *Wendell Phillips*, 41.

[6] Annie Fields, *Life and Letters of Harriet Beecher Stowe*, 59–60.

[7] Beecher, II, 118–19.

[8] George Clark to Weld, Oct. 10, 1884, Weld MSS; Fields, 2–3.

[9] Leonard S. Parker in *Oberlin Jubilee*, 71–72.

[10] Constance Rourke, *Trumpets of Jubilee*, 130; "Journal of Cyrus P. Bradley," 223.

[11] *Weld-Grimké Letters*, I, 138.

[12] For a list of Lane's first class with their birthplaces and their preparatory schools and colleges in so far as they are known, see Fletcher, *A History of Oberlin College*, I, 54–55.

[13] Beecher, II, 322–23.

[14] *Ibid.*, II, 332, 326–28.

[15] *Weld-Grimké Letters*, I, 78–87, 92–94.

[16] Beecher, II, 321.

[17] *Ibid.*, II, 289.

[18] P. Skinner to Weld, July 1, 1833, Weld MSS.

[19] *Weld-Grimké Letters*, I, 109–12.

[20] *Ibid.*, I, 114–17.

[21] *Ibid.*, I, 117–20.

[22] *Ibid.*, I, 121–23.

[23] Oliver Johnson, *William Lloyd Garrison and His Times*, 147–49.

[24] *Garrison*, I, 408–15.

[25] Johnson, 154–55.

[26] *Weld-Grimké Letters*, I, 121–24; Wright to Phelps, Dec. 31, 1833, Wright MSS.

[27] *Weld-Grimké Letters*, I, 124–30. The instructions warned: "Do not allow yourself to be drawn away from the main object to exhibit a detailed PLAN of abolition; for men's consciences will be greatly relieved from the feeling of present duty, by objections or difficulties which they can find or fancy in your plan. Let the *principle* be decided on, of immediate abolition, and the plans will easily present themselves." The abolitionists' insistence upon urging emancipation without offering a solution of the race problem which was certain to result from freeing the slaves was destined not only to evoke reproaches from their opponents but also to bring criticism from modern historical scholars. The criticism has a degree of validity, yet it should be noted in extenuation that if emancipation had waited upon the solution of the race problem, we should still have slavery today.

[28] *Ibid.*, I, 130–32, 136.

chapter 4

[1] Allan Nevins, *Ordeal of the Union*, I, 120–21

[2] Richard Hofstadter, "U. B. Phillips and the Plantation Legend," *Journal of Negro History*, XXIX, 109–24.

[3] Avery O. Craven, *The Repressible Conflict*, 37-40.

[4] Wilfred Carsel, "The Slaveholder's Indictment of Northern Wage Slavery," *Journal of Southern History*, VI, 504-20.

[5] Ulrich Bonnell Phillips, "The Central Theme of Southern History," *American Historical Review*, XXXIV, 30-43.

[6] William B. Hesseltine, "Some New Aspects of the Pro-Slavery Argument," *Journal of Negro History*, XXI, 1-14.

[7] Dwight L. Dumond, "Race Prejudice and Abolition," *Michigan Alumnus*, XLI, 377-78; Tyler, *Freedom's Ferment*, 501; Philip S. Foner, *Business & Slavery*, 1-15.

[8] *Autobiography, Memories and Experiences of Moncure D. Conway*, I, 177.

[9] Lewis Tappan to Benjamin Tappan, Nov. 13, 1835, Benj. Tappan MSS.

[10] Charles S. Sydnor, *The Development of Southern Sectionalism, 1819-1848*, 123.

[11] It has sometimes been contended that the South developed the argument that slavery was a positive good as a defense against the abolition attack. Actually the proslavery argument was fully developed before the antislavery assault of the 1830's began. Sydnor, 243; Nevins, I, 148-49; William S. Jenkins, *Pro-Slavery Thought in the Old South*, 48-81.

[12] Eugene Portlette Southall, "Arthur Tappan and the Antislavery Movement," *Journal of Negro History*, XV, 193.

[13] Dwight L. Dumond, *Antislavery Origins of the Civil War in the United States*, 6-9.

[14] *Garrison*, I, 1-240; W. Sherman Savage, *The Controversy over the Distribution of Abolition Literature, 1830-1860*. The Nat Turner insurrection brought on a frank and searching discussion of slavery in the Virginia legislature in which several legislators expressed the opinion that slavery was dangerous and detrimental to the South and should be abolished. Most of the advocates of this policy were concerned more for the welfare of the white man than for that of the Negro, however, and since there was no agreement upon the means of abolishing slavery, it was decided that for the present, Virginia should devote its attention to the problem of the free Negro. Sydnor 227-28.

[15] Barnes, *The Antislavery Impulse*, 57-58.

[16] Weld to Garrison, Jan. 2, 1833, William Lloyd Garrison Papers, Boston Public Library.

[17] Barnes, 50-52.

[18] Early L. Fox, *The American Colonization Society, 1817-1840*, Johns Hopkins University *Studies in Historical and Political Science*, XXXVII, No 3.

[19] Lewis Tappan's Diary, 67-68, Lewis Tappan MSS.

[20] *Garrison*, I, 293.

[21] *Liberator*, July 13, 1833.

[22] Amos A. Phelps, *Lectures on Slavery and Its Remedy*, vi-xi.

chapter 5

[1] Huntington Lyman, "The Lane Seminary Rebels," in *The Oberlin Jubilee*, 62.

[2] *New York Evangelist*, April 5, 1834; *Weld-Grimké Letters*, I, 132.

3 "Statement of the Faculty Concerning the Late Differences at Lane Seminary," *Liberator*, Jan. 17, 1835; Sidney Strong, "The Exodus of Students from Lane Seminary to Oberlin in 1834," *Ohio Church History Society Papers*, I.

4 *Weld-Grimké Letters*, I, 138.

5 *Emancipator*, March 25 and April 22, 1834.

6 John P. Pierce to Weld, Sept. 12, 1884, Weld MSS.

7 *Liberator*, April 5, 1834; *Emancipator*, April 1 and 15, 1834. Lyman's home was given as Louisiana, where he had been teaching, but he was a native of New York. One of the Lane students sent a copy of the society's constitution to the *Liberator*. "It is written by T. D. Weld," he wrote, "the great advocate of the rights of man, whose sole energies are enlisted in the cause of emancipation, and who, if he lives, will be a second Clarkson. I think that for power and effect, his eloquence surpasses that of any individual I ever knew." *Liberator*, April 26, 1834.

8 *Weld-Grimké Letters*, I, 132–34; *Emancipator*, April 8, 1834.

9 *Weld-Grimké Letters*, I, 135.

10 *Ibid.*, I, 273.

11 *Ibid.*, I, 134n.

12 Samuel J. May, *Some Recollections of the Antislavery Conflict*, 39–72.

13 *Liberator*, Jan. 17, 1835.

14 Beecher, II, 326.

15 *Weld-Grimké Letters*, I, 137–46; *Liberator*, June 14, 1834.

16 *Autobiography of the Rev. Asa Mahan*, 175–76.

17 *Annual Report of the American Antislavery Society, 1835*.

18 *Liberator*, Jan. 10, 1835.

19 On July 15, 1834, Elizur Wright wrote to Weld: "I drop this line to say that I have just forwarded you a box containing 400 copies of our An[nual] Report, 150 A[nti] S[lavery] Reporters & 73 handbills. We wish you set them all at work *without delay*. So far as you can sell them plan to do so . . . but give freely wherever there is a prospect of doing good. I have sent boxes to Pittsburgh & Western Reserve & have sprinkled a few copies over the valley by mail. Otherwise the whole valley is open to you. I suppose by the accurate knowledge of western men comprised in your Seminary you will be able to distribute the copies I send to the best effect." Weld MSS.

20 Lyman to Weld, Nov. 20, 1891, Weld MSS.

21 William Birney, *James G. Birney and His Times*, 3–54.

22 William Birney to Weld, April 14, 1884, Weld MSS.

23 *Letters of James Gillespie Birney*, I, 148.

24 *Ibid.*, I, 115.

25 Wright MSS.

26 Birney to Gerrit Smith, Nov. 14, 1834, James G. Birney MSS, William L. Clements Library.

27 *Weld-Grimké Letters*, I, 156; *Letters of James Gillespie Birney*, I, 115–22, 126, 127.

28 *Ibid.*, I, 127; A. T. Skillman to Birney, Birney MSS; Recollections of William Smith, Weld MSS; Lyman to Smith, April, 1884, Weld MSS. Birney's *Letter on Colonization* was printed in the office of the *Western Luminary*, in Lexington, Ky., and published in that paper beginning with the issue of July 15, 1834, and also as a pamphlet. Later

the American Antislavery Society also brought it out as a pamphlet.
[29] *Weld-Grimké Letters*, I, 157–58, 160–62.
[30] Wright to Beriah Green, July 10, 1834, Wright MSS.
[31] Biggs to F. Y. Vail, July 23, 1834, Lane Seminary MSS.
[32] See Fletcher, *A History of Oberlin College*, I, 155–57, footnote 14, for a list of Lane's trustees and their occupations.
[33] Minutes of the Executive Committee, Lane Seminary MSS.
[34] August 30, 1834.
[35] *Weld-Grimké Letters*, I, 168; *Letters of James Gillespie Birney*, I, 140.
[36] Birney's Diary, Sept. 15, 1834, Birney MSS, Library of Congress.
[37] *Ibid.*, Sept. 13 and 22, 1834.
[38] *Letters of James Gillespie Birney*, I, 130–34.
[39] *Weld-Grimké Letters*, I, 170–73.
[40] *Cincinnati Daily Gazette*, Oct. 22, 1834; Trustees' Minutes, Lane Seminary MSS. The Reverend Asa Mahan and two of his elders cast the negative votes.
[41] *Emancipator*, Oct. 28, 1834.
[42] *Cincinnati Daily Gazette*, Oct. 22, 1834.
[43] *Autobiography of the Rev. Asa Mahan*, 182–83.
[44] *A Statement of the reasons which induced the students of Lane seminary to dissolve their connection with that Institution* (Cincinnati, 1834). See also the *Liberator*, Jan. 10, 1835.
[45] Students' Request for Dismission, Oct. 15, 16 and 17, 1834. Lane Seminary MSS.
[46] James H. Fairchild, *Oberlin: Its Origins, Progress and Results*, 20; *The Oberlin Jubilee*, 66. Dr. Gama-

liel Bailey, later to be editor of the *Philanthropist* in Cincinnati and then of the *National Era* in Washington, taught the students physiology.
[47] *Letters of James Gillespie Birney*, I, 145–47; *Emancipator*, Nov. 4, 1834.
[48] *Liberator*, Jan. 17, 1835. Edward Weed, one of the Lane students, wrote to Weld: "The attack upon you . . . was written by Dr. Beecher after the rest of the statement was in type." *Weld-Grimké Letters*, I, 187.
[49] *Emancipator*, Oct. 14, 1834.
[50] Dec. 6, 1834, Wright MSS.
[51] Wright to Phelps, Dec. 6, 1834, Wright MSS.
[52] Fletcher, I, 184–185.
[53] Lane Seminary MSS.

chapter 6

[1] Fletcher, *A History of Oberlin College*, I, 85–116; and "Bread and Doctrine at Oberlin," *Ohio State Archaeological and Historical Quarterly*, XLIX, 58–67.
[2] D. R. Leonard, *The Story of Oberlin*, 215.
[3] Fletcher, I, 167–69.
[4] *Ibid.*, I, 170–71; *Autobiography of the Rev. Asa Mahan*, 190–94.
[5] In June, 1834, Weld had been offered the professorship of mathematics at Oberlin and declined for the same reason. *Weld-Grimké Letters*, I, 152–53.
[6] Leonard, 138–39.
[7] Fletcher, I, 175.
[8] *Memoirs of Charles G. Finney*, 324.
[9] Fletcher, I, 172.
[10] Fletcher, "Oberlin and Co-Edu-

cation," *Ohio State Archeological and Historical Quarterly*, XLVIII, 1–19.
[11] Fairchild, *Oberlin: the Colony and the College*, 56.
[12] Fletcher, I, 170–71.
[13] *Ibid.*, I, 177–78. The trustees divided evenly on the question, and John Keep, president of the board, broke the deadlock with his casting vote. MS Autobiography of the Reverend John Keep, 1781–1866, Library of Congress.
[14] *Liberator*, April 4, 1835; *Emancipator*, Jan. 13, March 10 and 24, 1835.
[15] Wright to Phelps, Nov. 27, 1834 and June 1, 1835, Wright MSS.
[16] *Weld-Grimké Letters*, I, 205–08, 237, 239.
[17] *Ibid.*, I, 178–94.
[18] *Ibid.*, I, 217.
[19] Thirty-two former Lane students were enrolled at Oberlin at one time or another, eleven of whom had formerly attended Oneida Institute. For a list of them see Fletcher, I, 183.
[20] *Liberator*, March 21, 1835.
[21] *Weld-Grimké Letters*, I, 270–74.
[22] Weld drew up the statement of purposes which announced: "We shall seek to effect the destruction of slavery not by exciting discontent in the minds of the slaves,—not by the physical force of the free States, not by the interference of Congress with State Rights; but . . . by ceaseless proclamation of the truth upon the whole subject, by urging on slave-holders and the whole community the flagrant enormity of slavery as a sin against God and man, by demonstrating the safety of immediate abolition, by presenting the facts, . . . by correcting the public sentiment of the free States. We shall absolve ourselves from political responsibility by petitioning Congress to abolish slavery and the slave trade wherever it exercises constitutional jurisdiction."
[23] *Weld-Grimké Letters*, I, 200n.
[24] *Ibid.*, I, 196.
[25] *Emancipator*, June 16, 1835.
[26] *Weld-Grimké Letters*, I, 221.
[27] Leonard, 272.
[28] *Weld-Grimké Letters*, I, 244–45.
[29] Fairchild, *Oberlin: Its Origin, Progress and Results*, 18, 26.
[30] *Weld-Grimké Letters*, I, 247–49.
[31] Wilbur G. Burroughs, "Oberlin's Part in the Slavery Conflict," *Ohio State Archaeological and Historical Quarterly*, XX, 269–334; Fletcher, I, 236–53.

chapter 7

[1] Huntington Lyman in *The Oberlin Jubilee*, 67.
[2] *Weld-Grimké Letters*, I, 298n.
[3] Birney's Diary, Oct. 23, 1834, Library of Congress.
[4] *Ohio State Journal* [Columbus], Oct. 9 and Dec. 4, 1835, quoted in Weisenburger, 371–72.
[5] Wright to Phelps, Sept. 4, 1835, Wright MSS.
[6] Stanton, *Random Recollections*, 46.
[7] *Weld-Grimké Letters*, I, 297.
[8] Frank A. Fowler to Weld, Feb. 19, 1887, Weld MSS.
[9] *Weld-Grimké Letters*, II, 879.
[10] Lewis Tappan to Benjamin Tappan, Feb. 13 and Nov. 4, 1839, Benj. Tappan MSS.
[11] Annie Heloise Abel-Henderson and Frank J. Klingberg, "A Sidelight on Anglo-American Relations,

1839–1861," *Journal of Negro History*, XII, 193. This valuable collection of letters exchanged by Lewis Tappan and various English abolitionists is referred to hereafter as Abel and Klingberg.
[12] *Weld-Grimké Letters*, I, 206–07.
[13] *Emancipator*, Oct. 20, 1835.
[14] Dresser's own account of the incident is in *The Oberlin Jubilee*, 236–50.
[15] *New York Commercial*, clipped in *Cincinnati Daily Gazette*, July 22, 1834.
[16] Robinson described the incident in a memorandum dated June 13, 1837, Marius R. Robinson Letters, Western Reserve Historical Society. See also Russell B. Nye, "Marius Robinson, A Forgotten Abolitionist Leader," *Ohio State Archaeological and Historical Quarterly*, LV, 138–54.
[17] *Weld-Grimké Letters*, I, 260–62.
[18] Weed to Mrs. Marius Robinson, Jan. 25, 1837, Marius Robinson Letters.
[19] *Emancipator*, Dec. 15, 1836; *Philanthropist*, April 22, 1836.
[20] Henry Howe, ed., *Historical Collections of Ohio*, II, 80–81; Norman Newell Hill, *History of Licking County, Ohio*, 446; Robert Price, "The Ohio Antislavery Convention of 1836," *Ohio State Archaeological and Historical Quarterly*, XLV, 173–88.
[21] Donn Piatt, *Memories of Men Who Saved the Union*, 100–01.
[22] W. Sherman Savage, "Abolitionist Literature in the Mails, 1835–1836," *Journal of Negro History*, XIII, 150–84.
[23] *Garrison*, II, 1–72.
[24] *Ibid.*, I, 451, 517–22.
[25] *Weld-Grimké Letters*, I, 318–20.
[26] *Ibid.*, I, 257.
[27] *Ibid.*, I, 287.
[28] *Ibid.*, I, 289. It is well to remember that many places which are cities today were towns and villages then. In 1830 the population of Cleveland was 1,076, of Columbus, 2,435. Cincinnati was a metropolis of 24,408, Albany's population was 24,238, Pittsburgh's 12,568, Rochester's 9,207, Utica's 8,323.
[29] Marius Robinson to Mrs. Emily Robinson, Dec. 29, 1836, Marius R. Robinson Letters; Theodore C. Smith, *The Liberty and Free Soil Parties in the Northwest*, 12; Archer H. Shaw, *The Plain Dealer, One Hundred Years in Cleveland*, 76.
[30] Wright to Green, Dec. 1, 1835, Wright MSS.
[31] *Annual Report, American Anti-slavery Society, 1835.*
[32] *Annual Report, American Anti-slavery Society, 1836.*

chapter 8

[1] Clipped in the *Philanthropist*, Jan. 22, 1836.
[2] *Weld-Grimké Letters*, I, 286–87.
[3] *Ibid.*, I, 241–45.
[4] Octavious B. Frothingham, *Gerrit Smith, A Biography*, 164–66.
[5] Garrison to Lewis Tappan, Feb. 29, 1836, Lewis Tappan MSS.
[6] Anne Warren Weston to Weld, Feb. 24, 1836, Weld MSS, Library of Congress.
[7] Weld to Anne Warren Weston, March 23, 1836, Weston Papers, Boston Public Library.
[8] *Weld-Grimké Letters*, I, 295–98.
[9] *Ibid.*, I, 309–10; *Philanthropist*, Oct. 21, 1836.
[10] *Weld-Grimké Letters*, I, 304–05.

[11] *Ibid.*, I, 305–08.
[12] *Emancipator*, April 22, 1836.
[13] *The Mob at Troy* (Troy, 1836).
[14] *Weld-Grimké Letters*, I, 310.
[15] *Friend of Man*, July 7, 1836; M. C. Younglove to Weld, Jan., 1891, Weld MSS.
[16] Wright to his parents, July 31, 1836, Wright MSS.
[17] *Weld-Grimké Letters*, I, 262–65, 287.
[18] *Ibid.*, I, 323. The plans of the national society contemplated the establishment of Negro schools and job training for Negroes as mechanics and farmers. Lack of funds forced discontinuance of these projects, but Wattles himself obtained money from wealthy individuals with which he purchased a tract of land in Indiana. Here he established a land office for prospective Negro farm owners. He founded a trade school and also taught free Negroes modern agricultural methods, until his removal to Kansas when the troubles broke out there. *Ibid.*, I, 90n.
[19] Wright to his parents, July 31, 1836, Wright MSS.; *Friend of Man*, Sept. 8 and Oct. 13, 1836.
[20] *Weld-Grimké Letters*, I, 330–34, 337–39.
[21] Lewis Tappan's Diary, 66, Lewis Tappan MSS.
[22] *Ibid.*, 66, 73, 113.
[23] *Ibid.*, 72.
[24] *Weld-Grimké Letters*, I, 323–29, 345.
[25] *Ibid.*, I, 338.
[26] *Ibid.*, I, 347–48.
[27] Catherine Birney, *The Grimké Sisters*, 161.
[28] *Garrison*, II, 116.
[29] *Emancipator*, Dec. 15, 1836.
[30] *Garrison*, II, 116.

[31] Birney, *The Grimké Sisters*, 159–60.
[32] Angelina Weld to her mother, July 15, 1839, Weld MSS.
[33] Nye, "Marius Robinson, A Forgotten Abolitionist Leader," *Ohio State Archaeological and Historical Quarterly*, LV, 148–49.

chapter 9

[1] *Weld-Grimké Letters*, I, 460–62.
[2] *Ibid.*, I, 436, 463–64.
[3] Samuel T. Pickard, *Life and Letters of John Greenleaf Whittier*, I, 214.
[4] *Ibid.*, I, 205–06.
[5] July 20, 1837, Wright MSS.
[6] *Weld-Grimké Letters*, I, 398–400.
[7] *Philanthropist*, July 14, 1837.
[8] *Letters of James Gillespie Birney*, I, 381–83.
[9] *Emancipator*, Oct. 5, 1837.
[10] Memorandum, undated, Weld MSS.
[11] Caroline L. Shanks, "The Bible Anti-Slavery Argument of the Decade, 1830–1840," *Journal of Negro History*, XVI, 132–57.
[12] *The Bible Against Slavery* (New York: American Antislavery Society, 1837). Weld's name did not appear as author.
[13] *Emancipator*, Dec. 28, 1837; *Philanthropist*, Nov. 28, 1837. For a moderately adverse appraisal see the Reverend William C. Wisner, *The Biblical Argument on Slavery, Being Principally a Review of T. D. Weld's Bible Against Slavery* (New York, 1844).
[14] Shanks, 135–36.
[15] *Emancipator*, March 1, 1838.
[16] Weld to Thome, April 5, 1838,

Oberlin College Library Autograph Letters.

[17] The full title was *Emancipation in the West Indies: A six months' tour in Antigua, Barbadoes and Jamaica in the year 1837*, by James A. Thome and J. Horace Kimball (New York: American Antislavery Society, 1838).

[18] *Weld-Grimké Letters*, II, 629.

[19] Barnes, *The Antislavery Impulse*, 138–39.

[20] New York: American Antislavery Society, 1838. The author was anonymous. Another production of Weld's was *Persons Held to Service, Fugitive Slaves, etc.*, published as Tract No. 5, New England Antislavery Tract Association (Boston: J. W. Alden, no date).

[21] Birney, *James G. Birney*, 334–46.

[22] *Emancipator*, Aug. 18, 1836.

[23] *Weld-Grimké Letters*, I, 196; II, 559.

chapter 10

[1] Catherine Birney, *The Grimké Sisters*, 94–96.

[2] *Liberator*, Oct. 25, 1834; C. B. Galbreath, "Thomas Smith Grimké," *Ohio State Archaeological and Historical Quarterly*, XXXIII, 301–12. Another brother, Frederick Grimké (1791–1863), graduated from Yale in 1810, practiced law in Columbus, and became a judge of the Supreme Court of Ohio. He was author of a penetrating study *The Nature and Tendency of Free Institutions* (Cincinnati, 1848).

[3] Birney, 19–20.

[4] *Ibid.*, 94–96.

[5] *Weld-Grimké Letters*, II, 602.

[6] *Ibid.*, I, 471; Birney, 70–74.

[7] *Weld-Grimké Letters*, I, 417.

[8] *Liberator*, Oct. 13, 1837.

[9] Birney, 55–56.

[10] *Ibid.*, 153–54.

[11] *Ibid.*, 120–31.

[12] Angelina became involved in a sharp controversy with Catherine Beecher, who asserted in *An Essay on Slavery and Abolitionism with Reference to the Duties of American Females* (Philadelphia, 1837) that the North was no more called upon to interfere with Southern slavery than it was to meddle with the press-gang system of England or the tithe system of Ireland. Angelina replied in the *Liberator* (from June through October, 1837), and her letters were later printed as a pamphlet entitled *Letters to Catherine E. Beecher in Reply to An Essay on Slavery and Abolitionism addressed to A. E. Grimké* (Boston, 1838). Angelina was aided by suggestions and editorial criticism from Weld.

[13] Julia Tappan to Weld, Aug. 30, 1888, Weld MSS.

[14] *Weld-Grimké Letters*, I, 354, 363; Birney, 170–71.

[15] *Ibid.*, 163.

[16] *Weld-Grimké Letters*, II, 586.

[17] *Liberator*, June 9, 16, 30, Oct. 6, Dec. 1, 1837.

[18] Tyler, *Freedom's Ferment*, 254.

[19] Birney, 186–87.

[20] Tyler, 444–45.

[21] *Weld-Grimké Letters*, I, 430, 468.

[22] *Letters of James Gillespie Birney*, I, 478–81.

[23] Sarah Grimké to Jane Smith, Jan. 5, 1838, Weld MSS.

[24] *Liberator*, Oct. 27, 1837, clipped from *Woonsocket Patriot*.

[25] *Liberator*, July 2, 28, August 4, 1837.

²⁶ Merle Curti, "Non-Resistance in New England," *New England Quarterly*, II, 35; Thomas Wentworth Higginson, *Contemporaries*, 332–33.
²⁷ *Weld-Grimké Letters*, I, 451, 454–57, 459–62.
²⁸ *Garrison*, III, 3, 225.
²⁹ *Weld-Grimké Letters*, I, 402.
³⁰ Birney, *James G. Birney and His Times*, 332; *Garrison*, III, 262–63.
¹ *Ibid.*, I, 269.
³² *Ibid.*, II, 182–91.
³³ *Ibid.*, II, 199–204.
³⁴ *Ibid.*, II, 145–48.
³⁵ Wright to Phelps, Oct. 29, 1837, Wright MSS.
³⁶ Curti, "Non-Resistance in New England," *New England Quarterly*, II, 34–57.
³⁷ *Weld-Grimké Letters*, I, 408, 447–48.
³⁸ *Ibid.*, II, 513–14.
³⁹ *Liberator*, Dec. 16, 1837.
⁴⁰ Wright to Phelps, Sept. 5, 1837, Wright MSS.
⁴¹ *Weld-Grimké Letters*, I, 423–27, 433–34.
⁴² *Ibid.*, I, 427–32.
⁴³ *Ibid.*, I, 434–36.

chapter 11

¹ *Weld-Grimké Letters*, I, 389.
² *Ibid.*, II, 524.
³ Andrew Combe, *The Principles of Philosophy applied to the Preservation of Health and to the Improvement of Physical and Mental Education* (New York, 1834).
⁴ *Weld-Grimké Letters*, I, 422.
⁵ *Ibid.*, II, 531–32.
⁶ Richard H. Shryock, "Sylvester Graham and the Popular Health Movement, 1830–1870," *Mississippi Valley Historical Review*, XVIII, 172–83.
⁷ Stanton, *Random Recollections*, 63.
⁸ *Weld-Grimké Letters*, II, 531–32.
⁹ The story of the courtship and bethrothal which follows is based on Weld's and Angelina's love letters printed in *Weld-Grimké Letters*, II, 531–670.
¹⁰ *Liberator*, April 6, 1838.
¹¹ Sarah's health was not the sole reason for her discontinuance of public speaking. The abolitionists were disappointed in several of her efforts, and Weld told her frankly that she should let Angelina do the speaking whenever possible. *Weld-Grimké Letters*, II, 604–06.
¹² Although Garrison was conspicuous at the wedding, he had misgivings about the match. Two days before the wedding he informed his wife: "bro. Wright and I visited our beloved friends the Grimkés, and had considerable conversation about the approaching marriage. I frankly told Angelina Weld's sectarianism would bring her into bondage, unless she could succeed in emancipating *him*. She heard my remarks very pleasantly, and trusted the 'experiment,' as she termed it, would prove mutually serviceable. How far she will feel it her duty to comply with his sabbatical notions, observance of forms, churchgoing worship, etc., I do not know. When I asked her whether she would join him in what is called 'family worship,' i.e. formal offering of prayer, morning and evening, she answered in the affirmative. If so I fear she will be prepared to go further. For I did hope that she had been led to see

that in Christ Jesus all stated observances are so many self-imposed and unnecessary jokes; and that prayer and worship are embodied in that pure, meek, childlike state of heart which affectionately breathes that one petition—'Thy will be done, on earth as in heaven.' " *Garrison*, II, 211.

¹³ Mrs. Fanny Garrison Villard, daughter of Garrison, recalled a meeting where Garrison and Burleigh spoke from the same platform and a lusty-voiced ruffian in the audience bawled: "Someone shave that black Christ and make a wig for Garrison." Once when Burleigh spoke in Cincinnati an auditor wrote: "The orator presently made his appearance and a most unfavorable one it was—the first characteristic being an intense amount of beard, covering his face and breast, so that you could see little more than his nose and eyes above the top vest button." C. B. Galbreath, "Antislavery in Columbiana County," *Ohio State Archaeological and Historical Quarterly*, XXX, 390.

chapter 12

¹ *Weld-Grimké Letters*, II, 511–12.
² *Ibid.*, II, 683–85, 701–02.
³ Birney, *The Grimké Sisters*, 245–47.
⁴ *Weld-Grimké Letters*, II, 698–99.
⁵ *Ibid.*, II, 787.
⁶ *Ibid.*, II, 713, 741–44. Weld's testimonial was subscribed by the Tappans, Garrison, Birney, Whittier, Gerrit Smith, Leavitt, Wendell Phillips, Giddings, May, Angelina Weld, Sarah Grimké, and other abolitionist leaders, and proved most

helpful to William Dawes and John Keep when they undertook the English mission in Weld's stead. William G. Burroughs, "Oberlin's Part in the Antislavery Conflict," *Ohio State Archaeological and Historical Quarterly*, XX, 276. Weld's draft as printed in the *Weld-Grimké Letters* is different from the final official text. R. S. Fletcher thinks it was "toned down" either by Weld himself or, more probably, by Dawes and Keep. Fletcher, I, 458n.
⁷ *Weld-Grimké Letters*, II, 773n.
⁸ Angelina Weld to James M. McKim, Dec. 15, 1841, James M. McKim Collection, Cornell University Library.
⁹ *Weld-Grimké Letters*, II, 772.
¹⁰ *Ibid.*, II, 937.
¹¹ Weld to Gerrit Smith, Sept. 16, 1839, Gerrit Smith Papers, Syracuse University Library.
¹² *Weld-Grimké Letters*, II, 795–96, 807–09.
¹³ Weld MSS.
¹⁴ Birney, *The Grimké Sisters*, 258–59.
¹⁵ New York: American Antislavery Society, 1839.
¹⁶ *Weld-Grimké Letters*, II, 752–53.
¹⁷ Clipped in the *Emancipator*, June 13, 1839
¹⁸ *Ibid.*, Dec. 12, 1839.
¹⁹ *Ibid.*, Jan. 9, 1840.
²⁰ *Ibid.*, Sept. 10, 1840.
²¹ *Ibid.*, Dec. 12, 1839.
²² Barnes, *The Antislavery Impulse*, 276.
²³ Joseph Sturge, *A Visit to the United States in 1841*, 106–07.
²⁴ Louise H. Johnson, "The Source of the Chapter on Slavery in Dickens' *American Notes*," *American Literature*, XIV, 427–30. A copy of

Slavery As It Is was listed in the sale catalogue of Dickens' library.

[25] *Weld-Grimké Letters*, II, 946.

[26] Thome to Finney, Feb. 3, 1840, Finney MSS.

[27] *Weld-Grimké Letters*, II, 823–24.

[28] The origin of the American and Foreign Antislavery Society is explained below, p. 188.

[29] Wright to Green, Nov. 21, 1837 and Dec. 22, 1838, Wright MSS.

[30] *Weld-Grimké Letters*, II, 835.

[31] *Ibid.*, II, 811–12.

[32] Sarah Grimké to Jane Smith, Jan. 24, 1839, Weld MSS.

[33] *Weld-Grimké Letters*, II, 746–48.

[34] Parker Pillsbury, *Acts of the Anti-Slavery Apostles*, 191–92, 204–05, 281; Louis Filler, "Parker Pillsbury: An Anti-Slavery Apostle," *New England Quarterly*, XIX, 323.

[35] Birney, *The Grimké Sisters*, 260–61.

[36] "A Home with a History," *Newark Evening News*, Dec. 26, 1894.

[37] Sarah Grimké to Jane Smith, March 14, 1840, Weld MSS.

[38] Sturge, 107–08.

[39] *Emancipator*, Dec. 15, 1836.

[40] *Weld-Grimké Letters*, II, 512–13.

chapter 13

[1] Birney, *James G. Birney and His Times*, 340.

[2] *Ibid.*, 340–42.

[3] Lewis Tappan to Benjamin Tappan, Nov. 4, 1837, Benj. Tappan MSS.

[4] *Philanthropist*, May 5, 1837.

[5] Birney, 345–46.

[6] *Letters of James Gillespie Birney*, II, 671–72.

[7] *Ibid.*, I, 481–83.

[8] *Garrison*, II, 270–71.

[9] *Letters of James Gillespie Birney*, II, 641–43.

[10] *Ibid.*, I, 481–83.

[11] Elaine Brooks, "The Massachusetts Anti-Slavery Society," *Journal of Negro History*, XXX, 323–29.

[12] Stanton to Phelps, June 18, 1839, Wright MSS.

[13] *Garrison*, II, 281n.

[14] *Weld-Grimké Letters*, II, 810–11.

[15] *Ibid.*, II, 755.

[16] Stanton to Phelps, June 18, 1839, Wright MSS.

[17] Barnes, *The Antislavery Impulse*, 161–70.

[18] For the abolition political movement in the Northwest see Theodore C. Smith, *The Liberty and Free Soil Parties in the Northwest*.

[19] *Emancipator*, Nov. 4, 1839.

[20] Abel and Klingberg, 62.

[21] *Garrison*, II, 344–48.

[22] June 5, 1840.

[23] *Emancipator*, May 15, 22, 1840; Harlow, 158–59.

[24] *Garrison*, II, 348–50.

[25] Barnes, 173–76.

[26] Birney, *James G. Birney and His Times*, 266–67.

[27] Abel and Klingberg, 121.

[28] Lewis Tappan's Letterbook, 1839–1840, May 4, 1840, pp. 390–91, Lewis Tappan MSS.

[29] Weld to Gerrit Smith, March 5, 1839, Smith Papers.

[30] *Weld-Grimké Letters*, II, 843.

[31] Sturge, *A Visit to the United States in 1841*, 107–08.

[32] Joseph G. Rayback, "The Liberty Party Leaders of Ohio: Exponents of Antislavery Coalition," *Ohio State Archeological and Historical Quarterly*, LVII, 165–78.

[33] On Jan. 30, 1844, Lewis Tappan wrote to John Beaumont, in London, that there was very little vigor in

the antislavery societies. "They seem to have performed the work for which they were organized. . . . The great body of the abolitionists in the land now belong to the 'Liberty Party' as it is called. They unite moral and political efforts for the abolition of slavery. The Garrison party is less numerous than it has been & is, I think, dwindling every day. It is so connected with other subjects that it has not the confidence of the moral & religious part of the community which abhors slavery. Were it not that many members of the Society of Friends are connected with it especially that part called Hicksites it would be insignificant." Abel and Klingberg, 174.

chapter 14

[1] *Weld-Grimké Letters*, II, 866.
[2] Weld to Gerrit Smith, June 30 [1841], Smith Papers.
[3] Sturge, *A Visit to the United States in 1841*, 109–10.
[4] *Weld-Grimké Letters*, II, 870.
[5] *Ibid.*, II, 868.
[6] Robert P. Ludlum, "The Antislavery 'Gag Rule': History and Argument," *Journal of Negro History*, XXVI, 203–43.
[7] Robert P. Ludlum, "Joshua R. Giddings, Radical," *Mississippi Valley Historical Review*, XXIII, 49–60; George W. Julian, *The Life of Joshua R. Giddings*, 11–46.
[8] Joshua R. Giddings, *History of the Rebellion: Its Authors and Causes*, 158.
[9] *Letters of James Gillespie Birney*, II, 643.
[10] *Weld-Grimké Letters*, II, 879–82. The executive committee of the American Antislavery Society had proposed to set up a Washington lobby as early as 1837. Weld was approached but refused to undertake the work because of his health. *Ibid.*, I, 478.
[11] Undated letter, Weld MSS.
[12] *Weld-Grimké Letters*, II, 883, 887, 914.
[13] *Ibid.*, II, 885–86, 889.
[14] *Ibid.*, II, 893–94, 903.
[15] *Ibid.*, II, 915–16.
[16] *Ibid.*, II, 936–37.
[17] *Ibid.*, II, 886–87, 888, 906.
[18] *Ibid.*, II, 889, 890, 893.
[19] Charles Francis Adams, ed., *The Diary of John Quincy Adams*, XI, 68.
[20] *Weld-Grimké Letters*, II, 899–900.
[21] *Adams' Diary*, XI, 70.
[22] Allan Nevins, ed., *The Diary of Philip Hone*, II, 583.
[23] *Weld-Grimké Letters*, II, 905; *Adams' Diary*, XI, 75–76.
[24] *Ibid.*, XI, 72–73.
[25] *Adams' Diary*, X, 409; *Diary of Philip Hone*, II, 547–48, 583.
[26] *Congressional Globe*, 27th Congress, 2d session, I, 171–76.
[27] *Diary of Philip Hone*, II, 581–82.
[28] *Congressional Globe*, 27th Congress, 2d session, I, 173–77.
[29] *Adams' Diary*, XI, 75–77.
[30] *Weld-Grimké Letters*, II, 909, 911.
[31] *Ibid.*, II, 905–06.
[32] *Adams' Diary*, XI, 83–86.
[33] *Ibid.*, XI, 87; *Congressional Globe*, 27th Congress, 2d session, I, 214.
[34] *Weld-Grimké Letters*, II, 913.
[35] Feb. 8, 1842, Giddings-Julian MSS., Library of Congress.
[36] *Weld-Grimké Letters*, II, 923.
[37] W. Sherman Savage, "The Ori-

gin of the Giddings Resolutions," *Ohio State Archaeological and Historical Quarterly*, XLVII, 20–29.
[38] *Weld-Grimké Letters*, II, 937–38.
[39] Sydnor, *The Development of Southern Sectionalism, 1819–1848*, 246–47.
[40] *Letters of James Gillespie Birney*, II, 684.
[41] *Ibid.*, II, 688.
[42] The congressional contest also served to accentuate the cleavage in the abolition ranks. While the political actionists strove to perfect their third-party organization, Garrison, stung to frenzy by Southern efforts to suppress the antislavery agitation, came out against the Union. On May 23, 1842, the *Liberator* printed a new slogan: "A Repeal of the Union Between Northern Liberty and Southern Slavery Is Essential to the Abolition of the One and the Preservation of the Other." At the annual meeting of the Massachusetts Antislavery Society on January 27, 1843, Garrison obtained the adoption of a resolution "That the compact which exists between the North and South is 'a covenant with death and an agreement with hell'—involving both parties in atrocious criminality—and should be immediately annulled."

chapter 15

[1] Weld to E. M. Davis, Jan. 7, 1842, Houghton Library, Harvard University; *Weld-Grimké Letters*, II, 941.
[2] Leavitt to Giddings, July 27, 1842, Giddings Papers, Ohio State Archaeological and Historical Society.
[3] Angelina Weld to Weld, undated, Weld MSS.

[4] *Weld-Grimké Letters*, II, 743.
[5] Giddings to Mrs. Giddings, January, 1843; Giddings Papers; *Weld-Grimké Letters*, II, 947–49.
[6] *Ibid.*, II, 953–54, 956, 958.
[7] *Ibid.*, II, 975–77.
[8] *Ibid.*, II, 975.
[9] Stevens was converted to abolition by the Rev. Jonathan Blanchard, one of the most successful of the agents that Weld enlisted and trained. *Ibid.*, I, 337n.; Richard Nelson Current, *Old Thad Stevens*, 34.
[10] *Weld-Grimké Letters*, II, 993–95.
[11] Tappan to Thome, Jan. 20, 1844, Lewis Tappan Letterbook, 1842–1844, 427.
[12] Tappan to Weld, Dec. 18, 1843, Lewis Tappan Letterbook, 367.
[13] Tappan to Leavitt, Jan. 9, 1844, Lewis Tappan Letterbook, 1842–1844, 404.
[14] *Weld-Grimké Letters*, II, 999.
[15] Sarah Grimké to Jane Smith, March 31, 1844, Weld MSS.
[16] *Weld-Grimké Letters*, II, 1002.
[17] *Ibid.*, II, 1003.
[18] A copy of the lecture is in the Lewis Tappan MSS. It is the only speech of Weld's that is preserved in full in the original language.
[19] Birney, *The Grimké Sisters*, 133–34.
[20] *Ibid.*, 250–51, 260.
[21] *Weld-Grimké Letters*, II, 917–18.
[22] *Autobiography, Memories and Experiences of Moncure D. Conway*, I, 330.
[23] Quoted in William S. Robinson, *"Warrington" Pen Portraits*, 190.
[24] *Annual Report, Massachusetts Antislavery Society, 1851; Annual Report, American and Foreign Antislavery Society, 1851*, 3–4.
[25] Undated letter, Weld MSS.
[26] Fields, *Life and Letters of Har-*

riet Beecher Stowe, 132, 205–06.
²⁷ Rourke, *Trumpets of Jubilee*,
95–97, 108–09.
²⁸ Harriet Beecher Stowe, *The
Writing of Uncle Tom's Cabin*, 6.
²⁹ Lewis Tappan wrote to the committee of the British and Foreign
Antislavery Society on Feb. 15, 1853,
that Mrs. Stowe had "availed herself
largely" of Weld's work in writing
her *Key*. Abel and Klingberg, 321–
22.
³⁰ "Mr. Theodore D. Weld," *Boston Herald*, Sept. 15, 1889.
³¹ Nevins, *Ordeal of the Union*, I,
411.
³² Sarah Grimké to Harriot Hunt,
Aug. 22 [1848], Weld MSS.
³³ Angelina Weld to Weld [Aug.
2, 1849], Weld MSS.

chapter 16

¹ Maude Honeyman Greene, "Rar-
itan Bay Union, Eagleswood, New
Jersey," *Proceedings of the New
Jersey Historical Society*, I, 1–20;
Katherine L. McCormick, "Rari-
tan Bay Union: The Story of the
Springs at Eagleswood." (A paper
read before the Kearny Cottage His-
torical Association on Nov. 18, 1943,
and presented to the Perth Amboy
Public Library.)
² Angelina Weld to J. M. McKim,
March 27, 1859, McKim Collection,
Cornell University Library.
³ For contemporary descriptions of
Eagleswood see Birney, *The Grimké
Sisters*, 272; Lillie Buffum Chace
Wyman and Arthur Crawford Wy-
man, *Elizabeth Buffum Chace, 1806–
1899: Her Life and Its Environment*,
I, 156–57.

⁴ Tuition and board cost sixty-five
dollars per quarter, with extra
charges of five dollars for Latin,
Greek, French, and German, ten to
fifteen dollars for instruction on the
piano, and fifteen dollars for violin.
"Prospectus of Eagleswood School,"
Weld MSS.
⁵ Barbara Bobichon to her father,
B. Leigh Smith, Nov. 20, 1857. Copy
furnished by the Perth Amboy Public Library.
⁶ Birney, *The Grimké Sisters*, 270.
⁷ Sarah Grimké to Harriot Hunt,
Dec. 20 [1854], Weld MSS.
⁸ Francis Bazley Lee, *New Jersey
as a Colony and as a State*, III, 299–
308.
⁹ James M. McKim wanted Weld
to move his school to Germantown,
Pa. Weld to McKim, April 22, 1855,
McKim Collection.
¹⁰ Ballou to Weld, Dec. 23, 1856,
Weld MSS.
¹¹ Sarah Grimké to Susan Wattles,
Dec. 27, 1858, Weld MSS.
¹² Caroline M. Kirkland, author of
highly successful Western stories,
moved to Eagleswood in 1856.
¹³ Birney, *James G. Birney and His
Times*, 380–81.
¹⁴ Later Mrs. Buffum had the body
removed to the family burial plot at
Rochester, N. Y. Weld to Elizur
Wright, undated, Wright MSS.
¹⁵ Lizzie and Henry B. Stanton to
Weld, undated, Weld MSS. Young
Green Smith took some managing.
Weld told his father he had an in-
genious capacity to deceive. He refused to work, broke furniture, and
wrecked the school privy before
Weld got him under control. Weld
to Smith, Dec. 1, 22, 1852, Feb. 5,
1853, Smith Papers; Harlow, *Gerrit
Smith*, 308.

[16] Samuel Wilkeson to Weld, Feb. 5, 1861, Weld MSS.

[17] The bloomer costume has been described as "a basque or coatlike waist surmounting a straight, short skirt that reached to the knees or a little below, and from underneath which mannish pantaloons, made of any preferred material, extended like loose, flappy pipes to the ankle." Wyman, I, 113.

[18] Eagleswood Prospectus of April 18, 1856, Weld MSS.

[19] Robert Collyer was a young Yorkshireman who migrated to America in 1850 and worked as a blacksmith near Philadelphia, reading and preaching in his spare time. At this time he was still a Methodist, but would soon be converted to Unitarianism by William Furness and Lucretia Mott.

[20] Green to Weld, Jan. 6, 1860, Weld MSS.

[21] F. B. Sanborn, ed., *Familiar Letters of Henry David Thoreau*, 333–38; Henry Seidel Canby, *Thoreau*, 408.

[22] Edward Palmer (1802–1886) had been a printer in Boston where he published pamphlets attacking slavery and capitalistic monopoly. Later he moved to New York, where he claimed that men should be motivated by higher ideals than monetary gain. He would accept no pay for anything he did, and lived on the barest necessities.

[23] For Thoreau's visit see also Bradford Torrey, ed., *Journal of the Writings of Henry David Thoreau*, IX, 134–39.

[24] Sanborn, 340.

[25] Other known visitors at Eagleswood were Moncure D. Conway, the young Virginia aristocrat, who was succumbing to abolition as he studied divinity at Harvard; and Edward Livingston Youmans, a self-educated writer and editor, a friend of Greeley and Walt Whitman, who, like Weld, had suffered a temporary blindness, but had now recovered sufficiently to study chemistry, evolution, domestic science, and education, upon all of which he delivered lyceum lectures. Two sisters of the Hungarian patriot, Louis Kossuth, also spent some time at Eagleswood, wearing on their wrists the iron bracelets they had vowed never to remove until Hungary was free.

[26] Sarah Grimké to an unidentified correspondent, March 8 [no year], Weld MSS.

chapter 17

[1] Sarah Grimké to Susan Wattles, Sept. 17, 1856, Weld MSS.

[2] Sarah Grimké to Susan Wattles, Dec. 27 [1856], Weld MSS.

[3] Sarah Grimké to Susan Wattles, Sept. 17, 1856, Weld MSS.

[4] Sarah Grimké to Susan Wattles, March 23 [1857], Weld MSS.

[5] *Ibid.*

[6] "John Brown's Men," *Perth Amboy Evening News*, Jan. 23, 1924 (one of a series of articles on "Perth Amboy in History" by H. E. Pickersgill).

[7] Birney, *The Grimké Sisters*, 283.

[8] *New Brunswick Sunday Times*, July 20, 1924. The bodies were buried at Eagleswood, but later disinterred and taken to North Elba, N. Y., to rest beside the body of John Brown.

[9] Fletcher, *A History of Oberlin College*, II, 846–66, 870–71.

[10] *Garrison*, IV, 79–80.

[11] L. B. Stowe, *Saints, Sinners and Beechers*, 285–86.

[12] Charles Stuart Weld to his father, June 2, Sept. 25, 1862, Weld MSS.

[13] *Reminiscences of Levi Coffin*, 619–50; *Garrison*, IV, 43.

[14] Eliza N. Bellows to Weld, Sept. 24, 1861, Weld MSS.

[15] Sarah Grimké to Frederick Grimké, May 3, 1862, Weld MSS.

[16] Birney, 288.

[17] Written by Weld in a corner of a letter from Sarah Grimké to an unidentified correspondent, July 30, 1862, Weld MSS.

[18] *Garrison*, IV, 21–22.

[19] *Ibid.*, IV, 32–33.

[20] Harlow, *Gerrit Smith*, 431–32.

[21] *Garrison*, IV, 34–35. On Dec. 31, 1861, the "covenant with death" slogan came down from the *Liberator's* masthead to be replaced with: "Proclaim Liberty throughout all the land, to all the inhabitants thereof."

[22] *Garrison*, IV, 31.

[23] *Ibid.*, IV, 45.

[24] *Garrison*, IV, 80–81.

[25] Weld to Garrison, Oct. 16, 1862, Garrison Papers; *Boston Globe*, Jan. 6, 1889.

[26] Sarah Grimké to "a dear Friend," Nov. 6, 1862, Weld MSS.

[27] *National Antislavery Standard*, Nov. 22, 1862; *Boston Evening Transcript*, Dec. 8, 1862.

[28] *National Antislavery Standard*, Nov. 22, 29, 1862.

[29] *Fitchburg Sentinel*, Nov. 28, 1862; *Worcester Daily Spy*, Dec. 6, 9, 1862.

[30] *Liberator*, Dec. 12, 1862, Jan. 2, 1863; *National Antislavery Standard*, Dec. 20, 1862, Jan. 3, 10, 1863.

[31] Pillsbury, *Acts of the Anti-Slavery Apostles*, 191–92.

[32] Nov. 30, 1862.

[33] Angelina Weld to Gerrit Smith, Nov. 20, 1862, Smith Papers.

[34] Randall, *Lincoln the President*, II, 232–37.

[35] Hesseltine, *Lincoln and the War Governors*, 308–09.

[36] Weld to J. M. McKim, Feb. 2, 1863, McKim Collection.

[37] *Liberator*, May 1, 1863.

[38] *National Antislavery Standard*, Jan. 31, Feb. 7, March 31, 1863; *Portsmouth Journal of Literature and Politics*, Feb. 7, 1863.

[39] Weld to McKim, Feb. 2, 1863, McKim Collection.

[40] Stackpole, *History of New Hampshire*, IV, 87.

[41] *Tribune Almanac and Political Register for 1864.*

[42] Angelina Weld to Weld, Feb. 25, 1863, Weld MSS.

[43] *National Antislavery Standard*, Feb. 28, March 7, 1863.

[44] *Liberator*, March 13, 1863.

[45] *Cleveland Plain Dealer*, March 12, 1863. The item from the *Oberlin News* was clipped in the *National Antislavery Standard*, March 28, 1863.

[46] Weld to "my beloved son," March 21, 1863, Weld MSS.; *Rochester Democrat*, March 25, 26, 1863.

[47] Weld to Garrison, April 28, 1863, Garrison Papers.

[48] Garrison to Weld, April 6, 1863, Weld MSS.; *National Antislavery Standard*, May 16, 23, 1863; *New York Tribune*, May 13, 1863.

[49] Morgan to Weld, June 29, 1863, Weld MSS.

[50] *National Antislavery Standard*, May 5, Nov. 8, 14, 1863.

[1] Birney, *The Grimké Sisters*, 286.
[2] Sarah Grimké to "Kate," Nov. 1, 1864, Weld MSS.
[3] *Garrison*, IV, 127–52.
[4] *Quoted in* Fletcher, *A History of Oberlin College*, II, 884.
[5] Sarah Weld to Weld, undated, Weld MSS.
[6] J. A. Thome to Sarah Weld, Aug. 18, 1865, Weld MSS.

chapter 18

[1] Sarah Grimké to "ma bien aimee," Nov. 14, 1863, and to Linus Yale, July 25, 1864, Weld MSS. The Weld address was 211 Fairmount Avenue.
[2] Mary F. Eastman, *The Biography of Dio Lewis*, 19–84; Eugene B. Vest, "When Dio Lewis Came to Dixon," *Journal of the Illinois State Historical Society*, XL, 298–312. The Rev. Moses Coit Tyler, later to be president of Cornell University, instituted Lewis' system of "light exercises" in England and endorsed his writings.
[3] Prospectus in Weld MSS.
[4] Eastman, 109–13.
[5] Weld to Garrison, Jan. 19, 1868, Garrison Papers.
[6] Angelina Weld to "Rebecca," undated, Weld MSS.
[7] On June 27, 1865, Dio Lewis wrote to Weld that he would pay him twelve hundred dollars for the next year and wished he could make it two thousand dollars. He does not feel right that he is headmaster while Weld is merely a teacher. Weld MSS. The usually accurate *Dictionary of American Biography* states that Weld was headmaster of Lewis' school, but this is incorrect.

[8] Birney, 289–95; *Boston Daily Globe*, Jan. 6, 1889.
[9] Angelina W. Grimké, "A Biographical Sketch of Archibald H. Grimké," *Opportunity: A Journal of Negro Life*, III (February, 1925), 45.
[10] Birney, 294–95.
[11] A. W. Grimké, "A Biographical Sketch of Archibald H. Grimké," 46.
[12] *Who's Who in Colored America, 1938–1940*; *Journal of Negro History*, XXX, 267. Francis James Grimké died on October 11, 1937, and Archibald Henry Grimké on February 25, 1930.
[13] File 30917, Probate Court, Norfolk County, Dedham, Mass. Angelina Weld Grimké was educated at Carleton Academy, Northfield, Minn.; Cushing Academy, Ashburnham, Mass.; Girls' Latin School, Boston; and the Boston Normal School of Gymnastics, and became a teacher and author.
[14] *Journal of Negro History*, XXX, 267–68.
[15] *Ibid.* See also the sketch in the *Dictionary of American Biography*.
[16] Clippings in the Henry A. Rich Collection, Hyde Park Historical Society, Hyde Park Public Library; also numerous letters and invitations in Weld MSS.
[17] *Eighth Annual Report, Hyde Park Library Board*, 57.
[18] Birney, 288.
[19] Sarah Grimké to an unidentified correspondent, June 1, 1872, Weld MSS.
[20] *Boston Herald*, March 8, 1870; *Boston Evening Traveller*, Feb. 21, 1870. Of course the ballots were not counted in the official returns.
[21] [Theodore D. Weld], *In Mem-*

ory, *Angelina Grimké Weld*.

[22] Birney, 309–13. Angelina left an estate of about seventeen thousand dollars to be divided between Theodore Weld and their three children. Sarah had left her estate to the children. Last Will and Testament of Angelina Weld, dated May 13, 1868, Weld MSS.

[23] Charles Stuart Weld became a teacher and writer. He contributed articles to the *Atlantic Monthly*, the *Radical*, and other periodicals. He was especially interested in the Isthmian Canals that the French government tried to construct, and in the life of Napoleon III. He died at Hyde Park on Nov. 8, 1901. *Hyde Park Gazette*, July 12, 1902. On Nov. 14, 1863, Sarah Grimké wrote: "Stuart thinks he shall go to France. He is so intent on being a frenchman, that I tell him the spirits of some of his Huguenot ancestors have certainly got possession of him & I suppose have some work for him to do there. It seems a strange mission for one whose parents are devoted to helping the cause of Humanity *here*, & whose country of-

fers, as we abolitionists think, the most glorious field for moral & intellectual labor and progress in the world." Weld MSS.

[24] P. G. and E. Q. Wright, *Elizur Wright*, 275, 283. Wright, after vicissitudes of fortune, became a consultant for life insurance companies. He was the first to put insurance on an actuarial basis and is sometimes called the father of life insurance.

[25] *Ibid.*, 311–22.

[26] *Memorial Services Upon the Seventy-fourth Birthday of Wendell Phillips*.

[27] *Boston Evening Transcript*, Feb. 4, 1895. Weld left an estate of approximately fourteen thousand dollars, most of it to his two sons, inasmuch as he had advanced considerable sums to his daughter and her husband, the Rev. William Hamilton, during his lifetime. The bequest to his colored nephew Archibald Grimké has been mentioned elsewhere. File 30917, Probate Court, Norfolk County, Dedham, Mass.

[28] Pickard, *Life and Letters of John Greenleaf Whittier*, II, 698–99.

Bibliography

BIBLIOGRAPHY

manuscript collections

The following are the chief manuscript sources that have been used in this book. No effort has been made to include scattered items, the location of which is given in the notes.

James G. Birney Collection, William L. Clements Library, University of Michigan, Ann Arbor, Mich.

James G. Birney Manuscripts, Library of Congress, Washington, D.C.

Letters of James G. Birney, designated as AC. 5508, Film Msc., Library of Congress.

Henry Cowles Collection, Oberlin College Library, Oberlin, Ohio.

Charles G. Finney Papers, Oberlin College Library.

William Lloyd Garrison Papers, Boston Public Library, Boston, Mass.

Joshua R. Giddings Papers, Ohio State Archaeological and Historical Society, Columbus, Ohio.

Joshua R. Giddings-George W. Julian Manuscripts, Library of Congress.

Lane Seminary Manuscripts, Virginia Library, McCormick Theological Seminary, Chicago, Ill.

Joshua Leavitt Papers, Library of Congress.

James M. McKim Collection, Cornell University Library, Ithaca, N. Y.
Oberlin College Library Autograph Letters.
Henry A. Rich Collection, Hyde Park Public Library, Hyde Park, Mass.
Marius R. Robinson Letters, Western Reserve Historical Society, Cleveland, Ohio.
Gerrit Smith Papers, Syracuse University Library, Syracuse, N. Y.
Benjamin F. Tappan Manuscripts, Library of Congress.
Lewis Tappan Manuscripts, Library of Congress.
Theodore Dwight Weld Collection, William L. Clements Library.
Theodore Dwight Weld Manuscripts, Library of Congress.
Weston Papers, Boston Public Library.
Elizur Wright Manuscripts, Library of Congress.

published sources

ABEL-HENDERSON, ANNIE HELOISE, AND KLINGBERG, FRANK J., "A Sidelight on Anglo-American Relations, 1839–1861," *Journal of Negro History*, XII, 128–329.
———, *A Side-light on Anglo-American Relations, 1839–1858, Furnished by the Correspondence of Lewis Tappan and others with the British and Foreign Anti-Slavery Society*. Lancaster, Pa.: The Association for the Study of Negro Life and History, 1927.
ADAMS, CHARLES FRANCIS, ed., *Memoirs of John Quincy Adams, comprising portions of his diary from 1795–1848*. Philadelphia: Lippincott & Co., 1874. 12 vols.
American and Foreign Antislavery Society, Annual Reports.
American Antislavery Society, Annual Reports.
ANDERSON, L. F., "The Manual Labor Movement," *Educational Review*, XLVI, 369–86.
APTHEKER, HERBERT, *American Negro Slave Revolts*, Columbia University *Studies in History, Economics and Public Law*, No. 501. Columbia University Press.
"A Pioneer Editor," *Atlantic Monthly*, XVII, 743–51.
A Statement of the reasons which induced the students of Lane seminary to dissolve their connection with that Institution. Cincinnati, 1834.

Baptist Board of Foreign Missions. *Third Annual Report*. Providence, 1831.

BARNES, GILBERT H., *The Antislavery Impulse, 1830–1844*. New York: D. Appleton-Century Co., 1933.

BARNES, GILBERT H., and DUMOND, DWIGHT L., eds., *Letters of Theodore Dwight Weld, Angelina Grimké Weld and Sarah Grimké, 1822–1844*. New York and London: D. Appleton-Century Co., 1934. 2 vols.

BALLANTINE, W. G., ed., *The Oberlin Jubilee, 1833–1883*. Oberlin: E. J. Goodrich, 1883.

BEECHER, CHARLES E., *Autobiography, Correspondence, etc., of Lyman Beecher*. New York: Harper & Brothers, 1864. 2 vols.

BEECHER, LYMAN, *Plea for the West*. Cincinnati, 1835.

BENNETT, CHARLES A., *A History of Manual and Industrial Education up to 1870*. Peoria: The Manual Arts Press, 1926.

Biographical Catalogue of Phillips Andover Academy, 1778–1839. Andover: The Andover Press, 1903.

BIRNEY, CATHERINE H., *The Grimké Sisters: Sarah and Angelina Grimké, the First American Women Advocates of Abolition and Women's Rights*. Boston and New York: Lee and Shepherd, 1885.

BIRNEY, WILLIAM, *James G. Birney and His Times*. New York: D. Appleton & Co., 1890.

BOYKIN, JAMES C., "Physical Training," U. S. Commissioner of Education, *Report, 1891–1892*, pp. 506–10.

BROOKS, ELAINE, "The Massachusetts Anti-Slavery Society," *Journal of Negro History*, XXX, 311–30.

BURROUGHS, WILBUR GREELEY, "Oberlin's Part in the Slavery Conflict," *Ohio State Archaeological and Historical Quarterly*, XX, 269–334.

CANBY, HENRY SEIDEL, *Thoreau*. Boston: Houghton, Mifflin Co., 1939.

CARRINGTON, HENRY BEEBE, *Theodore Weld and a Famous Quartet*. Hyde Park, Mass., 1904.

CARROLL, JOSEPH C., *Slave Insurrections in the United States, 1800–1865*. Boston: Chapman and Grimes, 1938.

CARSEL, WILLIAM, "The Slaveholders' Indictment of Northern Wage Slavery," *Journal of Southern History*, VI, 504–20.

COFFIN, LEVI, *Reminiscences of Levi Coffin*. Cincinnati: The Robert Clarke Co., 1898.

Congressional Globe, 27th Congress, second and third sessions.

CONWAY, MONCURE DANIEL, *Autobiography, Memories and Experiences of Moncure Daniel Conway.* Boston and New York: Houghton, Mifflin Co., 1904. 2 vols.

CRAVEN, AVERY, *The Coming of the Civil War.* New York: Charles Scribner's Sons, 1942.

——, *The Repressible Conflict.* University, La.: Louisiana State University Press, 1939.

CURRENT, RICHARD NELSON, *Old Thad Stevens, A Story of Ambition.* Madison: University of Wisconsin Press, 1942.

CURTI, MERLE E., "Non-Resistance in New England," *New England Quarterly,* II, 34–57.

——, *The Growth of American Thought.* New York and London: Harper & Brothers, 1943.

DUMOND, DWIGHT L., *Antislavery Origins of the Civil War in the United States.* Ann Arbor: The University of Michigan Press, 1939.

——, ed., *Letters of James Gillespie Birney, 1831–1857.* New York and London: D. Appleton-Century Co., 1938. 2 vols.

——, "Race Prejudice and Abolition," *Michigan Alumnus: Quarterly Review,* XLI, 377–85.

——, see also BARNES, GILBERT H.

EASTMAN, MARY F., *The Biography of Dio Lewis, A.M., M.D.* New York: Fowler & Wells Co., 1891.

EVARTS AND FARRIS, eds., *History of Oneida County, N. Y.* Philadelphia: J. B. Lippincott & Co., 1878.

FAIRCHILD, JAMES HARRIS, *Oberlin: Its Origins, Progress and Results.* Oberlin: Shankland and Harmon, 1860.

——, *Oberlin: The Colony and the College, 1833–1883.* Oberlin: E. J. Goodrich, 1883.

FIELDS, ANNIE, ed., *Life and Letters of Harriet Beecher Stowe.* Boston and New York: Houghton Mifflin Co., 1897. ⸜

FILLER, LOUIS, "Parker Pillsbury: An Anti-Slavery Apostle," *New England Quarterly,* XIX, 315–37.

FINNEY, CHARLES GRANDISON, *Memoirs of Charles G. Finney, written by himself.* New York: A. S. Barnes & Co., 1876.

FLETCHER, ROBERT S., *A History of Oberlin College from its Foundation through the Civil War.* Oberlin: Oberlin College, 1943. 2 vols.

——, "Bread and Doctrine at Oberlin," *Ohio State Archaeological and Historical Quarterly,* XLIX, 58–67.

———, "Oberlin and Co-Education," *Ohio State Archaeological and Historical Quarterly*, XLVII, 1–19.

FONER, PHILIP S., *Business & Slavery: The New York Merchants and the Irrepressible Conflict*. Chapel Hill: University of North Carolina Press, 1941.

FOX, EARLY L., *The American Colonization Society, 1817–1840*, Johns Hopkins University *Studies in Historical and Political Science*, XXXVII, No. 3. Baltimore: Johns Hopkins University Press.

FROTHINGHAM, OCTAVIUS BROOKS, *Gerrit Smith: A Biography*. New York: G. P. Putnam's Sons, 1879.

FUESS, CLAUDE M., *Men of Andover*. New Haven: Yale University Press, 1928.

GALBRAITH, C. B., "Anti-Slavery Movement in Columbiana County," *Ohio State Archaeological and Historical Quarterly*, XXX, 355–96.

———, "Thomas Smith Grimké," *Ohio State Archaeological and Historical Quarterly*, XXXIII, 301–12.

GARRISON, WENDELL P., and FRANCIS J., *William Lloyd Garrison, 1805–1879: The Story of His Life told by his children*. New York: The Century Co., 1885–1889. 4 vols.

GREEN, BERIAH, *Four Sermons preached in the chapel of the Western Reserve college*. Cleveland, 1833.

———, *The Chattel Principle the Abhorrence of Jesus Christ and the Apostles: or No Refuge for American Slavery in the New Testament*. New York: American Antislavery Society, 1839.

GREENE, MAUD HONEYMAN, "Raritan Bay Union, Eagleswood, New Jersey," *Proceedings of the New Jersey Historical Society*, Vol. 68, No. 1, 1–20.

GRIMKÉ, ANGELINA WELD, "A Biographical Sketch of Archibald H. Grimké," *Opportunity: A Journal of Negro Life*, III, 44–47.

HARLOW, RALPH VOLNEY, *Gerrit Smith, Philanthropist and Reformer*. New York: Henry Holt & Co., 1939.

HESSELTINE, WILLIAM B., *Lincoln and the War Governors*. New York: Alfred A. Knopf, 1948.

———, "Some New Aspects of the Pro-Slavery Argument," *Journal of Negro History*, XXI, 1–14.

HIGGINSON, THOMAS WENTWORTH, *Cheerful Yesterdays*. Boston and New York: Houghton Mifflin Co., 1898.

———, *Contemporaries*. Boston and New York: Houghton Mifflin Co., 1898.

HILL, NORMAN NEWELL, *History of Licking County, Ohio, Its Past and Present*. Newark, Ohio: A. H. Graham & Co., 1881.

HINTON, RICHARD J., *John Brown and His Men*. New York: Funk & Wagnalls Co., 1894.

HOWE, HENRY, ed., *Historical Collections of Ohio*. Cincinnnati: C. J. Krehbiel & Co., 1904. 2 vols.

Hyde Park, Mass., Library Board. *Eighth Annual Report*.

Hyde Park, Mass., Town of, *Sixth and Sixteenth Annual Reports, Jan. 31, 1874 and 1884*.

JENKINS, WILLIAM SUMNER, *Pro-Slavery Thought in the Old South*. Chapel Hill: University of North Carolina Press, 1935.

JOHNSON, LOUISE H., "The Source of the Chapter on Slavery in Dickens' *American Notes*," *American Literature, A Journal of Literary History, Criticism, and Bibliography*, XIV, 427–30.

JOHNSON, OLIVER, *William Lloyd Garrison and His Times*. Boston: B. B. Russell & Co., 1880.

"Journal of Cyrus P. Bradley," *Ohio State Archaeological and Historical Quarterly*, XV, 207–70.

JULIAN, GEORGE W., *The Life of Joshua R. Giddings*. Chicago: A. C. McClurg & Co., 1892.

LEE, FRANCIS BAZLEY, *New Jersey as a Colony and as a State*. The Publishing Society of New Jersey, 1903. 4 vols.

LEONARD, DELEVAN L., *The Story of Oberlin: the Institution, the Community, the Idea, the Movement*. Boston and Chicago: The Pilgrim Press, 1898.

LLOYD, ARTHUR YOUNG, *The Slavery Controversy, 1831–1860*. Chapel Hill: University of North Carolina Press, 1939.

LUDLUM, ROBERT P., "The Antislavery 'Gag Rule': History and Argument," *Journal of Negro History*, XXVI, 203–43.

———, "Joshua R. Giddings: Radical," *Mississippi Valley Historical Review*, XXIII, 49–60.

MAHAN, REV. ASA, *Autobiography, Intellectual, Moral and Spiritual*. London: T. Woolmer, 1882.

MARTYN, CARLOS, *Wendell Phillips: the Agitator*. New York: Funk & Wagnalls, 1890.

MAY, SAMUEL J., *Some Recollections of the Antislavery Conflict*. Boston: Fields, Osgood & Co., 1869.

NEVINS, ALLAN, *Ordeal of the Union*. New York: Charles Scribner's Sons, 1947. 2 vols.

———, ed., *The Diary of Philip Hone, 1828–1851*. New York: Dodd, Mead & Co., 1927. 2 vols.

NYE, RUSSELL B., "Marius Robinson, A Forgotten Abolitionist Leader," *Ohio State Archaeological and Historical Quarterly*, LV, 138–54.

Oneida Institute of Science and Industry, First Report of the Trustees, March, 1828. Utica: Hastings & Tracy, 1828.

PHELPS, AMOS A., *Lectures on Slavery and Its Remedy*. Boston, 1834.

PHILLIPS, ULRICH B., "The Central Theme of Southern History," *American Historical Review*, XXXIV, 30–43.

Phillips, Wendell, *Memorial Services upon the Seventy-fourth Birthday of*. Boston: James Cooper, 1885.

PIATT, DONN, *Memories of Men Who Saved the Union*. New York and Chicago: Belford, Clarke & Co., 1887.

PICKARD, SAMUEL T., *Life and Letters of John Greenleaf Whittier*. Boston and New York: Houghton Mifflin Co., 1894. 2 vols.

PILLSBURY, PARKER, *Acts of the Anti-Slavery Apostles*. Concord, N. H.: Clague, Wegman, Schlict & Co., 1883.

PRICE, ROBERT, "The Ohio Anti-Slavery Convention of 1836," *Ohio State Archaeological and Historical Quarterly*, XLV, 173–88.

RANDALL, JAMES G., *Lincoln the President: Springfield to Gettysburg*. New York: Dodd, Mead & Co., 1945. 2 vols.

RAYBACK, JOSEPH G., "The Liberty Party Leaders of Ohio: Exponents of Antislavery Coalition," *Ohio State Archaeological and Historical Quarterly*, LVII, 165–78.

ROBINSON, WILLIAM S., *"Warrington" Pen Portraits: a collection of personal and political reminiscences from 1848 to 1876*. Boston: Mrs. W. S. Robinson, 1877.

ROSS, EARL D., "The Manual Labor Experiment in the Land Grant College," *Mississippi Valley Historical Review*, XXI, 513–28.

ROURKE, CONSTANCE M., *Trumpets of Jubilee: Henry Ward Beecher, Harriet Beecher Stowe, Lyman Beecher, Horace Greeley, P. T. Barnum*. New York: Harcourt, Brace & Co., 1927.

SANBORN, F. B., ed., *Familiar Letters of Henry David Thoreau*. Boston and New York: Houghton, Mifflin Co., 1894.

SAVAGE, WILLIAM SHERMAN, "Abolitionist Literature in the Mails, 1835–1836," *Journal of Negro History*, XIII, 150–84.

——, *The Controversy over the Distribution of Abolition Literature, 1830–1860*. Washington: Association for the Study of Negro Life and History, 1938.

——, "The Origin of the Giddings Resolutions," *Ohio State Archaeological and Historical Quarterly*, XLVII, 20–39.

SHANKS, CAROLINE L., "The Bible Anti-Slavery Argument of the Decade, 1830–1840," *Journal of Negro History*, XVI, 132–57.

SHAW, ARCHER H., *The Plain Dealer, One Hunderd Years in Cleveland.* New York: Alfred A. Knopf, 1942.

SHRYOCK, RICHARD H., "Sylvester Graham and the Popular Health Movement, 1830–1870," *Mississippi Valley Historical Review*, XVIII, 172–83.

SIEBERT, WILBUR H., *The Underground Rail Road from Slavery to Freedom.* New York: The Macmillan Co., 1898.

SMITH, THEODORE C., *The Liberty and Free Soil Parties in the Northwest.* New York: Longmans, Green & Co., 1897.

SOUTHALL, EUGENE PORTLETTE, "Arthur Tappan and the Antislavery Movement," *Journal of Negro History*, XV, 162–97.

STACKPOLE, EVERETT S., *History of New Hampshire.* New York: The American Historical Society, 1916. 4 vols.

STANTON, HENRY BREWSTER, *Random Recollections.* New York: Harper & Brothers, 1887.

STEARNS, BERTHA-MONICA, "Reform Periodicals and Female Reformers, 1830–1860," *American Historical Review*, XXXVII, 678–99.

STEPHENS, JOHN VANT, *The Story of the Founding of Lane, address delivered at the Centennial of Lane Theological Seminary, June 25, 1929.* Cincinnati, 1929.

STOWE, CHARLES E. and LYMAN B., *Harriet Beecher Stowe: The Story of Her Life.* Boston and New York: Houghton Mifflin Co., 1911.

STOWE, HARRIET BEECHER, *A Key to Uncle Tom's Cabin: presenting the original Facts and Documents Upon Which the Story is Founded together with corroborative statements verifying the Truths of the Work.* Boston: P. Jewett & Co., 1853.

———, *The Story of Uncle Tom's Cabin.* Boston, 1897. *Old South Leaflets*, General Series, Vol. 4, No. 82.

STOWE, LYMAN BEECHER, *Saints, Sinners and Beechers.* Indianapolis: The Bobbs-Merrill Co., 1934.

STRONG, SIDNEY, "The Exodus of Students from Lane Seminary to Oberlin in 1834," *Ohio Church History Society Papers*, Vol. I.

STURGE, JOSEPH, *A Visit to the United States in 1841.* London, 1842.

SYDNOR, CHARLES S., *The Development of Southern Sectionalism, 1819–1848.* University, La.: Louisiana State University Press, 1948.

TAPPAN, LEWIS, *The Life of Arthur Tappan.* New York: Hurd and Houghton, 1870.

TANNENBAUM, FRANK, *Slave and Citizen: The Negro in the Americas*, New York: Alfred A. Knopf, 1947.

The Mob at Troy. Troy, 1836.

THOME, JAMES A., and KIMBALL, J. HORACE, *Emancipation in the West Indies: A Six Months' tour in Antigua, Barbadoes and Jamaica.* New York: American Antislavery Society, 1838.

TORREY, BRADFORD, ed., *Journals of the Writings of Henry David Thoreau.* Boston: Houghton Mifflin Co., 1906. 14 vols.

Tribune Almanac and Political Register for 1864. New York: The Tribune Association, 1864.

TYLER, ALICE FELT, *Freedom's Ferment: Phases of American Social History to 1860.* Minneapolis: The University of Minnesota Press, 1944.

VEST, EUGENE W., "When Dio Lewis Came to Dixon," *Journal of the Illinois State Historical Society*, XL, 298–312.

VILLARD, OSWALD GARRISON, *John Brown, 1800–1859: A Biography Fifty Years After.* Boston and New York: Houghton Mifflin Co., 1910.

WEISENBURGER, FRANCIS PHELPS, *The Passing of the Frontier, 1820–1850.* (The History of the State of Ohio. Carl Wittke, ed.) Columbus, 1941.

WELD, THEODORE DWIGHT, *First Annual Report of the Society for Promoting Manual Labor in Literary Institutions.* New York, 1833.

———, *The Bible Against Slavery.* New York: American Antislavery Society, 1837.

———, *The Power of Congress over the District of Columbia.* New York: American Antislavery Society, 1838.

———, *Slavery As It Is.* New York: American Antislavery Society, 1839.

———, *Persons Held to Service, Fugitive Slaves, etc.* (Tract No. 5, New England Antislavery Tract Association). Boston: J. W. Alden, no date.

———, *In Memory. Angelina Grimké Weld.* Boston: Press of George H. Ellis, 1880.

———, and THOME, JAMES A., *Slavery and the Internal Slave Trade in the United States.* London, 1841.

Whitesboro Seminary, Proceedings at the Fiftieth Anniversary of the Alumni Association of. Utica: Ellis H. Roberts & Co., 1878.

WISNER, WILLIAM C., *The Bible Argument on Slavery, Being Prin-*

cipally a Review of T. D. Weld's Bible Against Slavery. New York, 1844.

WRIGHT, G. FREDERICK, *Charles Grandison Finney.* Boston and New York: Houghton Mifflin Co., 1891.

WRIGHT, PHILIP G. and ELIZABETH Q., *Elizur Wright, the Father of Life Insurance.* Chicago: University of Chicago Press, 1937.

WYMAN, LILLIE BUFFUM CHACE and ARTHUR CRAWFORD, *Elizabeth Buffum Chace, 1806–1899: Her Life and Its Environment.* Boston: W. B. Clarke Co., 1914. 2 vols.

newspapers

Boston *Courier*
Boston *Evening Transcript*
Boston *Globe*
Boston *Herald*
Boston *Journal*
Boston *Traveler*
Cincinnati *Daily Gazette*
Cleveland *Leader*
Cleveland *Plain Dealer*
Collingwood (Ont.) *Enterprise-Bulletin*
Elucidator, The
Emancipator, The
Fitchburg (Mass.) *Sentinel*
Friend of Man
Hudson (Ohio) *Observer & Telegraph*
Hyde Park (Mass.) *Gazette*

Liberator, The
National Antislavery Standard
Newark (N.J.) *Evening News*
New Brunswick (N.J.) *Sunday Times*
New York *Evangelist*
New York *Observer*
New York *Tribune*
Norfolk County (Mass.) *Gazette*
Oneida (N.Y.) *Observer*
Perth Amboy (N.J.) *Evening News*
Philanthropist, The
Portsmouth (N.H.) *Journal of Literature and Politics*
Rochester *Democrat*
Western Recorder
Worcester (Mass.) *Daily Spy*

INDEX